Contents

Preface

This is a book about senior executives and the processes by which they seek to shape direction within their enterprises. We take it that senior managers matter; that they can and do make a difference. Few though they may be in number, it is often their interpretations of the enterprise and its environment – their *readings* – and their attempts to mould it in particular directions – their *'wrightings'* (for a definition see the beginning of chapter 2) – that have significant effects upon the companies' prospects:

> Managers may not fully agree upon their perceptions ... but the thread of coherence among managers is what characterizes organizational interpretation ... by which one really means, interpretation by a relatively small group at the top of the organization hierarchy.[1]

We take ourselves to be broadly part of the so-called 'upper echelons' perspective on the doing of managing which holds that 'experiences, values, cognitive style, aptitudes' of senior managers are important sources of variation on how organizations perform.[2] We say 'broadly' because we are not fully in accord with the kind of theory and research which underlies much of the writing deriving from this particular perspective. Most of it appears to be concerned with cause and effect: for example, the values of senior managers could be (and, indeed, are) conceived as acting on an organization to render it more or less effective. Our perspective is not of this ilk, in that we are much less concerned with *outcomes*; we are much more concerned with organiz*ing* and manag*ing* as processes, as activities about which we can all tell little stories, but stories with no conclusions, no punch line, stories which reflect the restless, inconclusive nature of interacting within enterprises, rather than stories which tell us definitively how such-and-such a thing comes about and may indeed be brought about.

Thus, the title of the book contains an important message about the nature of our data. We have a considerable amount of comment which depicts the doing of managing as a matter of active, purposive, deliberate and continu*ing* effort. It is not summed up by the word manage*ment*, as that, to us, suggests a somewhat static notion depicting a state of being or even a body of people. Likewise, simply calling what our respondents described as managing may be seen to describe a more passive and reactive state of affairs than that which we, and they, take to be the case. What our data describe is something much more dynamic and alive, in which act*ing*, choos*ing* and implemen*ting* are all fundamental ingredients. So while it may offend some, we choose to talk about the *doing of managing*, in an attempt to capture the restless quality of interpre*ting* and shap*ing* that appears to characterize our respondents and their 'doings'.

The data derived from some 47 senior executives to whom we talked about how it was they went about doing their jobs.[3] We transcribed the interviews, we reflected upon them, talked about them; we thought some more, followed up a few leads in the literature and wrote the book. The result, as will be seen, is a colloquy – a talking together – involving our respondents, ourselves and a handful of authors who have influenced us strongly: Chester Barnard, Michael Polanyi, Morse Peckham, Karl Weick, and to a lesser extent, Peter Sederberg and Jacob Bronowski. We make no claims that our respondents agree with our readings of their comments, nor with our wrighting (and writing up) of the material. This book is not an attempt to prove, test, predict or change anything. It is a genuine piece of *research*. Karl Weick has suggested that organizations act in order to discover what they are doing;[4] we conducted research and wrote this book in order to discover what it was (and is) about senior executives that interested (and continues to interest) us. The usual practice in a preface is to outline the delights to be found in the rest of the book. It is difficult for us to follow this practice since, as will be seen, we are committed to a wholistic perspective on the doing of managing. Therefore, even at this stage, to separate out the various strands is to run counter to our whole argument. The only way to find out what the book is about is to read it. Our headings, which we are content to preview here, can give nothing but the sketchiest of ideas of what is contained within each section. We begin with an overview of the process of the doing of managing and follow that up with a close look at the doing of organizing – how senior managers go about reading the circumstances they take themselves to be in, and how they attempt to wright the responses of others. Next we take a look at and comment upon teams and teamworking – our respondents spoke a great deal about 'working together' – and we follow this up with a section revisiting some of the ideas set out in the second part, this time in the context of relatively large-scale change. The final section revisits and extends some of the ideas introduced and developed in the rest of the book.

Prefaces are also the places where authors acknowledge their indebtedness to others. Foremost, thanks go to the executives (listed on the next page) who gave us their time and provided the raw material out of which we shaped the book. We appreciate the frank and thoughtful manner in which they responded to our inquiry and take this to be a mark of their strength. We are also grateful to the Economic and Social Research Council, who provided financial support for the project, and to Dr Sue Abbotson, who conducted some of the interviews and participated in the initial discussions. Our thanks are also extended to our respective families – Olive, Alasdair and Catriona Mangham, and Ian and (latterly) Rose Colville. Their patience and support, as well as critical observations and refusal to be easily impressed, have been invaluable in bringing this project to fruition. And, finally, our thanks to Joan Budge who, as always, has given unstinting help in preparing the manuscript.

I. L. Mangham and A. J. Pye
University of Bath

Introduction

The United Kingdom Economic and Social Research Council launched in 1985 a £1.5m research programme into the competitiveness and regeneration of British industry. The intention was to examine issues within firms, within the control of management, which influence industrial performance. Empirical investigations were carried out by 28 different teams in various British universities, polytechnics and other research institutes. Several related themes were pursued. These included the management of innovation, managing strategic change, the internationalization of business, the functioning of managerial labour markets, and the impact of design on competitiveness.

Much of the most significant and substantial research findings are being written up as monographs for this series. Other results, and interim findings, have been published as various journal articles. A complete bibliography of output from the programme may be obtained from the programme coordinator at The Management School, Imperial College of Science, Technology and Medicine, London SW7 2PG.

In this book, Iain Mangham and Annie Pye deal with the issue at the heart of company performance – how managers manage. The authors discuss conversations they have had with top managers in 13 leading British firms about how they manage those companies.

This is probably the most important and thoughtful book about the managerial process since Mintzberg wrote about the nature of managerial work in 1973. Mangham and Pye refuse to draw easy conclusions or suggest trite solutions. For them management is to be performed, not prescribed; it is an art or craft and not a science. Enhanced industrial performance, and a more competitive British industry, will not result just from the application by managers of new research findings about the relation between two variables, nor will it result just from inspirational paperbacks read on intercontinental airline flights. It can only be achieved if senior management possess and practise, at high level, the kind of craft skills which Mangham and Pye identify in this book. Such skills grow in the performance of them and cannot be learned simply from study. But most artists and craft-workers enjoy reading about their work. Not all skills are tacit. Training programmes involve words as well as example, precept and practice.

This book will therefore be of interest to all thoughtful managers who are trying to understand, and improve, what they are doing. It should also be required reading for those involved in making policy about, or providing, management education. The implications of this study for the design of management education and training are profound. And those whose academic specialism is organizational behaviour will need no persuasion that a book by Iain Mangham and his colleagues is an important contribution to their field of study.

Arthur Francis
Series Editor
Imperial College, London

Our Respondents

(Showing their positions at the time of the study)

Avon Rubber plc

J. Bradbeer	Finance Director, Avon Rubber
J. Hardwick	Group Personnel Director
D. Hudson	Managing Director, Avon Tyres
A. V. Mitchard	Managing Director, Avon Rubber
B. Stacey	Chairman, Avon Industrial Polymers

Beazer plc

B. C. Beazer	Chairman and Chief Executive
A. Chapple	Finance Director, Beazer plc
H. Rees	Director of Strategy Corporate Planning
T. Upsall	Chief Executive Homes & Property Division

BTR plc

Sir Owen Green	Chairman
N. Ireland	Formerly Finance Director

Coats Viyella plc

Sir David Alliance	Chairman
J. Ashton	Group Finance Director
J. Hewitt	Group Strategy Director
J. McAdam	Deputy Chairman and Chief Executive.

Consolidated Goldfields plc

R. I. J. Agnew   Chairman and Group Chief Executive

Glynwed International plc

G. Davies   Chairman and Chief Executive
D. Gripton   Chief Executive Glynwed Steels Ltd
R. Harris   Managing Director Glynwed
                                 Foundries Ltd
T. O'Neill   Chief Executive Glynwed Consumer
                                 & Building Products Ltd.
A. Price   Managing Director Aga Rayburn
D. Richardson   Chief Executive Glynwed Tubes &
                                 Fittings Ltd

Hanson plc

Lord Hanson   Chairman
J. H. Pattisson   Director
M. G. Taylor   Director

Lucas Industries plc

R. Dale   Managing Director Lucas Automotive
A. K. Gill   Chairman
Professor J. Parnaby   Group Director – Technology
B. Mason   Group Personnel Director
Dr A. Watkins   Managing Director Lucas Aerospace

Marks and Spencer plc

R. Greenbury   Chief Executive Officer

Metal Box plc

J. G. Armstrong   Group Personnel Director
Dr N. B. Smith   Chairman and Chief Executive
C. M. Stuart   Group Chief Executive

Prudential Corporation plc

K. L. Bedell-Pearce   General Manager Field Operations &
                                 Marketing
Sir Brian Corby   Chief Executive

G. F. Keeys

J. H. Sutcliffe

Reckitt and Colman plc

Sir Michael Colman
P. Knee
O. Parmenter

J. St Lawrence
J. West

TSB Group plc

P. Charlton
D. McCrickard
Sir John Read
D. Thorn

General Manager Prudential Assur-
ance plc
General Manager International Division

Chairman
Group Director North America
Group Director Development &
Human Resources
Chief Executive Elect
Chief Executive

Group Chief Executive
Chief Executive – Banking
Chairman
Chief Executive – Insurance
& Investment Services

1
The Doing of Managing

This chapter introduces the themes that will occupy us for the rest of the book. The larger themes, the dominant tunes, as it were, are those concerned with our view of the doing of managing as a *process* and our perspective on managers as *craftspersons and artists, improvisers of action*. Marginally less dominant, though still a swelling sound, are the variations around these themes: motifs, cadenzas and elaborations which we see as constituting the activities of senior executives as they seek to *maintain* the enterprises to which they belong.[1]

We begin with ourselves. What we have to say in the main body of the text is informed by our perspectives, our models, our frameworks, our bias and our prejudice. We collected the data, we listened to the tapes, we transcribed them, we read the transcripts, we discussed, and we present selected extracts from the interviews around themes that we have chosen. We take it that much of that activity (like much of any activity on the part of anyone) is informed by a particular way of seeing the world, which may or may not be widely shared. To the extent that we can determine how it is that we are seeing and shaping the data, we wish to be open about it. Those who use similar frameworks may well take what we have to say to be plausible; those who march to a different drummer may be tempted to break step or may stride on regardless.

The beat we march to, if at times somewhat haltingly, is that of the interpretative band; not a particularly well-known group, although many are now joining. Most scholars, consultants and writers, however, still trail along behind the long-established functionalist band.[2] The range of noise promoted within each of these ensembles is wide and, on occasion, cacophonous, but, broadly speaking, the two groups may be differentiated by the descants they perform on the objective–subjective theme. At the objective extreme are views such as behaviourism which view organizational reality as *concrete* and which treat organizational members as *responding mechanisms* who are *conditioned* by *stimuli* in the environment to behave in predictable ways. At the other, subjective, end of the range are phenomenological traditions which view what happens in organizations as a product of human *imagination* and which treat organizational members as transcendental beings who *create* and *shape* their worlds.[3] Some who write about organizations seek a position between these two extremes, seeking to march in both directions simultaneously; our stance, however, is a couple of paces from the subjective. We are not much interested in the so-called hard measures of organization; we do not present a range of figures to demonstrate the profitability of the organizations with which we are concerned in this book, nor do we speculate about the way technology or markets determine the actions that companies take. Nor, on the other hand, do we go quite as far as some of the phenomenologists in claiming that organizing is a matter of individual imagination: that there is nothing good nor bad but thinking makes it so. We are interested in the kind of sense individual managers make of their surroundings, but we take it that that sense will be influenced by the sense others construct. Order, for us, is improvised, to be sure, but it is an improvisation around values and beliefs (of which the individual performer may be more or less conscious), affected and effected – brought into being – by several performers.

As a consequence of adopting an interpretative stance on events, we tend to emphasize *process*; we take it that the doing of managing is one in which members engage in actions which shape and reshape what it is they take to be going on. Gareth Morgan captures something of our position:

The interpretive paradigm directly challenges the preoccupation with certainty that characterizes the functionalist perspective, showing that order in the social world, however real in surface appearance, rests in precarious, socially constructed webs of symbolic relationships that are continuously negotiated, renegotiated, affirmed or changed.[4]

A further consequence of our adoption of an interpretative perspective is a concern for seeing behaviour in context. Much of the research and a great deal of the writing that is produced about organizing seeks to uncover or discover patterns of cause and effect that are generalizable across contexts; ours has no such ambitions. Rather we seek to understand the unique dimensions of actions within particular situations. Our respondents talked to us about their organizations as they saw them at a particular time; for the most part they resisted generalizations and some were actively and understandably hostile to attempts to draw broad conclusions about organizing or managing. As one put it on our arrival, he would not contribute to any attempt to make 'academic claptrap out of the art and craft of managing'. What we have to say refers only to the individuals to whom we spoke and to the companies that employ them; it may resonate with what others think or do, but we make no claims that we have discovered principles or laws that are context free.[5]

Our final emphasis is upon pluralism and politics. Since we do not consider that there is an entity called the organization, we do not spend time seeking to find definitive statements about it. Our stance for a number of years has been that organizing is something that occurs between individuals (and groups), a matter of relating rather than a matter of a relationship or series of relationships. We are, therefore, interested in who is exerting pressure upon whom and in what particular direction with what perceived consequences at any particular time; since no one person can give us the perspective, we talk to several. Our interest is in what Barnard (more of him later) terms *the executive process,* which he sees as a matter of facilitating 'the synthesis in concrete action of contradictory forces, [reconciling] conflicting forces, instincts, interests, conditions, positions and ideals'.[6] We see the contradictory forces but we are much less sure about the notion of reconciliation and synthesis.

The Executive Process

It will be clear that our focus is a limited one. We are not interested in the manufacturing function, the finance function, the marketing function or the personnel function as *functions.* If the senior executives of a particular company spend their time selling the company products or sorting out problems on the line, they may well take that to be a good use of their time, but we would not take such activity to be necessarily a part of the executive process.[7] By this term we seek to refer to activities that are undertaken primarily, if not exclusively, for the purpose of establishing, maintaining or changing systems of coordinated effort:

The functions with which we are concerned are like those of the central nervous system, including the brain, in relation to the rest of the body. It exists to maintain the bodily system by directing those actions which are necessary more effectively to adjust to the environment, but it can hardly be said to manage the body, a large part of whose functions are independent of it and upon which it in turn depends.[8]

Our position is that managing is the process in and through which senior executives seek to promote and sustain coordinated effort.

We can and will talk about *aspects* of the doing of managing – indeed, to proceed we will have to distinguish between them – but in so doing we are following a heuristic procedure rather than attempting to state a truth. At the outset we wish to stress that the aspects (or functions, as Barnard somewhat unhappily terms them) are interrelated and interdependent, *not* separable in practice:

> The executive functions ... have no separate concrete existence. They are parts or aspects of the process of organization as a whole. This process in the more complex organizations, and usually even in simple unit organizations, is made the subject of the specialized responsibility of executives or leaders. The means utilized are to a considerable extent concrete acts logically determined: but the essential aspect of the process is the sensing of the organization as a whole and the total situation relevant to it. It transcends the capacity of merely intellectual methods, and the techniques of discriminating the factors of the situation. The terms pertinent to it are 'feeling', 'judgement', 'sense', 'proportion', 'balance', 'appropriateness'. It is a matter of art rather than science, and it is aesthetic rather than logical. For this reason it is recognized rather than described and is known by its effects rather than by analysis. All I can hope to do is to state why this is so rather than to specify of what the executive process consists.[9]

Amen to that. We will follow Barnard in our attempt to square the circle: to imply the importance of the whole whilst talking about selected aspects of it, aspects that can only make sense in terms of other aspects that, in turn, have a bearing upon each other and upon the whole. Our analysis is somewhat akin to talking about aspects of a picture or piece of music without ever being allowed to see it or hear it in its entirety. No amount of careful, detailed description of the colour, the brushwork, the perspective, or the pitch, tone and duration of the notes will lead to a full appreciation of the complete picture or the composition. Our enterprise, therefore, is doomed to failure: we will not and cannot capture the essence of the doing of managing in these pages. The best we can offer is some adumbration, some hazy outline of it, some signs taken for wonders.

The organization of this chapter, therefore, and indeed of the book as a whole, is arbitrary. The chapters bear titles and carry introductions which emphasize particular aspects of the doing of managing, but each runs into and overlaps with the others, so much so that, on occasion, the same example will be used to make several different points. This chapter has a similar character with the sections, on the doing of organizing, the doing of leading and the doing of organizing – again, merging one with the other.[10] We will conclude the chapter with a summary of our thoughts and further comments upon *the whole*. In subsequent chapters we will develop the themes we have introduced. In the meantime, we ask that it, *the whole*, the aesthetic integrity of the doing of managing, is borne in mind throughout the book.

The Doing of Organizing

Many of our respondents were much exercised by matters of structures and structuring. They appeared to devote large amounts of time to 'getting the organization right' and to securing the 'right' people for the 'top jobs'.[11] Many of our respondents took it that, without lines of authority in place, little else could be accomplished. Creating and dissolving positions or offices is a matter of deciding how to organize; it may be on a geographical, social, market, product, functional, customer or other basis.

I think another point that's worth making is that we have to be structured so that on both sides of the Atlantic decisions can be made very quickly, and we are able to react to events as they unfold. And by very quickly, that means in a matter of hours on occasion, irrespective of where particular people are.

The clear and obvious thing to do was to turn this business from being battleship run into being frigate run. So that meant that all the operating units that had had their head offices here on different floors ... we threw out. We said, 'Go away' and they said, 'Where?' and we said 'We don't care where, just go. You've got factories. You've got offices – just go. But don't stay here.'

Much of the strength of this business is in the form of our management organization. We have basically three levels of management ... and when you get down to the operating element, those companies are all very independent. They are left to run their own affairs, providing they produce what we require which is basically cash flow and profit. That is the strength of the group – its individuality, its independence, subject only to results.[12]

Whatever the design, the aim is to group activities to render them more capable of coordination. Putting the right people into the right jobs was seen to be a matter of selection, recruitment, development, retention, persuasion, incentives and rewards. Many of our respondents appeared to be very direct about the qualities and characteristics they expected of themselves, their employees and their colleagues:

I have boundless energy. I was born with magnificent health and I have retained it ever since. I have never had one half day away from work ever, other than for vacation. I was not born in an affluent community, we were never very poor but we were certainly not affluent. I was either given or created ambitious and I have the will to work. I personally arrive here or wherever I happen to be, I never start work later than seven in the morning, I never finish until nine at night, and I work six days a week, fifty weeks a year. And I have done so for the last thirty years. In addition to that I have sacrificed all my personal interests for the sake of my career, for whatever reason, and that's a big sacrifice. I have interests in history and theology, all of which you have to put aside to be involved in something such as this. And I have a reasonable degree of intelligence but I wouldn't say that it was a high level of intelligence. I can understand a number of technical issues, but again differing people have differing qualities. If you employ somebody to create for you an engineering solution for a deep water project, he needs a high degree of expertise in that field. I don't need those skills because I am not asked to do those things. At the end of the day, all success in business is only made by three issues, there are only three issues. One is hard work, that applies to every single business. If you are in a competitive world and are prepared to work twenty hours a day when Fred next door works three ... you will be more successful. That is an axiom that can't be altered. Those are the mathematics of life. So hard work is an essentiality. The second essentiality is economy of operation. Never spend a pound when 50p will do ... It's not your money – it's your shareholders' money. They put it up. They can demand to have a right of return. And it is dishonest not to give it to them. But the most important quality in business at my level is, sadly, neither of those things. And I say sadly because being a sort of Calvinist, I would hope that it was hard work and economy of operation. But it isn't – it's judgement. What is required is judgement. You have got to have judgement to be in the right things at the right time.

Well, you look for absolute talent, don't you? You are looking for people who have a proven track record of achievement, people who have got an ability to perceive problems and solve them rather than just worry about them. Anyone can take actions. It's achievement that you measure on. There is an illusion that dashing around is working. It's whether you actually do things. I always like to look for people who can conceptualize and have a sort of vision rather than just be reactive.

I like to think that they are all bright eyed and bushy tailed, that's the first thing. You must have people who really want to get on, who want to make money, who are ambitious ... The management at the sharp end, those people we hire, have got to be entrepreneurial in their outlook. I don't want Mr Milquetoast characters, I really don't, because it's a tough old world out there, it's difficult, so you've got to have people who are bursting out of their skins.

The development of the right people becomes the cornerstone of your success, because when you've got a huge business and you delegate more and more, you get to the stage where their ability and its being appropriate to the jobs you've given them ... is absolutely critical and the more you are delegating and the bigger the responsibilities they hold, the more important it is that you make the right personnel decisions. As you go international, it's obviously fundamental that you're appointing good people that are capable of doing the job because you are not going to be there holding their hands. And I would see personnel, the development of key people as being almost my most important job.[13]

Although none of us may 'know' precisely what it is that we expect of a senior executive in a particular position,[14] we appear to 'know' when he or she does not 'fit'. Consequently, a large part of the doing of organizing at a senior level consists in seeking to fit people to positions and positions to people. The selection, promotion, demotion and dismissal of appropriate persons for senior positions is of direct concern to the most senior of executives; upon the success of this exercise much of the rest of the enterprise appears dependent.

I suppose since I took the chair of this Executive Group, we must have spent 20–25 per cent of our management time as an Executive Group talking about management matters, management development, appointing people – now that is quite significant.[15]

If the enterprise is not successful, more often than not the failure is attributed to 'management' and in particular to its inability to come to grips with the demands of a particular situation; particular individuals in particular positions are said to be at fault. As a consequence, either 'reporting relationships' are changed or individuals are dismissed and others promoted/brought in to rectify matters.

Our respondents take it that selecting and promoting is a matter of securing a 'general condition of compatibility of personnel'. Again it is a matter of 'fit'. If the team is to be able to operate successfully, then members should be able to relate to each other; not necessarily in harmony. Some of our respondents stressed that compatibility did not mean conformity:[16]

And then there is the final thing which says 'How will he fit in with the group?' Now that isn't looking for conformity, it's looking for a guy that is prepared to put his ideas over and every now and then when his mates disagree with him he won't sulk or push off and do his own thing or go mad and so on.

The relationship between the four of us is very close because we all have trust in one another and we are able to talk freely. We are able to have a flaming row, because we don't agree with somebody else's view and then go and have a pint of beer afterwards which I believe to be healthy.[17]

Many stressed that informal organizing, the structuring of the top team, was as important as, if not more important than, the articulation of a formal organization.[18] Most of them appeared to recognize the interdependence of senior managers and appeared to place a heavy emphasis upon the compatibility of the most senior of their colleagues. The top team, in the sense of the group actively attempting to shape the organization, rarely appeared to be more than a handful of people and was frequently reported to be characterized by open communication and a large amount of trust:

I don't believe that you can have a company run by 20 people. If it's going to be effective, the smaller the number the better. One frequently says, somewhat in jest I suppose, 'The best number is two when one is away sick!' It is in jest, but I think it demonstrates the fewer the better, because I think you really can then get on and do it. If you've got to ring round ten other people before you can buy a pencil, then you get nowhere.

There is an atmosphere at the top that generates trust and friendliness and mutual support rather than everyone trying to climb on each other's backs to reach the top.

It works very well as a team and I think it's important that it should. One of the reasons perhaps that it does is a sense of common purpose and a sharing of a common vision between David Alliance and myself. We work in harmony and towards the same objectives and that is quite important in relation to the people down below in seeing things happen in that sort of way.[19]

Incompatibility at this level was seen to lead directly to poor coordination of effort elsewhere in the organization. If the people 'at the top' were seen not to be able to work together, then it was considered that those below would be uncertain as to what it was that would be expected of them.[20] Indeed, without a sound process of informal executive organization, without team work, it was often said to be 'impossible to secure effective and efficient cooperation'.[21] However, our respondents talked a great deal about teams *and* about individual effort. They praised individuals when something went well and criticized individuals when something went badly and, in virtually every case, they paid individuals and not teams on results. At the same time, occasionally in the same sentence, many of them stressed the importance of the team; clearly they saw no difficulty in switching from one focus to the other. Like many of them, we take teamwork to be central to the successful coordination of effort in an enterprise; indeed the sharpest image that remains with us from many of the enterprises we visited is that of a small group of senior managers seeking to shape events and activities, improvising the music and leading the dance for others to follow. In a subsequent chapter we will be devoting a substantial amount of space to the team.

We will also be following up on the comments our respondents made about 'the scheme of organization'; the system of offices that is put in place, according to Barnard, to facilitate coordination. It is our contention that the structuring of the organization and the selection of people for particular jobs are very powerful attempts to shape response within the enterprise. We take it that all attempts at structuring, all schemes of organization are, as it were, hypostasized explanations. Those doing the organizing, those suggesting the framework, declare in the very act of drawing up their little boxes and the lines of communication and decisions which link them and in the selection/rejection of individuals to 'fill the boxes' that this is the way the world is and, therefore, this is how we will organize to deal with it. Schemes of organization embody explanations.[22] Dr Brian Smith of Metal Box, for example, has an explanation which leads directly to a particular way of structuring his company:

I believe that the days of the battleship business have gone. By the battleship business I mean that you had a Goliath that could meet any weather or storm of economic disruption. You had the unique admiral on the bridge, who pressed the button to blast the opposition out of the water with his sixteen inch guns. And every member of the crew had a well-defined task. The admiral called the shots. Now the battleships were sunk off Singapore in 1941, and, symbolically, by the Japanese, and they've not been around since. I believe that you can't run a business like that now because the world is a much faster, much more complex place. What you do is set up your business as a lot of frigates, where every frigate has got a mission ... Now, you try and give the frigate all the resource and the fire power that you can and then you send them off out on missions ... It's important that the style of management that goes with that is compatible. So you have a small corporate Head Office and all the units operating to a degree independently.

This 'explanation' informs the organization which, in turn, power-fully communicates to those structured by it. Martin Taylor's (from Hanson) explanations are embodied in equally clear attempts at structuring. The concepts may well appear similar but the style and flavour of the response appears (to outsiders, at least) to communi-cate something different to that embodied in the structuring of Metal Box:

Oh, it's a very simple structure. We believe in full delegation of authority to the management team running the business. We want them to have the responsibility for running that business. We want them, therefore, to build confidence in their ability to solve their own problems without referring and deferring to us, because to do so would be, as it were, to allow us to make the mistakes for them without them having to feel responsible for the future success of their business. We're heavily involved in a financial control sense with what they're at. We're concerned with motivation and incentives. We're concerned with the selection of successor management. We don't insist that they trade with one another. They don't meet one another. We may move people about from time to time from business to business if they have financial skills. But rarely do we move a General Manager from one business to another. They are looked upon as having the task of performing better with the capital that they presently employ, coming to us to justify new capital that they might wish to invest in their businesses. They have no right to invest their capital in their business without our say-so, down to very small amounts, £500 in the UK, $1000 in the United States ...[23]

And so on. Our point is not that one attempt at structuring is better than another. Simply that both passages indicate the kind of beliefs and explanations that underpin the schemes of organization at that time: Brian Smith's structuring appears geared to some notion of flexibility, that of Martin Taylor appears geared to control. In both cases, the scheme of organization and the processes which give it life reflect the explanations that key figures hold of the world. Offices and the people who are selected to occupy them communicate directly and powerfully what the corporation is about and it is this aspect of structuring – the shaping of response – that we will be focusing upon in the next chapter.

The Doing of Leading

Our respondents have a great deal to say about the doing of leading. Part of what they have to say is concerned with their activities as propagandists and/or proselytizers: spreading the good news about their organizations to suppliers, customers, analysts, bankers and the public at large, not just to their own employees. Some of this propagandizing is general, both in its target and its effect:

The image we create is not good enough perhaps to win popularity prizes, but it certainly wins a lot of popularity prizes among the shareholders, and that's really all we think about. If we keep the shareholders happy and the customers happy, then all of us, all the 90,000 workers in the organization, all of us are going to be well paid and well looked after.[24]

Many of our respondents, however, seek to influence specific groups of people. Most spend a considerable amount of time in securing support, from the City.

Having brought the relevant individuals into contact with the organization, they seek to have them become identified with it by setting up regular and routine meetings. Persuasion, for the most part, appears to be a matter of offering information in return for support, but some of our respondents were very direct, for example with their brokers:

Hoare Govett, of course, who are a first division broker, weren't really for obvious reasons paying too much attention to Avon. So we turned to another broker and he placed our shares within two hours with a number of very good institutions. From memory, about half a dozen. So then we tackled Hoare Govett about this and said, 'Look, when we needed you, you weren't there. These other people did it for us. Are we too small for you? Are you interested or not?' Immediately they said, 'Well, we are interested. We like to think we can deal with small companies as well as big ones', and their whole attitude changed from that day – they were very much more positive – and relations have been extremely close ever since.[25]

Important though securing such relations are, our respondents recognize that securing effort from direct employees is crucial to the enterprise. Few are happy to settle for control; they do not want their colleagues or subordinates simply to do as they are instructed, they are looking for commitment. They appear to believe that every organization has to intensify or multiply the contributions which its members will make. They take it as important that employees show solidarity, display loyalty, are reliable, responsible, enthusiastic, concerned about quality and output; they aspire to producing circumstances in which they and those around them can feel proud to work, circumstances in which not only does the organization hold together but its manner of dealing with its constituents and its other stakeholders is morally sound. Again not something known by its parts – although a number of companies appear to believe that good public relations could change the image of their companies – but rather apprehended as a whole: 'A good company to work for ...', 'a good company to deal with ...'

In business, I am a great believer in personal integrity, because I think if you have personal integrity, you'll have commercial integrity and certainly in a business of our nature, commercial integrity is everything.

I think the biggest motivation is to be proud of what they are doing, to be proud of the company. Wanting to be recognized as a successful part of that particular company. This is the biggest motivation.[26]

Chester Barnard, as so often, has something to say on the matter and a couple of quotes from him will give the general flavour of what it is we will be attempting to outline and discuss:

Morals are personal forces or propensities of a general and stable character in individuals which tend to inhibit, control, or modify inconsistent immediate specific desires, impulses, or interests, and to intensify those which are consistent with such propensities. This tendency to inhibit, control, or modify inconsistent and to reinforce consistent immediate desires, impulses or interests is a matter of sentiment, feeling, emotion, internal compulsion, rather than one of rational processes or deliberation, although in many circumstances such tendencies are subject to rationalization and occasionally to logical processes. When the tendency is strong and stable, there exists a condition of responsibility.[27]

Barnard goes on to argue that responsibility is a key attribute of leading, holding that the persistence of an organization depends upon the quality of its leadership. One aspect of leading is the inculcation of an organizational morality which overcomes the 'centrifugal forces of individual interests or motives':

Without leadership in this supreme sense the inherent difficulties often cannot be overcome even for short periods. Leadership ... is an indispensable social essence that gives common meaning to common purpose, that creates the incentive that makes other incentives effective, that infuses the subjective aspect of countless decisions with consistency in a changing environment, that inspires the personal conviction that produces the vital cohesiveness without which cooperation is impossible.[28]

Many of our respondents displayed a sense of personal responsibility and sincerity, an integrity, which was an important factor, perhaps *the* important factor, in taking others along with them.

Personal integrity ... they conduct themselves in their lives in a proper manner. They don't bully people. They treat people fairly and squarely, they don't pass the buck when they're at fault. They don't take credit when the credit should belong to somebody else. They behave in a loyal and proper way towards the company, no matter how ambitious they are.[29]

It was rarely seen as sufficient. Commitment was underpinned, if not actually secured, by a host of incentives and inducements. A number of our respondents had a direct cash interest in their firm, paying substantial sums of money to attract and hold individuals, and, in many cases, themselves being tied to the enterprise in a similar fashion. All instituted and generally oversaw schemes of deterrents, supervision and control (often euphemistically called 'appraisal schemes'), inspection, education and training.

Whether selling the organization or directing it, we take leading to be an aspect of the doing of managing. This represents our none-too-subtle attempt to bring the concept back under control. The past decade has seen the growth of a vast literature on leaders and leading, much of it seeking to separate it out from managing. To our mind, this has resulted in nothing very much other than a vague feeling that managing is something rather mundane, looking after the nuts and bolts of the enterprise, and leading is something special and precious undertaken by the really important people in the enterprise. For us and our respondents, leading is not a separate and specialized activity, but simply an aspect, albeit a highly important one, of the doing of managing.

The doing of leading is largely a matter of managing meaning, shaping response. Managers have a responsibility to cause the entity to hang together, a responsibility they discharge through shaping and structuring communications within and without the organization. Barnard's phrase 'giving common meaning to common purpose' we find particularly resonant. Our respondents appeared to grab the attention of their colleagues and subordinates, they appeared to secure a high degree of commitment to a particular vision of the organization, but they rarely did this by simply promulgating a mission or a set of values as advocated in many a fashionable text. Rather they secured attention by what *they* paid attention to, by what *they* measured and controlled, by their own reactions to critical incidents and crises, by, in short, how it was *they* went about the daily, routine business of doing managing.[30] Tony Mitchard of Avon

Rubber, for example, provided clear direction by his response to a threatened strike:

We had one stoppage, and it was to do with tea breaks. What we said was that there would no longer be institutionalized tea and coffee breaks. We don't deny the people the need to have a cup of coffee, but somebody else has to be there to keep the machine running. We will not have the machines stopped during a shift ... Well, this was very unpopular, this business of not being able to stop the machines or go and have a smoke together and so on. And they announced one afternoon at about three o'clock that they were going to have a tea break. They were going to stop everything ... So, of course, we had to decide what to do. And I said to the management concerned, 'What do you think we ought to do?' and they said we ought to send them home. So I agreed. They duly went on their tea break and the management sent them home. So at four o'clock ... the whole place stopped. We had a meeting and decided that when the next shift came in we'd be there to ask them what they intended doing ... And they all announced to a man, they'd orchestrated it well, they were going to take a tea break. So we sent them all straight home. Anyway, the next shift came in and they did the same thing, so we sent them home, by which time it was the next day and there was a great confusion and concern on all sides.
We had a meeting involving a full time official of the TGWU. I started off by saying, 'I think that everybody's entitled to have a coffee break. Quite honestly, I don't think I could survive without a cup of coffee in the morning.' So I started off by adopting that sort of attitude, but I said, 'We are no longer going to have coffee breaks if it means that in having them, we stop machinery. I drink coffee,' I said, 'but I don't stop working. I keep working. I know that our people can't drink coffee and run machines at the same time, but you know that we've got procedures where machines can always be covered so that they don't have to stop.' ... Anyway, in the end the Union were very pleased to hear that I agreed that everyone was entitled to tea and coffee. They were very pleased to hear that. They understood that in this new competitive world and with Avon's new attitude, the machines had to be kept running, and after a lot of coming and going, normal work was eventually resumed.

Prior to this event, Tony Mitchard had sought to energize his managers, and had attempted to spell out the brave new world to the employees, but the former did not believe that 'when it came to the crunch this office (that of the Chief Executive) would support them ... we'd buckle, we'd compromise ...', and the latter just did not believe things would change. In this instance, and in many others told to us by our respondents, both words and actions were taken to be eloquence:

Where do you start? The man has set an example in every respect – Brian, in my view is someone of the utmost ability in any sphere. I think he's one of the few people that I've met who can do or knows something about everything. To the extent that he can go out, whether it's in the building industry, or building materials, whether it's in construction – he can talk on the subject. He has a wide grasp of the industry in every facet and I suppose … there's nothing to impress a person more than when you can take off your coat and do his job. He respects you for it. Brian, through his understanding, has the respect of everyone … There is little doubt that when it comes to motivation and incentivization, he has been the architect in taking the group where it is. Again, I think he is a man who looks for the opportunity, looks for the solution, touches on the problem but concentrates on solutions. He is a man who has a tremendous discipline in his way of life, in his approach to life, which has been an example to us all. He leads from the front. He is the first in and he is the last away. He travels more than any of us. He's the sort of person that everyone needs to take the whole operation forward. He leads from the front in every respect.[31]

These examples highlight, once more, the seamless nature of the doing of managing. It is not a matter of first doing this, then that, but in many many instances a matter of simultaneously doing many things. Our respondents are reading what is going on around them as and when they are seeking to wright (for a definition see the beginning of chapter 2) or shape what is going on round and about them. The aspect of the doing of managing concerned with purpose runs into that concerned with the securing of commitment which in turn has a bearing upon people and systems, jobs and offices, which in turn …

Again not a simple matter; not a question of either paying money or giving a moral lead, not a matter of commitment or control, but a heady mix of them all. In chapter 3 we will pick up on these points and extend them.

The Doing of Organizing – Again

The third aspect of the executive process, which we will address in chapter 4, is the most difficult to name. On the surface, what we are concerned about here is our respondents' thoughts about and comments upon themselves as would-be change agents. When our respondents talked of purpose and objectives it was often in the context of making changes, thus the doing of changing could be seen to shade into the doing of organizing and into the doing of leading.[32] But change implies persistence, something from which change arises or departs and change implies challenge and purpose. Many of our respondents recognized that the formulation and definition of purpose is a widely distributed and continuing process. Those 'at the sharp end' (the commanders of Dr Smith's frigates) apply personal energy to the definition and realization of highly specific objectives, those at the top (back at the Admiralty, as it were – largely our respondents) remain responsible for the formulation and promulgation of general, abstract, prospective, long-run ideas about where the company is going and for the overall 'indispensable' coordination of the whole.

I think basically it's what I've been describing. It's constantly saying, 'The world has changed'. And it's constantly challenging assumptions that don't recognize that.[33]

The fact that the formulation and definition of purpose is such an iterative and widely distributed process means that extraordinary effort has to go into it to ensure that the enterprise faces the rest of the world in as coherent and cohesive a manner as is possible. The senior managers of Hanson and a number of our other respondents see the necessity for 'indoctrinating those at lower levels with general purposes': 'Then there is an indoctrination process and it's constant actually. It's doctrination, it's not indoctrination. It's a total constant factor.'

Although not using quite the same terms, Brian Smith at Metal Box seeks to have all aware of the direction in which the company is heading. He and his colleagues do this by 'talking' back and forth, sharing ideas up and down the line with the overall purpose of generating 'excitement, energy and commitment': 'What is it that unites a team? Common purpose and a belief that you are winning. Nothing has a team more disunited than an unclear purpose and belief that you are failing.'

It is clearly not a matter of the top deciding and issuing instructions. It is an activity that demands sensitive systems of communication, a high but controlled degree of delegation and a sharp sense of imagination. Again Brian Smith illustrates our point:

Change the structure, get the budgeting done, get the first stage of strategy thinking, turn it back if it's not adequate, have another go, then let people run the strategies and get the confidence in them. Back end of last year, we pulled back in six or eight of the units because we felt the environment had changed, and we'd better have another talk. We also knew there was a rethink going on as to whether what they (a particular subsidiary company) had said was still right. It's not easy to come out with a strategy and then go off and try it, and get hit in the teeth and say, 'No, it wasn't right!' We've got the guys to relook – in any event they were already doing it and came and told us about it. So effectively now you can reckon that all the pieces of the business have operating control and know what they are trying to achieve, not just in the short term but also where they'd like to try and get to in the longer term if we will back them.

We would merely add 'for the moment'. Purposing is continuous. Our respondents, for the most part, did not have a mission, did not have a purpose, did not have a single set of objectives; many of them, however, were active in *missioning, purposing, objectivizing*.[34] That is to say, they were committed to the process of gaining clarity and commitment to particular and changing concepts of what kind of response they wanted from their employees.

The Whole and More

Three broad and overlapping aspects, then, constitute the executive process: the doing of organizing, the doing of leading, securing effort from those who can make a contribution to the enterprise whether within or formally outside it, and the doing of organizing again – none standing alone, each informing the other within a complex and ever-moving whole. And all a bit too pat. A tad too simplistic. A touch too analytic. To be sure, many of our respondents would recognize the terms that we have used and some would subscribe to them: they are involved in structuring, in securing effort and in purposing but, having said that, they sense something else beyond these terms, something less tangible but none the less meaningful. As do we. It is to these aspects of the whole – that which is recognized rather than described[35] – that we now turn, once more stressing that, as with the somewhat more readily assimilated notions outlined above, nothing stands in isolation and everything informs and is informed by everything else.

Barnard chose not to specify 'of what the executive process consists', but instead provided an interesting account of that by which it may be recognized. In a sense, this is what our respondents were also doing: by giving us examples they provided an account of their practice without, for the most part, seeking to prescribe of 'what it consists'. They take action to be their eloquence and by giving us descriptions of it, invite us to make whatever sense we can of it. They proceed by exemplification not out of wilful desire to obfuscate nor out of ignorance, but because meaning, for them, is expressed in the practical consequences of an event or action.[36]

But how do our respondents *know* what to recognize? If it, whatever it is, cannot be described, how are they so sure that it, whatever it is, has occurred? It is, they claim, a matter of experience, a matter of *intuition*.

In the common-sense, everyday, practical knowledge necessary to the practice of the arts, there is much that is not susceptible to verbal statement – it is a matter of know-how. It may be called behavioural knowledge. It is necessary to doing things in concrete situations. It is nowhere more indispensable than in the executive arts. It is acquired by persistent habitual experience and is often called intuitive.[37]

This aspect of the doing of managing is nicely caught in Lord Hanson's comment to us:

You have to have done your homework and know what you can do at the end … that means being very experienced not only in your own business and in the business world and having been around long enough to feel balanced, but also to know that instinctively when you look at a balance sheet, Gordon White excels in this particular field, when you look at a balance sheet, you can spot immediately that there's room for improvement. Basically you could just smell 'em a mile away, these companies.

Barnard loosely contrasts this conception of behavioural knowledge with what he calls 'scientific knowledge – explanations, concepts'. This duality, of course, is at the core of the well-worn dichotomy which has bedevilled the pursuit of knowledge over the years. On the one hand stands logic, reason, analysis and deduction and on the other tacit, intuitive understanding. Barnard sees the latter as subsuming the former; in effect he gives precedence to intuitive grasp over logical reasoning.

The dichotomy is the product of the tendency to think of objects, functions or processes as either one thing or another. The possibility that the focus of interest can be, at one and the same time, more than one 'thing' is rarely entertained. Yet the new physics tells us that all being at the subatomic level can be described equally well as 'either solid particles, like minute billiard balls, or as waves, like the undulations on the surface of the sea'.[38] What is more, quantum physics tells us that neither description is accurate on its own, that being is both particle like and wave like; that, in fact, this duality is the essence of being. The Principle of Complementarity claims that each way of describing being complements the other, the whole picture emerges only from the 'package deal'. In the present context, the doing of managing was not a process in which reason gave way to intuition or vice versa; both exist in a complex complementarity. They can be separated for analytical purposes, but, in practice, each informs the other at the point of action. Our respondents saw themselves as displaying rationality *and* intuition, rigour *and* feel.[39]

The dilemma in making this point is that while such different kinds of knowledge may be experienced as operating simultaneously, our description and the linear nature of the language of explanation that we must necessarily employ lead us directly to an implied separation. This problem is even more acute when trying to develop the notion of duality to embrace thinking and acting, reflecting and doing: acting thinkingly and thinking actingly. Again our respondents appear to deny that these activities need to alternate; that a bout of reflecting necessarily precedes a bout of acting.

There are two co-existing things going on. One is the feel, the intuitive feel, and the other is the formal planning running along with it. And to an extent behind it ... The intuitive thing was telling us that we were not only not as good as we thought, we were bloody awful, and that we had a lot of people in the organization who didn't believe that. So once we accepted that, we had to think about how we can use devices, plans, mechanisms to make people actually aware ... Forcing people to talk to each other and actually listen to each other, criticizing the organization and then defending their own patch, and being proved wrong.[40]

For us, and, more importantly, for many of our respondents, thinking may, on occasions, be said to qualify action. Executive action of any kind, walking the floor, writing memos, speaking into the telephone, holding forth at meetings, chewing out subordinates, placating customers, relating to colleagues – any action – can be done more or less thinkingly. Each of these activities can be undertaken with varying amounts of 'deliberateness, intention, care, control, and pertinacity'.[41] Such a perspective, as Karl Weick notes, involves treating *thinking* not as a verb but as an adverb. Thus our respondents may not spend a great deal of time sitting alone thinking, but they do spend time and energy doing things in a manner which they anticipate will be effective. When, for example, Gareth Davies of Glynwed Engineering convenes a meeting, he is reported to participate in it thinkingly: he is said to pay close attention to what is happening, apparently he tries to surface issues and to shape them and he is seen to keep a light but firm control on the process of the meeting. His acting is qualified by his thinking as and when he performs. To reinforce the point, it may be useful to consider its opposite, a meeting in which action is prosecuted *unthinkingly*, a meeting in which the Chief Executive Officer appears to act upon 'blind impulse', paying no attention to the setting or to others involved with him in it, giving off apparently random signals as to the direction he wants to take, and generally behaving in a mindless fashion. Our familiarity with such meetings means that such an exercise demands no great imaginative effort.[42]

Our respondents also appear to think actingly. When they *are* reflecting, when they *are* sitting alone, they appear not to pursue abstract thought for the pleasure such an exercise may bring. Most appeared to be Pragmatists, thinking things through to a decision rather than thinking things through to a conclusion.[43]

Pragmatists our respondents may be, but they do not appear to act without theme and direction. Their performance does not appear to be a matter of judging each and every situation as if it were distinct from all that has gone before. Indeed, in what they see themselves as doing and in the stories they recounted to us, there was a strong sense of unfolding, of immanence, of action started long ago coming together weeks, months, even years later. John West, Chief Executive of Reckitt and Colman, captures this symphonic development of themes in his comment: 'But one was in the fortunate position of inheriting a business with a lot of energy, that knew where it wanted to go. And all one had to do was to orchestrate that'. He was certainly not alone in seeing no radical discontinuity in the actions that he or his colleagues took. Like many others he saw action as a variation upon a corporate theme rather than the introduction of a completely new tune unrelated to anything heard before. Frequently an old theme underscores what is now being played, just as what will be heard a decade from now, whilst not completely predictable, will emerge from variations currently being rehearsed and performed.

Ah, but how do our managers know which variation to develop when?

The fine art of executive decision consists in not deciding questions that are not now pertinent, in not deciding prematurely, in not making decisions that cannot be made effective, and in not making decisions that others should make.[44]

Few of our respondents were of the opinion that they should call the tune; few of them held the 'implicit belief that they should make all the decisions of interest or as many as possible, the more and quicker the better'.[45] A number of them appeared to have cultivated the capacity to listen to the rhythms of their organizations – to sense and await the moment when actions could be effective. As in a piece of music or a play, an early passage suggests something that becomes more implicit in a later passage, which, in turn, presages a still later development, which, in turn, illuminates the very first passage, so in some organizations what occurs can be traced back, can be seen to be right, inevitable perhaps, in the context of what has occurred and what might occur.

The notion of immanence contains a powerful, continuing sense of unfolding drama in which there is a history and tradition which provide the backdrop against which scenes are played out; a sense of performance – a bringing to fruition. In this process, there is a sense of the timing, of temporality of action. It is a notion that presents problems for us as analysts and one that very often seems to be ignored. Research methods tend to allow only snapshot views of organizations and even longitudinal studies tend towards the fine detail of a chronology of events rather than a sense of temporality, of timing and 'rightness', inevitability even, in the unfolding of action. Timing appeared to be an important aspect of getting it right:[46]

That's my job. If you'd asked me before I'd started was this the agenda for change and was this the timetable (I would not have been able to answer), I'm not a textbook or a theorist, it's all feel of when the time is right for the next thing – because I find that you live in waves, and there are times when I go through what I would call an administrative period, when I just react to what's happening, and after a while you think, 'It's time now to make something happen. I can feel it.' And then you get the next initiative running.[47]

Temporality is difficult to deal with theoretically as it is frequently taken to imply linearity. We are after something more than a sequence, what our respondents imply is a circumstance where the past and the future are encapsulated in the present, something best expressed or embodied in Eliot's *Burnt Norton*:

> Time present and time past
> Are both perhaps present in time future
> And time future contained in time past ...

> Time past and time future
> Allow but a little consciousness.
> To be conscious is not to be in time
> But only in time can the moment in the rose garden,
> The moment in the arbour where the rain beat,
> The moment in the draughty church at smokefall
> Be remembered; involved with past and future.

Chance, in the words of Pasteur, favours the prepared mind. Opportunism is a characteristic of many of our respondents; events do not necessarily occur in the sequence that they would wish but when they do occur they are prepared to take advantage of them. Assigning opportunity to randomly chosen members of the population would not do the trick. To exploit an opportunity one must observe the phenomenon and understand what it implies. A naive manager cannot have insights into situations simply because having insight implies the recognition of familiar features in unfamiliar settings; without the required degree of familiarity – itself the product of experience and education – cues would not be taken to be cues. Hanson and White's ability to 'smell' the companies that could benefit from their approach to managing is based, ultimately, upon experience and know-how.

We take it that much of what occurs in the doing of managing is the product of both careful, rational thought, and of 'persistent, habitual experience'. Intuitive understanding, sensing the whole in the part and acting accordingly, appeared to our respondents to be a matter of experience. Many claimed that they had been exposed to managerial challenge and responsibility at early stages of their careers and that this experience was invaluable to guiding their subsequent actions. As Huxley pointed out, though, 'experience is not what happens to a man, it is what a man does with what happens to him'.[48] Here, once more, we catch the echo of simultaneity: what a man does with what happens to him, indicating a sense of learning while doing.

Polanyi described this as 'an active shaping of experience ... in the pursuit of knowledge'.[49] In the process of actively shaping experience (wrighting it, in the terms used earlier), so knowledge is built up and continually reformed, both by logical reasoning and inference as well as intuitive grasp and understanding. These processes cannot be rendered explicit; at least not in their conjunction. Heisenberg's Uncertainty Principle tells us that while both wave and particle descriptions are necessary to give us a complete grasp of what being is, only one of these descriptions is available to us at any one time. Either the exact position of something like an electron can be measured in its manifestation as a particle, or its momentum as a wave can be measured. We can never have a measure of both exactly at the same time. The position is complicated by the fact that 'most electrons and subatomic entities are neither fully particles nor fully waves but some confused mixture of the two known as a "wave packet"'.[50] We take it that the position with regard to the conjunction of rational thought and intuitive understanding is even more uncertain. One element of the process, intuitive understanding, resists analysis and tests our powers of description. In Polanyi's terms, to reflect on an intuitive performance changes the essential nature of such 'knowing', rendering it no longer something tacitly occurring, but instead a more stepwise logical reasoning from particulars to the whole: '... an unbridled lucidity can destroy our understanding of complex matters'.[51] He goes on to argue, as do we and, implicitly, many of our respondents, that the 'belief that, since particulars are more tangible, their knowledge offers a true conception of things is fundamentally mistaken'.[52] There is, indeed, more to the doing of managing than we can analyse.

Few of our contributors would claim that knowledge of particulars could give a true conception of the whole. Each suggested that there was more to the doing of managing than they could tell and than they wanted to tell, since 'unbridled lucidity' may well destroy the very nature of what it was they were about.

Tacit knowledge may not be accessible but it informs action. We take our respondents to be artists of the floating world of enterprise. Like artists everywhere, they conduct a kind of covert conversation with that which they create as it emerges. The American painter, Ben Shan, makes the point for us: 'Painting is both creative and responsive. It is an intimately communicative affair between painter and painting, a conversation back and forth, the painting telling the painter even as it receives its shape and form.'[53] On the one hand, therefore, we have the encounter with the object of attention (this may be a partially completed painting, a piece of music, a stretch of prose, a set of figures, a strategic plan, a half articulated problem) and on the other a performance of whatever insight may emerge from this encounter, a performance which fully expresses the insight and tests it. That test provides further insight, in turn expressed and so on. The doing of managing, like the doing of painting or the doing of composing, is an iterative, restless, never quite finished process. It is clearly not random behaviour since it may be said to be guided towards some form by the implicit notion of 'fit'. All fields of activity organize experience through the evolution of norms by which subsequent experience is ordered, and which are themselves developed by the activities they mediate. These norms are necessarily tacit; we cannot describe 'fit', the best we can do is to talk about 'misfit' or 'lack of fit'. We cannot say what constitutes a good performance even though we can recognize it. It is much easier to enumerate that which constitutes a poor performance even though we may be aware that the rectification of each and every one of these failings will not necessarily lead to a good performance. Thus a manager approaches a circumstance with a set of tacit criteria which are activated when some specific action is found to be inconsistent with one of them. A particular action arises from the interplay between these tacit norms, these 'oughts', and critical reactions to them given the context within which the manager takes himself/herself to be called upon to perform. Action may conform to the norm or go beyond it and, in so doing, contribute to its development or its demise.

A coherent performance by an actor, artist, composer or manager requires that the performer both apprehends that which underlies whatever he or she is confronting and simultaneously embodies his or her response to it. Both apprehension and embodiment require expression in a manner that at once utilizes and transcends the currently accepted language of painting, acting, composing, managing or whatever. An inspired piece of managing, no less than an inspired piece of painting or composing, has a mix of the universal and the idiosyncratic, the expected and the novel.

For example, at Coats Viyella, following the merger between Vantona and Carrington Viyella in 1983, the Executive decided to invest heavily in shirt factories. No one else in the UK, and certainly no one in Northern Ireland, was prepared to put large amounts of money (some £13 million) into shirt factories and equipment at that time. Indeed, pundits were suggesting that the UK textile industry was beyond redemption, facing relentless competition from cheap imports.

But until you actually do it, you can not be sure that you can actually do it. And you are also talking about quite major organizational changes in the process of actually doing it. But anyway, as that work was being done, it gave confidence that it wasn't just words on paper – that it could be made manifest.

A firm belief held by Vantona Viyella executives and a sense of possibility, together with a commitment to demonstrating that belief, led them to take some key decisions which ran counter to what at that time was received wisdom. As analysts, we might say that this illustrates a paradox of both thinking and doing: that is, of thinking which sets off in the opposite direction to everything else and doing which runs counter to all informed prediction. Again, though, we have to stress that this would only be the construction of analysts. Our respondents were aware that their decisions and actions ran counter to received opinion, but none the less persisted since they believed it was necessary action.

Clearly there are many interpretations one might construct around this example. Strategists would see it as a particular stage in the overall strategy of becoming a world-class textile company. Financial analysts might see it in terms of risk evaluation and payback potential. We can see the sense of such interpretations, but would suggest that it illustrates the kind of counter-cyclical thinking and doing that is characteristic of some artists and scientists and some of our respondents. At some point each of them has taken action which appeared to run counter to what has gone before and to what commentators and analysts might predict.

However, the way in which these episodes are described in our data is not in terms of contradictory forces or opposing dimensions; not in terms of aspects to be resolved in some way or other. Still less are they depicted as circumstances in which someone or other must take a heroic stand, hazard all on a single throw. Rather the descriptions tend simply to convey a powerful sense of Pragmatism, the 'philosophic method that makes practical consequences the test of truth'.[54] For the Pragmatist (and all artists are pragmatic), the emphasis lies in identifying that shifting ground of potential practical consequences of action. And this ground shifts daily according to individual issues, yet it has to be judged at a particular time under particular circumstances. Reading and wrighting are inseparable.

They seem to lie at the heart of the executive process and are well evidenced in the accounts of action that were presented to us. It is much more than that which is implied by notions such as tolerating ambiguity or coping with uncertainty. It is a very active, positive, almost existential sense of doing managing. And while such relentless continuous activity might imply a strong practical and tangible core of action, it is given focus and significance by much more elusive notions such as awareness of particulars bearing on the whole, a sense of possibility and immanence, underwritten by a simultaneity of knowing, thinking and doing.

The ultimate irony of studies of successful organizations or managers is that they seek to define the impossible: there can be no absolute notion of managerial or organizational success. In each case, the doing of managing is judged against previous actions and organizational achievements. 'Today's excellence is tomorrow's competence.'[55] A successful performance, a good fit, changes the context for everything that has gone before and everything that is to come.

We conclude with some further thoughts from Chester Barnard which summarize what it is we have attempted to outline in this chapter:

Most men whose judgement I respect take plenty of time on major problems and make time if possible. They do not decide until it is necessary to do so. They 'think it over' carefully but not necessarily logically. What I have tried to emphasize is the insufficiency of logical processes for many purposes and conditions and the desirability of their development in intelligent coordination with the nonlogical, the intuitional, even the inspirational processes which manifest mental energy and enthusiasm. This is by no means easy. To rely upon 'feeling', to give weight to first impressions, to reject logical conclusions and meticulous analysis in favour of an embracing sense of the whole, involves an inconsistency of attitudes. It means developing the artistic principle in the use of the mind, attaining proportion between speed and caution, between broad outlines and fineness of detail, between solidity and flexibility ...[56]

A number of our respondents manifested the kind of *feeling mind* tht Barnard saw as the key characteristic of effective senior managers, the mind that senses amongst the welter of competing interests and special pleadings the end result, the net balance; the singularity of spirit that perceives the concrete parts yet can also grasp the intangible whole.

Barnard's injunction to cast some light upon the parts within the whole is one which we take seriously. We recognize that we cannot pull it off, we cannot square the circle since, as we have argued, knowledge of the parts cannot reveal the whole; but we think the attempt may be illuminating. This chapter has introduced some of the themes, some of the motifs, which run through our data. The rest of the book extemporizes on these themes and motifs.

2
The Doing of Organizing

In the many hours we spent seeking to find an appropriate way of organizing our data, we tested a number of metaphors. Despite our declared interpretative stance we tried out metaphors from other bands and even experimented with those that depicted organizations as machines, or systems, or organisms. We also played around with the less popular, such as those which compare organizations to jungles, theatres and markets. Each revealed something and, at the same time, concealed some other thing. Of course, no metaphor can be judged definitively 'right' or 'wrong'; they are not 'mirrors' of nature, but are more like 'portraits' which show some features whilst neglecting others.[1] We settled, finally, upon the notion of the executive as artist/scientist/craftsperson, someone who 'reads' the circumstances in which he or she find himself/herself and someone who 'wrights' in the sense that a playwright 'wrights' and a ship-wright 'wrights'. Someone, that is, who shapes the material with which he or she works; someone who operates hands on in an activity that is palpable, someone who inherits and is shaped by a tradition and yet remains capable of going beyond that tradition and shaping *it*; someone whose work reflects his or her understanding of the world at a particular moment in time, whose work, however, is never finished, always evolving. We went further and took it that an artist/scientist/craftsperson's work may be seen as a communication; we can (and do) treat the works of such people as if they represented some particular perspective on activities or events. So, gently push-ing the analogy, it seemed to us reasonable to consider organizations as if they too were artefacts, as if they too embodied attempts to communicate. It seemed even reasonable to assume that a respon-dent who set up a framework of reporting within his enterprise that caused senior managers to spend considerable amounts of time talking to customers had a different perspective on the world to one who created structures that caused managers to spend considerable amounts of time in the office or on the line attending to costs. We took it (and take it) that enterprises are not usually haphazard arrangements of offices and people; the way they are set up and the people who are selected to occupy the offices communicate the wrighter's perspective on the world, his or her explanations of the way things are (or should be). In this chapter, therefore, we intend to treat our respondents as if they were artists/scientists/craftspersons, readers and wrighters, and to consider what they have to say about their enterprises and, in particular, what they say about how they structure them; we will treat them, that is, as if their stories and their designs were communications and explanations.[2]

You Scratch My Back...

Following up on the ideas of Morse Peckham and Peter Sederberg, we take it that organizing is a matter of sharing meaning, of elaborating and sustaining patterns of mutually expected response.[3] This may entail little more than temporary interaction as in a queue for a bus or a taxi, when relations between those queuing are relatively transitory (depending upon the service), non-hierarchical and largely unregulated, or it may involve relatively stable interaction between office holders whose relations are coordinated by someone capable of enforcing compliance.[4]

Being organized is a matter of knowing roughly what to expect in one's encounters with one's fellow workers; any enterprise may be reduced to the responses of those who constitute it. These responses, however, are unlikely to be unexpected; we know, roughly, what to expect from others in the enterprise in which we work and they know, roughly, what to expect from us. What they do and what we do, therefore, is shaped by these mutual expectations. The entire enterprise is created and sustained through a dialectical process, with our responses both creating and being created by the responses of others.

All enterprises organize the same thing: patterns of mutually expected response. As Peter Sederberg puts it: 'Whatever other tasks they [organizations] undertake – producing toasters, collecting taxes, conquering neighbors – organizations depend upon the structured responses of those who comprise them. By routinizing responses, organizations establish shared meaning by guaranteeing mutually fulfilled expectations.'[5]

He goes on to argue that explanations also attempt to control shared meaning by channelling response. Explanations make something intelligible, they create a circumstance in which we know how to respond to some phenomenon or other. Thus we may offer an explanation of an eclipse which declares it to be a manifestation of heavenly power or one which declares it to be a predictable, astronomical occurrence governed by the laws of physics. Each explanation asserts a form of response. Scientific explanation strives to structure what it takes to be appropriate response through appeals to logic and empirical evidence, while other forms of explanation draw upon different means to control the range of response.

Organizing is a matter of explaining and organization is an explanation or set of explanations made manifest. Thus, presently in our enterprise – a university – a number of explanations contend to structure responses but only one is made manifest in the structures and procedures with which 'the management' seeks to routinize behaviour.[6] An explanation which holds that universities are places where scholars can pursue knowledge wherever that pursuit may lead them struggles with one which holds that universities are answerable directly to the wider society for the supply of vocationally trained graduates and for the prosecution of research that is of direct and immediate use to industry. The patterns of response implied by these explanations differ: the former stresses collegial relations, peer evaluation of scholarship, and places little emphasis upon hierarchy, the latter implies reporting relationships, subservience to overall univer-sity objectives, a willingness to be monitored, more time to be spent with students, less with one's own scholarship, and so on. Different explanations, different structures, different processes.[7]

Not every explanation, not every attempt to structure response, becomes an organization, but every explanation and every attempt to structure response is a potential organization. Explaining the environment in terms of costs, declaring that numbers of students, articles, books or whatever rather than the quality of any of these are the measures of success may not succeed in convincing anyone that this is indeed the case. This being so, the desired response will not be forthcoming, old patterns may persist even when formal structures are put in place.

We can claim that organized behaviour exists when specific responses fit into a pattern, when, that is, responses match expectations. But, as we have hinted above, commonly organizing is a matter of finding a way through competing explanations. In any given enterprise it would be unusual not to find several explanations contending as to how people ought to respond. In such circumstances, it would be folly to claim that the explanation offered by the most senior of those doing the managing determined the responses of any other member of the enterprise. Although our focus is upon the top handful of executives in the enterprises we studied, we do not claim that their perspectives hold throughout their companies; what we do claim is that their explanations are attempts to structure response and that structuring response, offering explanations, shaping meaning is central to executive process.

In Their Own Wright

Our respondents attempt to wright their enterprises in line with what they take to be good practice; the explanations they offer, the patterns they seek to inculcate derive from their own experience of doing managing and the observations they make of others engaged in the same trade. How, that is, they *read* the situation. What they read or read into situations depends upon how literate they are and upon what they notice. A literate manager or executive will notice more cues in the environment and will be able to read these cues better than an illiterate manager or executive. No manager or executive, however, can notice and respond to everything. As William Starbuck and Frances Milliken point out in their review of how it is that executives make sense of their circumstances, the one thing that 'an intelligent executive does not need is totally accurate perception'.

Such perception would have no distortion whatever. Someone who perceived without any distortion would hear background noise as loudly as a voice or music and so would be unable to use an outdoor telephone booth beside a noisy street, and would be driven crazy by coughs and squeaks at symphony concerts ... The processes that amplify some stimuli and attenuate others, thus distorting raw data and focussing attention, are perceptual filters.[8]

While we agree with the gist of what they are saying, we demur from the idea(l) of 'totally accurate perception'. Inasmuch as we are talking about readings people make of situations, there can be as many different perceptions as there are different people. If there is any notion of accuracy to be attributed, it will go to those who share the most commonly held view. Clearly, filters cut out some data and allow through only that which is deemed relevant. Thus an executive who chooses to focus upon certain ratios to the exclusion of others will only 'see' those that he or she takes to be of interest. Those who 'look out' for certain types of individual to develop and promote will only 'see' them. After a while filtering has the characteristics of being intuitive; it occurs without apparent reflection and is resistant to elucidation.

A number of writers, including Starbuck and Milliken, make a distinction between *noticing* and *sensemaking;* the former neatly captured in this piece of doggerel by R. D. Laing:

> The range of what we think and do
> is limited by what we fail to notice.
> And because we fail to notice
> *that* we fail to notice
> there is little we can do
> to change
> until we notice
> how failing to notice
> shapes our thoughts and deeds.[9]

We fail to notice that we have failed to notice because we have become all too familiar with that which surrounds us. However, noticing and sensemaking are not easy to distinguish and indeed, for some writers, noticing is part of the process of sensemaking.[10] Many of our respondents, for example, have been with their companies for many years; they have grown accustomed to their surroundings and to each other and the things that they initially noticed about Glynwed, Beazer, Reckitt and Colman or wherever have faded into the background. On the other hand, this very familiarity has also caused them to notice and make sense of things which, as novitiates, they may well have missed or dismissed. Such things are foregrounded through conditioning, learning and experience. Systems evolve and/or are set up to collect and monitor foreground data and meetings are often convened to 'make sense' of the data. What is noticed and how what is noticed is processed is a matter of such systems.

Implicit in what we have written above about what our respondents notice is the possibility/probability that their associates influence what it is that they notice. Sir Geoffrey Vickers talks of culture as a 'shared appreciative system' and we find the idea attractive. He goes on to mention that culture is a 'set of readinesses' to distinguish some aspects of situations rather than others, to classify them and value them in a particular way.[11] People who share a culture share a set of readinesses. Time and again in going through the transcripts we found respondents from the same company talking in very similar terms about their company and the environment within which it operated. Metal Box executives, for example, *appreciated*, paid attention to, were ready to notice, flexibility and a willingness to tolerate ambiguity in their managers:

What it does mean is that you can no longer have managers who are just good at their own unique professional discipline. If you are a production manager now, you've got to be infinitely more alert about the outside world, because it can obsolete you overnight.

We are looking for managers who can understand and work comfortably with that high level of change and flexibility. We are looking for managers, too, who don't see role in specialized terms. We want people to have worked in several different staff functions, several different line areas.

We're in a process of change. We're looking for a very high tolerance of ambiguity. We're looking for a capability to absorb a concept of continuous change and continuous improvement. That the world is never going to be like it was.

Reckitt and Colman executives appreciated (paid attention to, talked about) themselves as the decision makers, the small group at the heart of the company:

We have the Chief Executive in Committee. We study all the common strategic issues and strategic problems. We act as a management group, irrespective of geographical boundaries ... but Head Office is essentially very small.

We prefer to be a small organization, we think that we are more effective that way. John West has made substantial savings in the hierarchy of the organization. The tendency under his direction has been to move towards a more economic and more focused sort of hierarchy.

I'm not saying it's right, but it's consistent with our current organizational attitude of saying that we really want to have a very small corporate office.

Not only would Metal Box executives notice (and indeed actively seek out) evidence of flexibility and tolerance for ambiguity, not only would such attributes be foregrounded for them, but the act of framing such attributes implies a shared categorization of behaviour – a reading – common to them all. As at Metal Box, so at Reckitt and Colman, the shared appreciative system stimulates a readiness to look at things in terms of how they will affect the size and potential authority of the Head Office. Senior executives at Metal Box and at Reckitt and Colman, as elsewhere, talk to each other and in so doing create appreciative systems, readinesses to perceive and to respond in a particular manner. In turn these systems and readinesses serve to ensure that those party to them notice and process similar kinds of data. Thus what an executive reads is influenced by the vocabulary he or she brings to the event, a vocabulary, in turn influenced by mentors and colleagues.[12]

The Language of Managing

Some vocabularies are more general than others; some have a currency and an influence well beyond particular companies in particular settings. One of the appreciative systems that might be thought to inform the explanations and actions of our respondents is that which has been termed 'scientific management'. It is an appreciative system, a way of seeing the world and an explanation of it that has developed strongly in the twentieth century. This explanation holds that there are laws and principles which if discovered and followed would enable the enterprise to manipulate its environment. The procedures for rendering the world predictable and manipulable are akin to those used in the layman's understanding of 'proper' science and place a heavy emphasis upon rationality, precision, discipline, reliability, calculability and impersonality.[13] This explanation translates into specific attempts to structure response within an enterprise. For example, scientific managers hold that there should be clarity of objective, widely shared, there should be a hierarchy of responsibility with roles and authority clearly delineated, there should be a high degree of specialization into staff and line tasks, a limited span of control, and so on.

If scientific method does indeed delineate the most systematic exploitation of the links between explanation, experimentation and feedback (as many in the twentieth century would claim), perhaps it would not be surprising to find that many who would like to be thought of as running effective and systematic organizations would parallel scientific procedural controls in their explanations and their enterprises. A highly developed enterprise, from this perspective, would resemble a rigorous scientific experiment.[14] From business laws or principles, a clear and coherent vision would be developed and communicated which would be given flesh in a strategy which, in turn, would inform a cascading series of objectives. These objectives could be monitored to provide feedback against which the original strategy could be tested and, where necessary, revised. Finally, and the parallels with scientific endeavour in general are blindingly obvious, this evaluation and revision could be used to guide further refinements in specific objectives.

As we have indicated earlier, our respondents must be considered individually but none of them could be considered wholly and exclusively scientific managers. However influenced each may have been by the general vocabulary of science to which he was heir, none failed to wright it in his own fashion. To be sure some Chief Executives created structures and procedures that appeared to be primarily concerned with measurement and control. Indeed, some appeared to believe that the tighter the control the more calculable and predictable the results, so effort was expended in setting up and monitoring aspects of performance. Lord Hanson was as explicit about this as about every other aspect of his managing:

On the other hand, at the top of the tree, you have to be aware of all that's happening and have to be able to pick out those who are failing you, who are not up to their job.

The managers at Metal Box, on the other hand, appeared to be subject to less control, they were asked to experiment. They were invited to open their cages and stimulated to fly. Brian Smith and his colleagues talked of a structure and set of procedures that encouraged experimentation; one that acknowledged the possibility of failure. Behind these structures and procedures was a more or less explicit reading about how Metal Box could become more competitive: it should become less bureaucratic, less concerned with the protection of individual fiefdoms, and more flexible and innovative in its thinking and its actions. Stimulating individual managers to let go, to break out from their cages (in many cases seen to have been erected by the inhabitants) was perceived as a test of the reading: if managers are provided with a greater degree of freedom and responsibility, they and the organization will perform better.

Both examples, however, are misleading. Attempting to read our respondents using a general vocabulary, be it that of scientific management or any other, is not easy and is probably not worthwhile. Our data proved recalcitrant. The doing of managing is not necessarily a matter of either/or thinking; either one encourages freedom or one goes for calculability and control. Many of our respondents appeared to encourage freedom *and* to insist upon tight controls. Most set up structures which pushed accountability for results down the line. And most, at the same time, kept a sharp eye on what those with the accountability did. In Brian Smith's terms, many had commissioned destroyers in the last few years and mothballed the battleships, but many (including Brian Smith and colleagues) remained in strong radio contact with their fleet. In effect they signalled to the commanders of their individual ships, 'Yes, the command is yours but the battle plan is ours. We are monitoring you on our highly efficient radar. Please keep in touch.'

Our respondents no less than ourselves have to live with complexity and contradiction. As Simon points out the 'principles of administration ... are like proverbs, they occur in pairs. For almost every principle one can finds an equally plausible and contradictory principle'.[15] He seems to be suggesting that there are two sides to every argument and we have no trouble with that. But a reading that stresses that an enterprise works 'best' when the span of control is limited runs directly up against a reading that holds that it works 'best' when there are few levels. And this describes the essentially paradoxical nature of the doing of managing, although it still makes it no easier to analyse or describe.[16]

It is probable that some of our respondents have both wider and more complex vocabularies than others, thus enabling them to make multiple readings of their situations. It could be that they are able to switch from one explanation to another, emphasizing as they do, different aspects of their circumstances. We have no direct evidence that this is indeed the case, although we can surmise that it may be so given the differing perspectives advanced by various of our respondents. It does not follow, however, that those able to make many readings are able to act decisively or 'better' in the light of these readings. Starbuck and Milliken hold that:

The ambiguity and complexity of their worlds imply that perceivers may benefit by using multiple sensemaking frameworks to appraise events; but perceivers are more likely to act forcefully and effectively if they see things simply.[17]

This perhaps sounds like a case of being unable to see the wood for the trees – one of those tantalizing statements that makes us wish that we could manipulate our data so as to come to some sort of conclusion one way or another. Unfortunately, we are in no position either to refute or support this opinion. What we find described by our respondents, however, is an ability to do both and, again, it often seems simultaneous: that is, in 'using multiple sensemaking frameworks' to appraise events, they also *read* a simplified explanation which is necessary for action.[18]

Beliefs and Values ... Believing and Valuing

We have to be careful about the implications of the terms like 'reading' and 'explanation'. To be sure, we are claiming that the structures and the procedures that managers set up and sustain are reflections of their understanding of the world and are attempts to control and channel response. However, we are not claiming either that managers are necessarily aware of what they are doing as they do it, or that each and every action they take is a matter of calculation. Perhaps only exceptionally is a manager (or anyone else) conscious of making a reading and manipulating responses. We are not proposing that any of our respondents sat at his desk thinking about the principles of scientific management and then putting them into practice (although at some time in the past one or two of them may actually have done so). Nor are we suggesting that any of them sat with any of their immediate colleagues, carefully articulating a set of categories into which they would fit the behaviour of their subordinates. What we are proposing is that in their daily interactions our managers, no less than managers elsewhere, sustain appreciative systems or improvise readinesses which reflect their values and beliefs which, in turn, are likely to be influenced by and to influence received ideas about the doing of organizing. We hold that much of the doing of organizing is either a matter of running through a *script* or an instance of *improvisation*, and that both of these activities relate to readings which have reference to appreciative systems which are, in turn, reflections of deeply held beliefs and values. These readings, systems, readinesses, values and beliefs may be similar to ones which underpin scientific management, they may reflect other approaches and/or they may be a mishmash of individual experience and reflection. Whatever they are and whatever their origin, they may well have a profound influence upon the doing of organizing and the doing of organizing may well have a profound influence upon them.

Donald Hambrick and Gerard Brandon define a value as a broad and relatively enduring tendency to prefer certain states of affairs and a belief as a matter of knowledge or assumptions about future events.[19] Essentially, in their analysis, a value has to do with what is desired or desirable, whereas a belief has to do with what is thought to exist or, more usually, thought likely to happen. Values deal with what should be, beliefs with what is (or ought to be). However, we find it very difficult to make such distinctions in our material. For example, many of our respondents may well value materialism and believe that everyone works better if provided with incentive compensation. Facts, information, results may cause this belief to be shaken, even substantially revised or abandoned, without in any way affecting the pleasure any one of them would take in wealth and possessions. But we must stress that this example is merely conjectural. We scoured our data to find more substantial support, but our respondents speak a different language. They talk a lot about believing: indeed, they speak with much force and passion about what it is they believe. And it is from this that we infer some system of beliefs and evidence of values: demonstrations of believing and valuing.

Our respondents appear to hold a variety of beliefs and preferences, at least in so far as these are revealed in their comments to us.[20] Some, perhaps many of them, appear to rank rationality as a key value. Reason appears to permeate their accounts and explanations but few made explicit statements about it:

The Managing Directors of the companies, the senior managers, the general managers, have got to have some appreciation of financial expressions. They've got to be able to think of the activity in financial terms. We've never had a successful manager who had absolutely no financial language. He has to be able to converse, if necessary, in financial terms, because there is no other language common to all disciplines.

The financial controls are now fairly sophisticated. Everybody is on the same reporting system, method and timetable ... We know what our priority areas are ... it's decided that that product group is the one we want to go for and that message goes round the world.[21]

Several rate novelty highly and are explicit about it:

One of the strategic issues clearly now is organic growth. We need acquisitions but we need to innovate and get our growth rate, internally generated growth rate, going up faster.

There's a big stress now on innovation and creativity ... You can't just focus on optimizing returns on your core business. You have got to be creative in generating new business innovations.

I've started a number of processes in the last couple of years ... One of those was innovation, to try and see if we couldn't develop a more innovative, imaginative ... whatever. Innovation ... I don't like the word particularly ... We are saying 'Let's be more imaginative. Let's be more creative...'[22]

A few comment on or imply notions like loyalty and duty:

Total commitment – I've said before and I'm not alone, I've only ever had three loves in my life, Avon comes first, I'm afraid the family comes second and cricket third. I'm sure that most would say that that's the wrong order. Family ought to come first, then the company and then one's hobby. But I think a lot of us would put the company first.

He's unusual in the sense that he works 18 hours a day. It sounds a lot but I speak to him very regularly on the telephone in the United States at five o'clock in the morning his time. But that's nothing to him. He's all about the business and he works seven days a week. He's a very unusual man. You can't ever imitate that sort of thing, because it's unique. But he sets a fair pace. He doesn't expect anybody to be a carbon copy of him but his view is simple. We are here, we are paid high salaries, and we occupy very senior positions in a very large organization within the British industrial structure, and as such we've got to earn it. And if we think we can get here at nine o'clock in the morning and go home at five o'clock and clear off every weekend and forget it, that's not on. There's no way you can do that. It's very rare I leave here before eight o'clock at night, very rare...

I've never in our company come across politics ... I've never experienced a political situation, not on our Board and not underneath our Board. I suppose because we are very open in our government that it just hasn't been required. But I talk sometimes about loyalty and I express the rather quaint and perhaps eccentric view that loyalty has to be demonstrated downwards, but it shouldn't be relied upon, it should neither be sought nor felt necessary – upwards ... I suppose I am talking about loyalty to people rather than just to the company. So I say to our people, 'Show loyalty downwards, that's absolutely important – collective responsibility, but don't expect it upwards'.[23]

Many value relations with colleagues and employees:

The great majority of people with the proper motivation and hopefully with the proper leadership can do things which they on the whole never thought they were capable of.

I am a great believer at always looking to identify people coming up who will ultimately do the job better than you do it today. I think that is absolutely key. Never be afraid of the man who is going to do your job better than you do it.

You gradually get it into the shape you want. You obviously don't fire them. Or ask them to resign, or something like that. It takes time.

My belief is always in people, if the people are secure, if they like what they are doing and they know why they are doing what they are doing, and given the responsibility and challenge, they will deliver in 99 cases out of 100.

Our success is based upon a set of business principles established many years ago and which, although we occasionally forget them, we always come back to – they're the platform on which the business bases everything it does. One of them would be that you must give very high quality and the best possible value to customers and good service ... I think our relationship, what we call our partnership with our suppliers is the cornerstone of our success ... And we believe it's important to treat your staff well and motivate them. We have always believed it is important to have a satisfied, happy, well motivated, well paid staff.[24]

And most clearly value what, for some might be called power, and for others such as Barnard, executive responsibility – the control of people and situations, more often than not exercised with a 'light touch':

It's a process of encouraging people to do what they should be doing anyway. And if they are not enthused by that, then they are probably not quite the right people. And there's a bit of shifting out ... so it's an open door ... (best done) ... with a light touch and not with a heavy hand. Not least because this industry is still very short of skilled management at many levels and it would not be the right use of resource to disenchant the experienced people we have got. We have to build on that and guide along the route. Signpost the route rather than use a steamroller, because there is not a sufficient pool of talent to give rise to any other options anyway.

You give people a new sense of purpose and they feel that they are part of a larger whole and they are certainly in charge of their own businesses. We create an environment in which they can operate effectively. We leave the operation very much to them, although there is a great deal of cajoling and encouragement.

It's people skills and some people are born with it and some can be taught it, but not everybody has it. But at the end of the day, in this job, you have to impose your will on people. And if you can actually do that without them knowing that it's happening – then that's the ideal.

We now get raw data direct from the businesses and we are much better informed than we were before. That is mischievous, I think, having separate areas, sources of power around the world. At the end of the day, they have to come back here if it's anything that is important. But we do actually give all our businesses habitually a great deal of freedom. Once they have agreed their annual plan and we know what the game is, they are free to go about it.

We almost obsessively resist corporate dictat in all that we do. If we think that something is going to sound like a top-down corporate dictat, we generally don't do it if we can possibly avoid it. Not to the extent of allowing total *laissez-faire*. But it's 'Wouldn't it be a good idea if we did something, don't you think?' rather than, 'Well, we have decided that the best way to run the business is ...'

We want our people to believe that we are in control of the situation. We are in control of everything.[25]

Theorists attempt to distinguish between different values and integrate them into some overall system, in some form of hierarchy, such that certain values take precedence over others. They also debate such finer details of value-intensity and relative strength of different values.[26] Our data clearly do not allow us to make such claims and, indeed, we have no desire even to try. What we are seeking to demonstrate is that *believing and valuing* form the subtext for much of the action which occurs within enterprises. That is, whether one calls it perceptual filters, a hierarchy of values, a belief system, a 'set of readinesses' or, in Barnard's terms, the 'moral factor',[27] action is informed by a code of what is considered acceptable or appropriate behaviour. Certainly, there may be codes, overlapping codes, shared codes or even competing codes – within one individual as well as between individuals – and they may well change with time and situation. The point we wish to stress, though, is that there is some sense of codes of appropriate conduct underwriting our data, but these are known through *practice* rather than abstract conceptualization. They are demonstrated through the whole doing of managing. Thus the daily actions of senior managers in Lord Hanson's enterprise *appear* to be informed by a set of preferences which clearly value control, *appear* to be materialistic, *appear* to value rationality and duty whilst placing less value upon novelty and showing less regard for people as members of a system. The daily actions of senior managers in Metal Box *appear* to be informed by a set of preferences which value novelty, rationality and people with a lesser emphasis upon power and control, materialism and duty. This is not to say that novelty and people are not valued at Hanson nor that control is out of favour at Metal Box; it is simply to state that neither *appears*, from our data, to be as *salient* as those that we take to be the preferred modes.

What they believe will influence their particular doing of managing. To stay with our examples, if our analysis is correct (and remember it relates to a particular period of time), at Hanson routine interacting was (perhaps is) concerned with control, at Metal Box

with change, the new and the different. Scripts – patterns of behaviour run off without reflection – may embody both control and
novelty, but will favour one over the other. Improvisation – the
casting around for a precedent or referent that will enable someone to
deal with a circumstance for which no script appears to be immediately to hand – too will favour either control or novelty. The referents – the underlying beliefs – at Hanson and Metal Box may well
change over time, and/or a particular manager may find himself/
herself in conflict with them, none the less, at the time of enactment
all action – scripted or improvised – is informed by a preference for a
particular state of affairs. However difficult to discern in practice, it is
probably reasonable to assert that certain associations may be expected to exist between executives' beliefs and organizational attributes. And this is likely to affect the organization's competitive
actions, how decisions are made and by whom, what kind of
structure is put in place and who gets the jobs.

So by believing in particular ways of doing managing, demonstrating preferences for particular kinds of behaviours, it is possible to
infer codes of conduct which influence action. For example, some of
our respondents may appear to have strong materialistic values and
would be likely to support incentive schemes whether or not the
evidence revealed that they ensured greater effort and commitment.
Indeed strong values tenaciously pursued can surmount any amount
of evidence. In this mode a manager 'sees what he/she wants to see'
and 'hears what he/she wants to hear'. Thus, to return to our
example, the manager strong on materialism (but not as strong as the
person likely to exert a direct influence upon action) would tend to
notice or look for evidence that incentives increased effort and to
discount (or turn a blind eye to) evidence that did not support his/her
position. A manager strong on novelty would come to believe that
change was essential to the survival of any enterprise and would be
much less interested in evidence that suggested that stability was an
attribute of successful enterprises.

˙And, of course, once more it is not as simple as that. Our process
orientation alerts us to the fact that what any executive is capable of
achieving is highly dependent upon the responses of others. Thus
our highly materialistic executive is only likely to achieve satisfaction
of this particular value if others allow him/her the discretion to deploy
it. It is unusual for any executive, even a Chief Executive, to find
himself/herself in a situation in which it is possible to exercise
complete discretion. Some of our respondents clearly had more
discretion to act than had others, but even those with the most
individualistic of orientations appeared to be constrained to some

extent by what their colleagues were prepared to tolerate and/or support.[28]

The notion of process is, perhaps, most clearly demonstrated in the debates that many of our respondents appeared to be conducting around the issue of centralization versus decentralization. Virtually every one of them signalled a strong desire to distance themselves from their subordinate companies:

We still feel quite passionately that the right way to go is to encourage smaller business units, competent management, to do their own thing, and if they want a lot of help and they can show that it is justified, then the corporation will super-resource them.

My father would interfere with other managers and I think that I did not like that. And at a later date, I said that if ever I was in a position to control the firm, I would devise an organization where that is impossible. And it really is impossible in this organization to interfere with other people's business, provided they perform.

The group philosophy is very much one of decentralization. The managing directors of the individual businesses, being, as David Alliance describes them, the gaffers, are running their businesses, taking full responsibility and accountability for these businesses. The individual companies are run on a decentralized autonomous basis with as loose a control as possible consistent with the financial control which has to be exercised in order to make sure that we run the total business responsibly.

The Divisional Directors have enormous authority, because ... the chairman and myself haven't the time to be making decisions for them, and they must get on with it, and learn to stand on their own two feet, so to speak.

But we do actually give all of our businesses habitually a great deal of freedom. Once they have agreed their annual plan and we know what the game is, they are free to go about it.

A BTR type structure in which the operating groups operate. The centre here we keep small, as small a number of people as we can.[29]

Careful scrutiny of these quotes will confirm that most of them carry two messages: our companies are free to go ahead and operate *and* we, at the centre, control them. Some, as we have seen, are explicit about control:

I would say that they can get on with the job but they know damn well everything is being monitored.

And then we're going to go back and we're going to change the culture of the business. We're going to make everybody follow a certain pattern, a policy line that we're going to lay down. We are actually going to be a lot more active in that area, calling for standards to be improved. It's not going to happen in a week, it will take a year or two.

But we set the pattern. We set the standards, we make the demands. It is a very demanding standard and I don't hesitate to criticize somebody if something goes wrong. I don't hesitate to take the blame for them if it does go wrong, because that is a company decision. But on the other hand, if they have slipped up on something, then they know about it from me.[30]

It is perhaps useful to consider these quotes as examples of the kind of distinction it is necessary to draw between *operational authority* and *true authority*. Lawrence Mohr argues that the former applies to the delegated right to carry out certain assignments without close supervision – within, say, the guidelines provided by a plan and the intermittent oversight of superiors – and the latter term refers to 'ultimate' authority, the kind of authority that delegates and withdraws delegation.[31] As Sir David Alliance of Coats Viyella puts it: 'I don't believe there is anyone born that can know all the ramifications of a group's different companies in different countries round the world.' Thus, on the one hand, there is a move to cede as much operational authority as is necessary to run the overall company effectively and, on the part of the operating units, to wrest as much true authority as they can. What results is part independence (since no supervisor can possibly supervise everything) and part joint decision. In effect the centre says 'this far and no further' (where 'this far' may be quite a high degree of independence) and the subordinate companies may well say 'just this little bit farther'. Whether or not that little bit farther is ceded or willingly offered is a matter of the perceptions those with ultimate authority hold about particular people, values (the more democratic will see value in spreading participation), size and stage of development of the company. The Brian Smiths, Lord Hansons, Brian Beazers of this world choose to cede degrees of authority and choose to withdraw authority, but their choice is influenced by their perceptions of what is necessary, their perceptions of what can be delivered, and by the skills, competencies and perceptions of others including those attributed to their subordinates.

Whatever a manager wrights, therefore, is not necessarily – and certainly not always – wrighten in his/her own fair hand. To be sure it is shaped and fashioned by the beliefs held by that individual, but it is also to a greater or lesser degree constrained by the beliefs of others; some of whom are directly present in the situation, some whose ideas persist long after their death. Whatever is wrought, however, either in terms of structures, procedures or daily actions is an attempt to shape meaning and channel response.[32]

Response and Stimulus

As individuals, and particularly as managers, we take it that each of us spends a considerable proportion of our working day in attempting to structure the social world so that it remains or becomes relatively comfortable for us to inhabit; we want Tom, Dick or Mary to agree with us about the nature of the circumstances we find ourselves in and we want them to behave in a way which we can all take to be productive (or, at the very least, predictable). For the most part we do not wish to face every eventuality as if it were one off. Once we have determined how to structure events, once significant aspects of our interactive arrangements become mutually expected, we have the beginnings of a 'structure'. Such patterns tend to become objectified and to assume a 'reality' that appears to transcend any particular one of us (or group of us) and we, severally and individually, come to take ourselves to be subject to that which we, severally and individually, create and/or sustain.[33]

And this is very much what we find in our data where 'doings' are commonly shared and mutually constituted. Sticking with the Hanson group for our illustration, long ago and far away,[34] a set of principles and practices were developed which are still used to guide and control the businesses:

So, yes, I think certainly in my time with the company since '69 the policy has been absolutely unchanged and it arises I think very much from the family experience of James Hanson. His family business had gone back into the middle of the nineteenth century in the transport industry, which is very much a service related industry, very much an industry where you have to rely on the man running the transport depot from which the horses are pulling the cloth across the Pennines the following day to determine what the right price is, so you have to learn how to delegate, learn that every business you are in is effectively a marketing business rather than a manafacturing business ... And so that preparedness to delegate was very much endemic, if you like, in the Chairman's family.

Within Hanson, this preparedness manifests itself as:

Oh, it's a very simple structure. We believe in full delegation of authority to the management teams running the business. We want them to have the responsibility for running that business. We want them, therefore, to build confidence in their ability to solve their problems without referring and deferring to us, because to do so would be, as it were, to allow us to make the mistakes for them without them having to feel responsible for the future success of their business. We're heavily involved in a financial control sense with what they are at. We're concerned with motivation and incentives. We are concerned with the selection of successor management ... They (the general managers) are looked upon as having the task of performing better with the capital that they presently employ, coming to us to justify new capital that they might wish to invest in their businesses. They have no right to invest their capital in their business without our say-so, down to very small amounts, £500 in the UK, $1000 in the United States.[35] So that's effectively the cost of the free form management approach that we've adopted, and has really been left unchanged since 1965 when James Hanson became the Chairman of the company.

A common feature of all our accounts was the way in which our respondents were able to simplify the past; to strip it down to bare essentials and describe a particular key pattern of events and actions which helped to explain and guide understanding of the immediate present and the possible future. Working for Hanson is summed up in these few phrases, encapsulated in the story of the Chairman's family business. To the extent that these stories continue to be told, and to be believed, and to be unquestioned, to that extent will the interaction persist in the patterns of behaviour implied within the tale. A good Hanson company man or woman understands the myth and recreates it daily in his/her every action.[36]

The meaning of anything – a word, an action, a story – lies in the response to it. If Hanson managers accept the Chairman's definition of freedom and behave in line with it, then his meaning for the term has clearly prevailed. The doing of managing is a process of shaping and sustaining mutually expected response, of controlling shared meaning. The very notion of *an organization* implies relatively stable interaction among a fairly well-defined group of people who know, roughly, what to demand and expect of each other. In the beginning was chaos. In such a circumstance, organizing would be a matter of reducing the incidence of random response, of elaborating patterns of mutually expected response. Building and sustaining an enterprise is a matter of bringing people together who in an evolving dialectical fashion construct and reconstruct patterns of response such that mutual expectations are fulfilled. The role of the senior manager in seeking to bring this about, in seeking to reduce random response to minimum levels, in seeking, that is, to achieve an optimum degree of coordination, is crucial.

Achieving an optimum degree of coordination is a matter of structuring rather than simply structure, of process rather than simply procedures. Not that structures and procedures do not shape response; they clearly do. But structures and procedures must be continually sustained or revised. Stories may be told, explanations offered but different managers in different settings or the same managers at different times may well respond to them differently. Since the shaping of response is such an important aspect of the doing of managing, it may be worth examining in some detail how a particular effect occurs.

Consider the following passage. The speaker is Tony Mitchard, Chief Executive of Avon Rubber:

I remember in February 1982 having announced all these redundancies, being asked by the Union on the Friday before the Sunday when they were going to have a branch meeting if I would be prepared to go and address them and I said that of course I would, although some of the management were distinctly unhappy about it. So they said, 'Well, we'll have to raise it at the meeting, so could you sit by the telephone?' So I said 'yes' and it was a typical February morning, it was pouring with rain, and I wasn't feeling exactly on top of the world, and the telephone rang and on the other end was Eric Bates, who was chairman of the Union Branch and, incidentally, our branch in those days was the biggest single branch of the Transport and General Worker's Union in the West of England, which had been in existence for many years. Anyway, I got the telephone call, I got into my car and I drove over to the Assembly Hall at Melksham, which is a hall which, if quite a lot of people are prepared to stand up, holds about a thousand people. As I drew up, the leaders of the Union were there to meet me and asked me if I would get my message across in about 20 minutes. So I got up there on the stage, got the microphone and there was this mass of faces. I would think 90 per cent male, 10 per cent female, and many were standing. The meeting had already been going on for about an hour, so I stood up with the microphone and basically said to them, 'Look, I'm convinced that we can secure the future of this company but it does mean, I'm afraid, that we are going to have to do things that in our wildest nightmares we could never have imagined would be necessary and I'm going to have to ask for a reduction of about 600 jobs.' Anyway, I spoke, I suppose, for about 20 minutes and then answered a number of questions of which only a couple were hostile, all the others were very pertinent questions. Anyway, I must have been on the stage for about 50 minutes altogether and Eric Bates, who chaired this large meeting extremely well, he said, 'Well, that's it now, brothers and sisters. Mr Mitchard has been good enough to answer your questions.' So I said to them, 'Thank you very much for listening to me in the way that you have. All I will say to you again is that if we can grasp these nettles together, I feel sure that we can pull through.' Not that I was wholly convinced myself! Anyway I handed the microphone back to Eric Bates and as I was going down the steps from the stage, to go out the side door, I was suddenly aware of all this noise – applause, would you believe?

Now this response was not entirely predictable. How was it achieved and what can we learn about the shaping of response through examining this example? Odd though it may seem, we believe that we can best learn through comparing what happened in this draughty hall on this wet Sunday morning in February with experiments that occur in a psychologist's laboratory and with performances of plays in a theatre.[37]

What occurs in these settings is a presentation of a limited set of stimuli; none of the events encompasses 'reality' as it is fully experienced on a daily basis. Each is an abstraction, each is focused. The meeting in the Assembly Hall is not concerned with mundane aspects of working for Avon; it is highly specific. Similarly in the laboratory, the stimulus to be presented is highly specific; the experiment is set up to test a limited hypothesis. Theatres deal only with selected aspects of reality, they do not, and indeed cannot, truly reproduce a 'slice of life'. Furthermore, each event presents its respective stimuli for selected audiences. The theatre audience is not a random selection of those passing in front of its doors. It is made up of those who for some reason or another fancy a night out at the theatre. Judging from comments heard recently at The Theatre Royal, Bath, the reasons can range from an intense interest in the work of a particular playwright, company, director or actor, through a desire to be part of a playgoing group, to a seat as a refuge from a particularly wet evening. A variety of interests, but a selected variety. In a similar, perhaps more rigorous, fashion, an audience or set of subjects is selected for a psychological experiment. Indeed, subjects for psychological experimentation are often drawn from a very narrow population: students. If anything, the participants in particular enterprises are even more rigorously selected. Those in the Assembly Hall are all employees of Avon, those who have turned out are the ones who are concerned about the future of the company and the future of their jobs.

So we have select audiences for select performances: in each case, theatre, laboratory and enterprise. Furthermore, in each situation there is an individual or group of individuals who manage the presentation of the stimulus. In the theatre there is a whole gaggle of them: playwright, set designer, lighting director, casting director, producer, director, stage manager and so on. In the laboratory, the experimenter takes on a range of similar functions. He or she designs the experiment including the setting; great care is taken to exclude every stimulus but the one that is to be tested. As director, the experimenter sets it all up. In the Assembly Hall, the event was set up and managed by both the Union members and Tony Mitchard. We do not know precisely what was said before the Chief Executive took to the stage, but we can reasonably infer that some attempt to shape expectations had been done by the Union officers. Tony Mitchard had thought out what he was going to say and had geared himself to perform in a particular fashion. He was going to be direct and non-evasive, no doubt reckoning that this would be the best course of action, although by no means sure that it would be received well. Indeed, as he told us, 'some of the management here did not want me to do it ... he [one of the very senior managers] pleaded with me not to do it. And I said, "Well, if they want me to do it, I'm going to do it."'[38] Doing it, in this case, meant presenting the workforce with the facts (as the then Operations Director saw them) and outlining the solution – the loss of 600 jobs. It also meant presenting himself as a no-nonsense, honest, credible manager.[39]

As in the theatre and the laboratory, this involves the manager in predicting how the subjects (audience) will respond to the stimulus. In other words, just as the director of a play anticipates and attempts to bring about a particular effect, as the experimenter anticipates and attempts to bring about a particular response (having, of course, set up the experiment to 'prove' or 'disprove' a hypothesis), so the manager attempts to have his/her audience respond appropriately to his or her message. However surprised he may have been by the applause, Tony Mitchard anticipated that there was a chance that they would respond positively if he presented the facts directly to them, otherwise he would not have agreed to go to the meeting. He structured what he had to say in this belief. Furthermore, like the theatre director, the manager attempts to read the audience to see how the message is being or has been received. Tony Mitchard knew that he was likely to be successful when the questions that he received were 'mostly very sensible'. If there is no dominant response, if the audience is confused as to how it should respond, then the manager, just like the cast and the director in the theatre, may have a flop on his/her hands. As in the enterprise and the theatre so in the laboratory; if there is no dominant response or the dominant response is different to the one anticipated, then the experimenter has 'failed', something has 'gone wrong', the experiment may have been badly designed. On occasion, however, flops can be transformed, experiments which go wrong can produce insight, and managers who fail to sense a particular response can learn from the event. Flops and mistakes are as much attributions as are notions of getting it right and success, and, as such, are equally subject to revision: today's mistake or failure may be tomorrow's success. At the very least, error – a matter of social invalidation – may provide an opportunity for learning.

Again we must stress the interactive nature of such events, be they in the theatre, the laboratory or, as in this case, an assembly hall. In each of the settings, the audience plays a part in shaping the meaning of the event. It may know that it is an audience. If so, it becomes an audience to itself. In the theatre, many are aware that they are to be exposed to certain patterns of behaviour to which they are expected to respond. They know their responses will affect the performers (the other performers – those on the stage) and they know that their responses will be examined by the director/cast and by themselves. In the interval, they talk to themselves, they articulate their responses, give feedback to themselves and to each other: 'What do you think of it so far?' 'It's all terribly RSC, isn't it?' These interim responses go on to have an effect upon the next act. As in the theatre so in the laboratory. Participants know they are subjects and may well anticipate the kind of behaviour desired of them – going along with it or not as the mood takes them. Something of the same occurs when 'management' attempts to 'get its message across'; elaborate structures and procedures may well be set up, heightening the awareness of employees that they are audience to this presentation and, in effect, inviting them to play their part wholeheartedly but at the same time the effort may do little more than cast the employees in the role of critics. Mitchard's audience heard him in silence; there was no booing, no barracking, no foot stamping. Effectively they were either cast into this role by their leaders as part of the management of the message, or they cast themselves into attentiveness and silence, or Tony Mitchard's performance cast them into silence (or, of course, some admixture of all three performances). It could well have been very different. As in the theatre, claques and cliques could have disrupted the performance and contributed to the shaping of a very different response on the part of both the work-force and the management.

Both the director in the theatre and the experimenter in the laboratory seek to avoid flops and failures. They do so by seeking to concentrate the minds of their respective audiences/subjects upon selected stimuli. An attempt to reduce randomness of response is made by seeking to deprive audiences/subjects of alternative sources of stimulation and, thus, alternative modes of response. Great efforts are made to protect both audience members and experimental subjects from irrelevant stimulation. Watching a play involves going to a special kind of building, milling about in a foyer with other like-minded souls, entering a carefully decorated space, sitting in seats which, although reasonably comfortable are not excessively so, thus reducing the possibility of dozing off, watching a specially lit stage in relative darkness and relative silence.[40] Everyone is expected to concentrate and all the signals proclaim: 'You are now in for something really special.' Taking part in an experiment has something of the same quality. The setting is bare, but unusually so. It is clearly not the kind of setting in which one would normally find oneself. It is stripped of all stimulation that may interfere with the experiment. It is a special place: a laboratory; somewhere where scientists test things out. You are in the company of like-minded souls (there, no doubt, for the fee), and you are about to be involved in something special, something different. Taking employees away from the line or the office to participate in a special meeting, to listen to the Managing Director or the Chairman, has something of the same quality. In the present instance, the fact that the Chief Executive was prepared to attend a Union meeting and speak directly to the labour force signalled to all involved that this was indeed an unusual and special event.[41] In the theatre, the laboratory and the management conference (or extraordinary meeting), the setting and the separating off of the experience from everyday routine serve to heighten responsiveness.

In effect what the theatre director, the laboratory scientist and the manager are up to is an exercise in sensory deprivation. Each, in his/her own manner, selects the kind of response that he or she wants and attempts to achieve it by focusing upon the stimulus that may well produce that response. In the case of the example from Avon, simply being there, demonstrating his willingness to talk, focused attention on Mitchard's message. He presented a single stark scenario and a single solution to the problem that he outlined. In highlighting this we do not wish to imply that his behaviour was manipulative, that he set out to deceive his audience or put one over them. He them the facts as he saw them and trusted that they would accept his message. At this stage, all we are interested in establishing is that the absence of any other stimulation enhanced the impact of his presentation. Whatever discussion there was going to be was concentrated upon his presentation of the problem and his solution to it. But also their response shaped his response.

I think this was one of the most important experiences of my life because not only did it put some more steel in my spine, it certainly indicated that if you are prepared in the most direct way to tell people the facts of life, you will not only get a fair hearing, but the majority will support you.[42]

Randomness or perversity of response is reduced by depriving the audience of alternative modes of stimulation and, thus, of response. Perhaps it is not surprising that managers have begun to borrow ideas from the theatre; it has a long tradition of shaping response. Theatre directors and actors know what kind of stimulus produces what kind of response; they can make audiences laugh and cry. They can, by careful positioning of the actors and careful setting of the lights, cause the audience to focus on a very narrow aspect of the performance. In a sense, such a staging is echoed in the cinema where the close-up eliminates the irrelevant; and in the company video or the Chairperson's address, where the lights isolate the leader whilst the text on the screen picks out the essence of his/her message. And here, in our example, the bare stage, the rain bucketing down, the serious demeanour of the supporting cast of Union officials, the simple statement of the issue by the Chief Executive concentrated minds wonderfully.

It can, of course, go wrong. The audience, or part of it, can focus upon the irrelevant. Groucho Marx illustrates this point well in his response to marks upon Julie Harris' legs in a stage performance of *I Am A Camera*; 'At first we thought this had something to do with the part and we waited for these scratches to come to life. But ... it was never mentioned in the play and we finally came to the conclusion that either she had been shaving too close or she'd been kicked around in the dressing room by her boyfriend.'[43] The Chairperson can deliver his/her message unaware that the slides are upside down on the screen behind him or that one of his colleagues on the platform has fallen asleep. Random response can never be entirely eliminated, but it can be controlled to a degree and the director of a theatre, the laboratory scientist and the manager are all in the business of response prediction and response control.

This extended analogy between theatre, laboratory and company can lead to a number of conclusions, all of which are important to the case we are seeking to outline in this chapter. Neither the theatre nor the laboratory nor the special management event is similar to ordinary everyday interaction. Each select what they take to be stimuli from other situations and circumstances and place them in quite different situations and circumstances. They do not in so doing *isolate* stimuli, they simply place them in another equally complex stimulus configuration – a configuration which is designed to heighten response. Theatres, laboratories, art galleries, cinemas, classrooms, courts, palaces, assembly hall meetings, management conferences may be seen as events or settings which are designed to or likely to heighten excitation, to put the audience into a state of readiness to receive a message. As a consequence, all of them ordinarily result in the dominance of a single response or a small group of responses. The setting – the lights, the music, the heightened speech in the case of the theatre and, increasingly, of the management conference, the bare walls, the austerity, the white coats, the scientific talk in the case of the laboratory – produces a piling-up effect that focuses and shapes response. Each seeks to reduce the potential randomness of response; each seeks to signal what is to be taken as the appropriate response. And this, of course, is what organizing is about; organizing is about inculcating appropriate behaviour; organizing is about setting up and sustaining a *culture* that renders collective activity relatively predictable. Tony Mitchard's meeting is an attempt (a highly successful attempt, it has to be said) to constrain response, but in and of itself it illustrates a culture in which workers are conditioned (or if you prefer less tendentious phrasing, are prepared) to accept the authority of the Chief Executive, are conditioned/prepared to listen, are conditioned/prepared to behave as though the interests of the shareholders are paramount, and so on. In other words, they operate within a culture – a set of readinesses to respond in a common fashion, a set of directions for behaviour – of which this extraordinary meeting is but one manifestation. Each of our respondents is in the business of creating and sustaining such cultures. To understand this aspect of the doing of organizing we need to spell out the kind of assumptions which underpin it.

Containing Random Response

Perhaps the most basic assumption of the many that we have made in writing the last few paragraphs is the one that holds that in the absence of channelling, response is likely to be random. This is decidedly the position of Morse Peckham, but we are less keen since we take it that few responses can be completely random; virtually every way that we respond is informed by some experience and some learning. We agree with his assertion that for human beings the world consists of signs and that it is impossible for us to consider any aspect of it, including ourselves, from a position that does not depend upon signs; we cannot take a metasemiotic stance to what we perceive or to what we do. The various attempts to define our relation to the world, including all that we have written so far, are but words. They are verbal behaviour and thus implicitly normative. In effect, all that we have written (and all that we will write), is an attempt to have our explanation prevail; it says this (or that) is the way everyone *ought* to see and to respond to the world. Whether or not these oughts are acceptable oughts is a matter of social validation. In the final analysis, all attempts to determine what science is, what art is, what managing or organizing consists of, are based upon what is *accepted* as science, art or managing by those who are taken to be the best judges. In the present case, our responses to the data that we collected will be weighed not against some universal standard of truth, but against what others, our readers and critics judge to be appropriate.

What is taken to be appropriate, therefore, is not something that is genetically transmitted. Rather it is something that is learned and, frequently, something that is taught. In a formal teaching situation the student is encouraged to respond. Any response is welcome initially, but the random response is generated, only then to be selected and shaped by the teacher. Learning is a matter of interplay between random and shaped response. Human beings can and do both respond randomly and select and validate one of the random responses. Thus innovation is always a possibility. Less so in circumstances where the definition of what is appropriate is strong, where channelling of response is continuous, where, that is, control is effective. The Hanson corporation, it will be recalled, established and maintained a structure for its organization and a set of procedures which constantly reiterate the required response. Hanson's is not a one-off announcement of intent, it is a shaping of response that is repeated frequently and in many different forms. In every aspect of organizing, subordinate managers are reminded of the desired response. They know and are advised by every means possible of both the width of their responsibility, the depth of their accountability and the limits of their authority. Thus the structure, with its separate line for reporting financial results and its absence of 'barons' on the main board, signals at one and the same time that the individual managing directors are the ones who must come up with the plans for their own enterprises but, equally, that they are under constant surveillance. What is more, the procedures for capital expenditure signal that, whatever else they are free to do they are not free to spend what is taken to be the corporation's money. The response that James Hanson wants from his managers is clear: 'We want them to have the responsibility for running that business. We want them, therefore, to build confidence in their own ability to solve their own problems without referring and deferring to us, because to do so would be, as it were, to allow us to make the mistakes for them without them having

to feel responsible for the future success of their business.' The
desired response is channelled by structures and procedures and by
incentives: 'You see, we motivate them – and I mention motivation
as a very important part of the role – each business has a separate
incentive plan devised each year which is set up to improve profits on
the one hand and return on capital on the other, which hopefully
directs the management to what we think is important.' *To what we
think is important.* A clear unequivocal and, given the frameworks out
of which senior managers at Hanson are operating, wholly
appropriate attempt to shape and control response.

What Hanson senior executives do, and what many others do with
a greater or lesser degree of success, is to heighten the possibility of a
desired response on a daily rather than an occasional basis. Through
their procedures and structures, their surveillance and their communications, they constantly reiterate their general expectations to their
subordinate managers. Reiteration is necessary to establish and
maintain a pattern of response. Everywhere there are signs, indicators of appropriate readinesses which are taken as instructions for
behaviour. These signs constitute the *culture* of the organization, their
repetition an embodiment of the principle of cultural redundancy:[44]

I would spend at least one day a week, including a half day on Saturday, in
the stores with goods and with the customers, actually getting the feel as to
what is happening and why it's happening. So that's about twenty per cent of
my week. Then I would spend certainly one day a week with our suppliers,
so that's another twenty per cent ... because at the end of the day we are as
good as they are – it's a partnership. And in both cases you are listening and
watching and hearing what people have to say.

We are the centre but we try very hard not to have that concept. Basically the
organization itself is so mobile, we don't have organization charts for
example, we don't have an organization manual. We have all sorts of people
who have got split responsibilities, different bosses, and we've got people
pulled into project teams all the time. People working under chairmanship of
others who might be more junior than they are in the organization in grade
terms. We have a fair amount of that going on.

One of the reasons we quite deliberately avoided setting up a bureaucracy at
the centre was that there was a danger that if I said, 'This is what your job is.
This is what we want you to do', if we had set up a control section at the
centre, they wouldn't actually have believed it. I deliberately moved into this
office a year ago ... to make it clear that I wasn't involved in the day-to-day
work any more ... as a gesture, if you like, a symbol, I just moved upstairs.[45]

Culture

A great deal has been written lately about culture. Some of our respondents used the term themselves, not necessarily in the sense that we have used it above. In line with a generation of interactionists, and acknowledging the influence of others such as Peckham and Barnard, together with our own struggle to infer from beliefs some code of values or appropriate conduct, we take culture to be a matter of signs and signals through which patterns of behaviour are controlled over time. We take it that human beings have very little of their behaviour genetically transmitted, therefore what is to be passed on is transmitted and sustained by culture. Human beings initiate, learn and maintain behaviour through the manipulation of signs and symbols. To establish a particular pattern of response, a strong culture, in an enterprise as anywhere else, is to control performance through 'semiotic redundancy systems'. To succeed, that is, in establishing a shared set of readinesses to respond in predictable and acceptable ways.

The beginnings of the channelling of response are observable in the situation in the Assembly Hall that we have used to illustrate this chapter. The Chief Executive asserts that the world is such and such a shape and that, therefore, a particular course of action has to be followed. His message is appreciated, his audience is successfully cast into generally agreeing with his diagnosis and his solution. He cannot and does not leave it there. Cannot because the memory of what he has to say will not necessarily persist (dramatic though his speech may have been). Does not because his general message needs to be translated into the shaping of specific responses. He recognizes that reiteration is necessary if he is to be successful in bringing about a particular response. Thus the message that he wishes to transmit is reinforced in every action he and his managers take: productivity must go up and costs must be reduced. Thus numbers of workers must go down and practices long established such as tea breaks and washing up breaks must be stopped. Every day in every way the desired response is shaped and sustained.[46]

Likewise at Metal Box, the input to change was relentless. It was not simply a case of redefining all the subsidiaries as frigates and leaving them to set off for the horizon, it was backed up in every possible way and at every possible point. Indeed, they even talked about 'experiments' to try to reinforce the message; and 'retraining thinking programmes' to 'get people clear as to what they have to achieve'; developing a team incentive scheme which the team must apportion individually – 'it makes people think what their real targets are. The bonus is generated by the operating results of the business ... (but) individual performance is judged against these other tasks which are not usually quantified, they are subjective – like strategic objectives rather than today's operating objectives. But they are the issues that determine whether a company is moving forward.' Several respondents describe this as 'like water dripping'; the constant reiteration of 'instructions for behaviour' by which learned behaviour is maintained and made reliable.

In effect, each of these examples is a way of reminding people that this is the desired response at the point where that response is desired. If managers want to effectively channel response, they must constantly reiterate their message and, on occasion, be prepared to enforce it. Force is the ultimate sanction for securing or maintaining a particular response. Those who cannot or will not accept the message, those who are manifestly oddballs or misfits and more particularly those who actively work against the inculcation of a particular response will be dismissed. Such data are implicit rather than explicit in the comments made by our respondents, but there is no doubt that 'letting people go' is a strategy for sustaining a particular response. For example, one of Brian Beazer's 'three rules' of taking over a company is: 'that any changes you are going to make in an organization, you should make immediately you acquire it. If you are going to get rid of people, you need to do it immediately so that you can say to the rest of the staff, "Fine, that's it, you are all now in a secure job and employment and environment, providing you perform." And that at least removes the uncertainty.'

Such men (and women) that have to be released, are those who are strongly identified with a particular system of cultural redundancy. Thus, for example, a group of senior managers may be seen as strong promoters of the kind of relationship between themselves and the work-force that emphasizes a particular form of bargaining. One that signals, 'Yes, we will go through the rituals, we will each threaten the other, but in the end nothing very much will change and a suitable compromise willl be found.' Their structures, systems and actions, if consistent with their beliefs, would be such that everyone knew what was expected. A take-over of this company, or the assumption of the role of Chief Executive by someone determined to, say, raise productivity, would signal a period of conflict which would, ultimately, be resolved by force. The old system of redundancies verbal and non-verbal would need to be replaced with a new one. Radically opposed directions for behaviour (cultures) could not exist in parallel and one would have to go. Either those who persisted in attempting to sustain the old or, perhaps, those who attempted to bring in the new would have to go. To be successful, the new management would have to remove all signs that pertained to the old culture. In effect they would have to indulge in 'cultural vandalism'.[47] Take-overs and acquisitions and, on occasion, succession are often marked by periods of extraordinary turmoil; periods in which old meanings, old readinesses are attacked and new meanings elaborated and tested, underpinned by a set of beliefs or codes of appropriate conduct.[48]

Celebrating Randomness

As some of our respondents pointed out, establishing and sustaining a response, maintaining and elaborating a culture is by no means easy. All cultures are threatened with disintegration, with undermining, with impoverishment. Culture channels behaviour through time, but even the most tightly controlled culture admits of some deviance. Morse Peckham sees this as 'the fundamental condition of human behaviour'. To the degree to which any behaviour pattern is poorly transmitted, 'to that degree there will be a spread of deviancy from the culturally defined norm'. Given that next to nothing is known about the doing of managing at a senior level and that what is taught appears to be related to that which occurs on the ground (thus providing only the weakest set of readinesses to the would-be senior executive), it is hardly surprising that the 'delta effect' is great. Managers lacking clear direction are condemned to innovate.[49] On the other hand it is possible to argue that there is an optimum level of deviance (however difficult it may be in practice to discover what this is). A considerable degree of consistency of behaviour is important to the survival of the enterprise, but so is an incidence of innovation, of random response, of deviance. The theory of evolution can be held to suggest that in any given population there are those who are perfectly adapted, those who are well integrated in the interactional behaviour of their society, enterprise or whatever and those who are less well adapted: the oddballs, the alienated, the misfits. When, however, the situation to which a group is highly adapted undergoes a significant change, the best adapted go under simply *because* they are so well integrated to the old order. The survivors are likely to be drawn from the ranks of those who did not fit the previous conditions, some of whom may well find a better fit in the changed circumstances. A strong culture, one which successfully integrates everyone, assuming that it could be created, let alone sustained, may be one that would ensure the demise of the enterprise; the skill of some of our respondents lay in sustaining a culture with just the right degree of imperfection, in keeping some of the oddballs, sustaining some of the misfits, encouraging a degree of alienation.[50]

And in Conclusion ...

In concluding this chapter, we need to spell out some of its implications. Our argument is that culture controls behaviour and that culture consists of a series of signals – semiotic redundancy systems.[51] Such signals are both a part of and an attempt to predispose us to respond appropriately. Managers (or any-one else, for that matter) seeking to shape the responses of colleagues and/or superiors, peers, subordinates, customers, suppliers – whoever – do so primarily through words. Talk, talk, talk. They (like the rest of us) talk in order to effect some control over their environment (and we may be part of that environment just as they may be part of ours); they wish us to respond in line with their plans and their intentions and, accordingly, present us with certain signs – verbal and/or non-verbal. Control depends upon the meanings attributed to these signs; smooth interaction depends upon each of us reading the signs in a similar fashion, depends upon each one of us accepting the fiction that meaning is immanent. But it is not, it is ascribed. Much of the time, however, many of us sustain the fiction. We collude one with another in pretending that the meaning inheres somewhere outside our good selves; that 'the truth' is discoverable rather than something that is created intersubjectively.[52] It's a nice pretence, it saves face and it reduces the incidence of open conflict but, in the final analysis (which we rarely wish to reveal, let alone invoke) victory goes not necessarily to the executive with the better explanation (most plausible) but to the one who has the bigger stick. There is no metasemiotic ground upon which we can stand to judge the value of particular fictions or readings. For some, the only way of asserting an appropriate response is force: either you accept my definitions or you leave. Force may certainly increase conformity and reduce deviance, but such behaviour does not necessarily contribute to survival. Few, if any, of our respondents saw any value in resorting to force; on the contrary a few delighted in alternative fictions, exploited cultural incoherence and appeared to positively value instability. Others, perhaps the majority, appeared to be the kind of manager who sought to shape response, sought some stability, some predictability and yet tried to remain open to new readings, new, perhaps more promising, fictions. Pragmatists, perhaps?[53]

3
The Doing of Leading

As elsewhere in this book, we take it that the measure of any piece of behaviour is the response to it: following is the measure of leading, and leading the measure of following. Neither makes any sense in the absence of its effects. We take it to be crazy to assert, as some do, that the leader did a brilliant job but was let down by his/her followers; a point neatly highlighted by Brecht in his comments on the East German regime:

> After the uprising of the 17th June
> The secretary of the Writers' Union
> Had leaflets distributed in the Stalinallee
> Stating that the people had forfeited the confidence of the government
> And could win it back only
> By redoubled efforts. Would it not be easier in that case for the government
> To dissolve the people
> And elect another?

It would be equally crazy to claim that the following was spot on, but the leading was inadequate. We take some particular activity to be an example of good leading by *the followers* playing their parts; a good piece of following is known by a *leader* playing his or her part. This truth we take to be simple and self evident.[1] Acceptance of it, of course, implies that leading/following is not simply a matter of individuals and roles, but also an instance of process. Acceptance ensures that none of us is likely to be wholly satisfied with the fashionable and romantic simplification which holds that a single charismatic individual can, alone, work wonders for an enterprise.[2]

This chapter, therefore, will not be concerned with roles, but with process and will focus upon that which occurs *between* people rather than upon heroes, villains and fools. We intend to take our respondents seriously when they claim, as many of them do, that they are but part of a senior management group, at best first amongst equals.

This is not to deny, however, that some of them, some of the time, attribute and have attributed to them almost superhuman powers whereby they take others to be or are taken themselves to be the one and only cause of wonderful events. Occasionally our respondents even discern these qualities in themselves. We shall have occasion to comment upon such attributions later.[3]

No organization can persist without the willingness of persons to contribute their individual efforts to the system. The doing of leading, particularly at the most senior levels, is about securing that personal, individual contribution. The previous chapter was concerned with general notions of creating and shaping response, this one addresses issues of incentive, inducement, individual and shared leadership, talk, trust, dancing, marksmanship, improvising, creating, imagining and consensus, with a mention of Spinoza and a brief disquisition on the behaviour of chickens.

There is little that is original in our first theme. It was quietly fingered out by Barnard many years ago in his thoughts upon 'securing essential services from individuals':

Membership, nominal adherence, is merely the starting point: and the minimum contributions which can be conceived as enabling retention of such connection would generally be insufficient for the survival of active or productive organization. Hence every church, every government, every important organization has to intensify or multiply the contributions which its members will make above the level or volume which would occur if no such effort were made. Thus churches must strengthen the faith, secure compliance by public and private acknowledgements of faith or devotion, and secure material contributions from their members. Governments are concerned with increasing the quality of the citizenry – promoting national solidarity, loyalty, patriotism, discipline and competence. Other organizations are similarly occupied in securing loyalty, reliability, responsibility, enthusiasm, quality of efforts, output. In short, every organization to survive must deliberately attend to the maintenance and growth of its authority to do the things necessary for coordination, effectiveness, and efficiency. This depends ... upon its appeal to persons who are already related to the organization.[4]

Barnard and quite a number of our respondents hold that the energy of the organization comes from individuals who yield it because of incentives of one kind or another. 'The individual,' he writes, 'is always the basic strategic factor in organization. Regardless of his history or his obligations he must be induced to cooperate, or there can be no cooperation.' It follows that it is individual motives which determine the success of any enterprise; if individuals do not

feel that they, individually, are getting anything out of the association, they will put less and less into it. Hence incentives and
inducements of one kind or another appear to be fundamental to the
doing of leading. As Brian Beazer summed it up:

People want to be rewarded for their own efforts, ingenuity, integrity and
ability. The idea that mankind will slave for the common good, it may exist,
but ... I've rarely seen it.

Some of our respondents were convinced of the need to provide
material incentives (money, cars, medical insurance, shares, housing
benefit, etc.).[5] One or two companies did not see material reward as
the way to stimulate effort in senior executives: 'We have never
wanted to motivate through money',[6] others regarded such incentives as ineffective beyond a certain level. The trick, of course, is in
recognizing that 'certain level'.

Beyond this level, however (and, for some, well below it), other
non-material personal inducements appeared to be important in
securing commitment to the enterprise. Standing out as reasons why
the executives we talked to stayed with their enterprises were issues
of power, personal fulfilment and what we can only term the
pleasures of associating with each other or collegiality. Working at
senior level for Glynwed, Beazer, Avon or wherever afforded our
respondents, above all, opportunities to influence events and to
shape the destiny of their enterprises. Most gave the impression of
enjoying these opportunities and of relishing the demands made
upon them.

Who Shapes Whom?

Some take it that it is up to the Chief Executive Officer to shape the
enterprise. No doubt there are occasions when this is so, when the
strong leader succeeds in telling others what to do. Some of our
respondents, some of the time (including those who also talk about
consensus) appear to hold that leading is not so much a matter of
sharing ideas but of being *inspired* by the charismatic individual. It is
important to note that they (and we) talk of *individuals*; organizations
are not considered charismatic, nor are teams, it is individuals who
lift ordinary people to extraordinary heights:

I think that Tony was the new broom and he brought a renewed energy.
Always fairly energetic anyway, the moment he had the reins he brought his

own personality to bear on the company. Tony brought this new dynamic approach – he's made mistakes, of course, we all do – but the thing that's respected right across the group is that there's dynamism, enormous energy, immediate, sometimes almost too immediate decisions but people would sooner have a decision that is wrong than no decision, so enormous following.

The truth is that there are just people who are marvellous at it, outstanding ... You'd follow them anywhere. You're not quite sure why but you would. And you can go a long, long way on charisma and the ability to motivate the troops and carry them with you in your policies, there's no question about that.

I think his quiet confidence and his ability to instil confidence in everybody around him. He can convince people that things are achievable that on first sight may appear not to be. I think that is his greatest ability and to be able to talk to people and ... lead by example. By the fact that he has proven to all of us that he knows the way and the way things should be done.[7]

Again we wish to stress that we know such people by their effects – charisma lies in response, not in intent. None of us can take to the corridors today determined to be charismatic. As Robert House puts it: 'Charismatic leaders are those who have charismatic effects on their followers to an unusually high degree.' These effects are seen in: follower trust in the correctness of the leader's beliefs, a similarity of follower's beliefs to those of the leader, unquestioning acceptance of the leader, affection for the leader, willing obedience to the leader, identification with and emulation of the leader, emotional involvement of the follower in the mission, heightened goals of the follower, and a feeling on the part of followers that they will be able to accomplish whatever is demanded of them providing they have the support of the leader.[8]

Although neither House's theory nor our research addresses the issue directly, it is not difficult to argue that the kind of responses that we have outlined implies the *dependence* of followers on leaders. Following such a line implies that independence would be rare in organizations where charisma is attributed to the leader and that interdependence would be very much a matter of following in the leader's footsteps. Such a conclusion falls too easily into either/or thinking: either one has a charismatic leader or one has interdependent, shared leadership. Our data suggest that such thinking is simplistic. Some of our respondents reported charismatic *and* interdependent relations:

We (colleagues) don't overlap and we can't do a lot for each other because we do live in our own world, but the attitudes which you have gathered from me this morning, the work ethic, the obsession with growth and results, is exactly the same. It is infectious you see. It comes from Gareth. We are what we are because we respond to him. I mean he rang our chimes and together we did it.[9]

Those who worked for Metal Box, Coats Viyella or Hanson, no less than those who worked for many of the other enterprises we studied, enjoyed inspired leading, but this should not be taken to imply that as followers they were submissive or craven, victims of some kind of corporate Svengali. Charismatic leaders were seen to perform an essential function for the organization; they were hailed as the person who made the difference, pulled it all together, made us what we are today ... They were taken to have played a crucial role in creating a vision and setting the style for the enterprise, but they were not taken to have done the managing or the leading on their own:

We are all looking for the Messiah! And I actually believe that the Messiah is within us all – within the team not within the individual.[10]

Taking on all comers alone was rarely commented upon by our Chief Executives. Many saw their activity as a matter of teamwork, of securing commitment by widening participation in decision making and a matter of stimulating and reconciling differences rather than imposing views upon others. Generally they appeared to feel uncomfortable with notions of force and compliance, at least when applied to their relations with immediate colleagues:

One generally shuns the coercive label like the plague, takes pains to deny that he is bribing others when he offers them inducements, and represents himself as a persuader – if possible someone using rational persuasion.[11]

Issuing formal instructions was not seen by our respondents as the way to secure essential effort, other than in the most extraordinary of circumstances and only then when sanctioned by those subject to them.

I very rarely have to say, 'That's what we are going to do.' They all think in terms of Glynwed ... generally they participate and we will come to a conclusion as a Board without there having to be a single-minded decision taken by me. That is very rare. That style goes down the organization. So we have teams of people all working together, knowing what they have to achieve and trying to identify how to achieve it. Autocratic management is not a style which is often successful.[12]

Our respondents were clear that, for the most part, shaping the organization was a collective responsibility. Those we talked to, almost to a man, saw their work as team work; stressed that decisions were jointly arrived at and jointly implemented. It appeared clear to them that no single manager could formulate, define/redefine, break into details and decide on the innumerable and simultaneous and progressive actions that are the 'stream of syntheses' constituting purpose of action. The responsibility must be shared; if, as Barnard asserts, 'responsibility for abstract, generalizing, prospective, long-run decision is delegated *up* the line,' and 'responsibility for definition, action, remains always at the base where the authority for effort resides'; if, that is, there is a need for 'up-and-down-the-line coordination', then some group or other must become the focus, must interpret what is going on in and outside the organization and determine, broadly, what action needs to be taken.

The team does value that it is a team. I don't think that we are a bunch of individuals ... There are (of course) political situations, by which I mean that there are some people who are trying to advance their own causes and trying to get support for those. That does happen. But I think we are aware of them and give them as much currency as they are worth and no more.

We formed the Lucas Executive and then forced that group to tell each other the truth. We'd got to try to bury – to destroy the politics by having that sort of requirement that people should be outspoken and share their problems as well as their opportunities.

We've always kept a very small, tight acquisition team. I was reading somewhere that at some of the meetings of the Guinness people, they had about twenty people sitting round the table. We've never had more than six people, ever, sitting round this table, and usually about four of us. That was another feature that I would say in BTR was rather important, that we had worked together for 26 years. We knew what each of us was strongest at and we didn't bother to re-explore those avenues. And that saves a lot of time.

We are interchangeable. Several of us would feel that we could do several other people's jobs. And we have worked together for a long time. It makes a big difference. And we are unpolitical in relation to one another. We are not power seeking ourselves which leads to politics and we are not insecure which is another thing which leads to politics. Not insecure about our jobs ... we are a very close team at the centre.

After four or five years one becomes conscious that you are achieving a lot and you are starting to work as a team. It's taken you a long time to get a shared common purpose and when you've got it you can delegate between yourselves the actions to achieve that common purpose.[13]

Our respondents acknowledged that they had disagreements, even that they had serious rows, but their sense of collegiality or community – as, in most cases, no more than a handful of executives – overcame most of the problems. If, as Barnard maintains, the function of the executive is to facilitate the 'syntheses in concrete action', then those who do the synthesizing are those who display the differences.[14] There is no ducking it, harmony will not always prevail; men and women will differ about what steps ought to be performed and will fight to have their patterns prevail; successful *executive* action consists in exerting control and influence – deliberate, conscious and specialized control – upon 'the purposes, desires and impulses of the moment'.[15] This may be done *ex cathedra*, decisions and directions may be handed down from on high, and/or decisions may be the resultant of teamwork. The former may reflect an attempt to deny that differences exist or an attempt to cut through them in an authoritative manner, the latter (of which many of our respondents spoke) may be seen as a recognition of and celebration of difference and diversity.

Many asserted that it took teamwork to identify and to reconcile differences; that an agreed meaning emerged from talking rather than from simply deferring to the most senior person in the enterprise.[16] To be sure, on occasion discussion apeared to be limited, appeared to be informed by strongly held views powerfully expressed perhaps by one individual (not necessarily the most senior); on other occasions more than one had strong views to contribute and on still other occasions it was noted that no one person claimed expertise or superior knowledge and the discussion was much more exploratory and fragmentary. The overall impression many of our respondents left us with was one of sessions in which attempting to shape the discussion was taken up and dropped by members as seemed appropriate. Not every leader wishes to be seen as a star; not every Chief Executive feels the urge to sing, conduct the band and play the drums. Many of our respondents were reported to adopt a somewhat more androgynous approach to the doing of managing, involving immediate colleagues in discussions and decisions not only because it appeared to them impossible to do otherwise, but also because they appeared to be convinced that sharing secures better decisions and even greater effort from those with whom one shares influence.[17]

The image of the doing of leading that springs to mind, therefore, is not that of a colossus bestriding his colleagues, but of a circle, to be more specific of Poussin's painting in which the Seasons, hand in hand, tread in rhythm, 'stepping slowly, methodically, sometimes a trifle awkwardly, in evolutions that take recognizable shape: or breaking into seemingly meaningless gyrations.'[18] Each of the dancers is an individual, each has something to contribute, but none can perform alone. We take it that no one person can impose meaning upon the enterprise; he or she may attempt to lead the dance but if no one takes up the steps, or key performers persist in setting their own patterns, no agreed figure will emerge from their gyrations. Given differing cognitive styles, differing experiences, differing responsibilities, it is likely that in many circumstances those who constitute the most senior group in the enterprise will have differing perspectives on what the issues are that need resolution and what needs to be done about them. In some circumstances one individual may successfully call the tune, in others the tune arises from differing individuals elaborating competing tunes and, eventually, agreeing upon some pattern distinct from what any person or group initially contributed.

Talk

Coordinating was a daily achievement for our respondents; as testament they remained in being, edging forward in time, giving the dance some recognizable shape most of the time. How was this achieved? Largely through talk. Talking made the enterprise go round. And round. And round. Our respondents spend a substantial amount of their time talking; to themselves and to others inside and outside the organization. They talked to themselves when they ran up ideas in their heads or jotted their thoughts down on paper. They talked to each other in meetings, in chance encounters in corridors, in planes, trains and automobiles; on video and telephone links, in memos, letters and reports – talk, talk, talk. Words, words, words.

The way of finding out or declaring what a particular enterprise is about is through building some form of dialogue.[19] Order and coordination is discovered and created through the very act of seeking consensus on what needs to be done. To be sure, there are occasions when it is obvious to all what needs to be done, but at other times no one is sure about the issue, let alone its resolution. Problems do not arise fully articulated and packaged for instant decision. Although our respondents are able *now* to articulate more or less clearly the issues that they faced and resolved, many note that *at the time* events were not clear cut. Some found it difficult to recall how problems were defined, how resolutions arose and how consensus emerged (assuming that it did) because members' perceptions and understandings of the issues and the process were formed in and through the restless, continuous dialogue which constituted the medium through which obfuscation and clarification occurred. Engaging in talk was itself transformative. Our respondents were able to refer to a number of occasions where the outcome of a discussion was different to outcomes or preferences any of them had expressed before they talked. The resultant was a genuine discovery to all concerned. They talked themselves into trouble and out of it. Their dialogue revealed the issue in all its complexity, their pooled ideas stimulated the exploration of still more possibilities, shaped and reshaped the initial perceptions and then led, circuitously, to a resolving of the issue. Like our dancers, they wove in and out, now looking inwards, now out, now dissolving into apparently meaningless exchanges which, however, sparked new patterns, new intricacies developing a consensus, a shared awareness of the whole in all its variety.

All this talking cannot but help in bringing about a shared 'appreciative system', a common 'set of readinesses', as, picking up on Sir Geoffrey Vickers, we termed it in the last chapter. Teams develop and sustain 'language' through which they filter their experiences; they develop a series of collective cognitive structures which determine what it is that they, as a team, will regard as worthy of attention.

They acquire this language individually through selection, assignment, development, appraisal and collectively through talking to and listening to each other. Thus, when some element of external or internal reality changes, the team is likely to react collectively to it, is likely to 'perceive' it in a similar fashion and is likely to come up with ways of dealing with the change that fit their common language, fit the way that they habitually talk about things. Alice Sapienza makes some important points about the impact of 'language' upon the way teams conceive of and implement strategy:

The language of organizational strategy is both an outcome of the reality construction process and an input to it. It is an outcome because it is determined by the culture of the speech group in which it is used ... Words, phrases, acronyms and stories repeated in organizational communications reflect the values and beliefs that make that speech community unique. Language is also an input: words and syntax are repeated in conversations and writings. Managers hear and see this language and make it their own (meanings are implied and validated by trial and error until connotations become stable). Language thus becomes part of – that is, input to – managers' collective cognitive structures.[20]

She goes on to argue that 'images' often influence the way events are perceived and strategies are constructed and cites Lakoff and Johnson in support of her contention: 'We draw inferences, set goals, make commitments, and execute plans, all on the basis of how we in part structure our experience, consciously and unconsciously, by means of metaphor.' It is not our present intention to enter into a lengthy disquisition upon the nature of metaphor, all we wish to do is to comment upon one or two of the images or metaphors which appeared to find favour with two or three of our respondents. It is our contention that such images are indeed outputs and inputs into the strategies that the respective teams pursue; outputs and inputs which both facilitate and restrict action. Thus at Metal Box, the shared language appears to be that of flexibility, rapidity of response:

I think that Brian Smith's contribution to the company has been to unhook us from rigidity. To unhook us from a rigidity of process which we had at the time and to force people to think about their businesses.

We still feel quite passionately that the right way to go is to encourage smaller business units, competent management to do their own thing.

The clear obvious thing to do was to turn this business from being battleship run into being frigate run.

The image of the frigate is a striking one, and one against which all matters will come to be perceived within the top team – what does this or that mean for our desire to devolve responsibility:

I think that we mustn't say 'Thou shalt' – I think that we can say, 'We observe it may not be too clever. This is what it could be costing you, us, if we're not very careful. We recognize that we can't tell you to do these things but you should be aware of them and you should probably, if you are looking at decisions on balance, you should probably lean this way rather than the other. But ultimately the decision is yours and see if that works.' Because I don't think it's worth destroying the advantages of independence we've got, as they are considerable.

The image at Glynwed is notably different and just as widely shared in the top team:

We have what we call controlled autonomy. They all have autonomy but they operate within parameters – fairly tight parameters and fairly tight controls, but they do have autonomy.

We in Glynwed have, as you have probably already discovered, a very specific formula in terms of measuring our day-to-day or month-by-month progress and we call it the Glynwed treatment. That is very important to Glynwed.

The financial controls here are very very tight and ratios are strictly adhered to.

The respective master images of Glynwed and Metal Box are strongly contrasted in the next couple of quotes:

The first function in management, it applies to any manager going to a new job, is to have an organization that he understands, that he needs and that other people understand. Publish it. Stick it on the wall so that other people can see what their job is and what they are entitled to do and what their role is, they can see what other people's responsibilities are. Having established that, then you develop trust.

Basically the organization itself is so mobile, we don't have organization charts for example, we don't have an organization manual. I've refused to have them ... So we have all sorts of people who have got split responsibilities, different bosses, and we've got people pulled into project teams all the time. People working under the chairmanship of others who might be more junior than they are in the organization in grade terms. So we have a fair amount of that going on.

Now again, we are not saying that Glynwed is a better organization than Metal Box or vice versa; what we are saying is that the language of the one differs from the language of the other and that there are likely to be consequences to that fact. Glynwed executives will tend to process issues in terms of control and Metal Box executives in terms of flexibility. The executives of each of our companies talk the language of that particular company; part of that language is readily transferred from one company to another, part is not. And language affects both perceptions and action. It reflects and facilitates (or inhibits) trust and contains and expresses the core values of the company.

And Trust

Our respondents spoke also of trust. The term cropped up with remarkable regularity from interview to interview:

I've known Brian now for twenty-four years. Terry Upsall has been here for nineteen years, Hugh Rees for twelve years, and what we have developed over the time is absolute trust in one another. And we don't go around checking up on what each other does, we all know what our jobs are within the organization, because they have developed over a long time.

There's an atmosphere at the top that generates trust and friendliness and mutual support rather than everyone trying to climb on each other's backs to reach the top.

I suppose our strength is in our confidence. No one is going to find anything out [he didn't know]. Nobody is doing anything that is wrong ... I suppose it is trust really. We do trust each other.[21]

The trouble with the notion of trust is that it is difficult to define. It is covered by a wide range of literature and an even wider range of application in everyday usage. This makes it rather difficult to find some general statement which will find ready acceptance. Starting with the dictionary we can include phrases like: 'confident expectation', 'worthiness', 'integrity'. Most clearly, however, trust seems to imply some sort of faith, a belief in someone or some thing. Simmel's comments on confidence seem to suggest that trust is a blending of knowledge and ignorance:

Confidence, evidently, is one of the most important synthetic forces within society. As a hypothesis regarding future behaviour, a hypothesis certain enough to serve as a basis for practical conduct, confidence is intermediate between knowledge and ignorance about a man. The person who knows completely needs not trust; while the person who knows nothing can, on no rational grounds, afford even confidence. Epochs, fields of interest and individuals differ, characteristically, by the measures of knowledge and ignorance which must mix in order that the single, practical decision based on confidence arise.[22]

Some of our respondents appeared to feel that they were pretty close to knowing completely how their colleagues were likely to deal with issues. In this respect trust was not necessary. There were, however, circumstances in which they could not be totally sure and here trust was taken to be appropriate. They did not *hope* that their colleagues would do the right thing:

Trust is only involved when the trusting expectation makes a difference to a decision: otherwise what we have is simple hope ... one who trusts takes cognizance of the possibility of excessive harm arising from the selectivity of other's actions and adopts a position towards that possibility. One who hopes simply has confidence despite uncertainty. Trust reflects contingency. Hope ignores contingency.[23]

Another cluster of terms relating to trust as used by our respondents includes such notions as respect, solidarity, loyalty and commitment. In a sense, usage in these ways does not add much to our understanding of what is meant by trust. Rather, they expand on the idea of belief and confidence by implying some sense of values. By placing trust in someone, one is showing respect, loyalty and solidarity and indicating one's commitment to the person (or to the cause). On the other hand, although our respondents do not make the point, it is possible to trust without associating these values, particularly where trust is shown towards the system rather than to a person. Our respondents, for example, probably trust money to represent a certain system of exchange and value, although, in so doing, this trusting does not necessarily imply loyalty or respect.

The next cluster of terms employed by our respondents raises similar questions: cooperation, mutuality and coordination. Behind some of what some of them said lurked the idea that through mutual expression of trust the group cooperates, enabling greater coordination of efforts in defining and solving problems. This moves the question of what is meant by trust on to a different level: the level where it is more a question of what is meant by *trusting*.

Our final cluster of terms is also more directed towards the process of trusting. These include expectation and anticipation, taking risks and showing vulnerability. From the ideas about confidence and belief, there is a clear implication that trust relates to some future event or decision: to trust someone is to have confidence that they *will* ... In anticipating future events through trusting someone, one is taking a risk and in so doing becoming vulnerable, should trust prove to have been misplaced.

Luhmann points out that without trust, one would never get out of bed, such would be the potential chaos ahead. His whole analysis of trust is based around the idea of reducing complexity and is very much part of his theoretical perspective:

The world is being dissipated into an uncontrollable complexity; so much so that at any given time people are able to choose freely between very different actions. Nevertheless, I have to act here and now. There is only a brief moment of time in which it is possible for me to see what others do, and consciously adapt myself to it. In just that moment only a little complexity can be envisaged and processed, thus only a little gain in rationality is possible.

Additional chances of a more complex rationality would arise if I were to place my trust in a given course of action of others. If I can trust in sharing the proceeds, I can allow myself forms of co-operation which do not pay off immediately and which are not directly visible as beneficial. If I depend on the fact that others are acting, or are failing to act, in harmony with me, I can pursue my own interest with more rationality.[24]

This is very much the position many of our respondents appear to be in – they cannot act alone, they need each other to handle the complexity that surrounds their every move. In anticipating future events through trusting someone, one is taking a risk and in so doing, becoming vulnerable, should that trust prove to have been misplaced. Again, these ideas move on to imply something of what is meant by trusting, although they do help to expand what trust can be taken to mean.

From this brief introduction to ways of thinking about trust, it appears to be easier to talk about what else might be associated with trust or what is meant by trusting, than it is to give a simple definition of the concept, trust. Indeed, we have yet to find one. Instead, most definitions refer to trust in terms of behaviour and trusting. For example, Luhmann's work begins from a simple statement of behaviour: 'To show trust is to anticipate the future. It is to behave as though the future were certain.'[25] Deutsch seems to have provided the foundation for much of the literature around the subject, and his definition seems to expand on that of Luhmann.[26]

Trusting behaviour ... is defined here as consisting of actions that (a) increase one's vulnerability (b) to another whose behaviour is not under one's control (c) in a situation in which the penalty ... one suffers if the other abuses that vulnerability is greater than the benefit ... one gains if the other does not abuse that vulnerability.

The last part of this definition seems to imply some kind of exchange process which involves a potential costing of benefits against penalties. It adds a rather mechanical, distinctly non-mutual flavour to the idea of trusting behaviour which conflicts with some of the points Zand goes on to make in his paper. It does not seem to reflect the sense in which trusting behaviour is referred to in our contributors' accounts either, although the notion of vulnerability is implied in what they say. By and large their accounts of trust lack the notion of calculation. They appear to be for each other in a much more whole- hearted fashion than implied in Deutsch's definition.

One key conclusion from the discussion so far is that to seek a definition of trust is an artificial challenge. It seems that even from our data, while contributors talk about trust, it is expressed in terms of trusting others or trusting behaviour rather than some abstract thing called trust. Whatever else it is, trusting behaviour seems to our respondents to be a key to group achievement. And they are not alone in coming to that conclusion. There are many examples in the group process literature of trust forming a basic foundation on which to develop a common/shared view of group aims and group task as well as facilitating the achievement of the group goal. High trust groups are generally seen as better able to solve problems or derive more valuable learning experiences than low trust groups.

Trust seems to imply some sense of mutuality or collegiality in group situations. Our respondents spoke of it. And our friend, Chester Barnard, also has something to say on the issue, although he chooses to use the term communion:

It is the feeling of personal comfort in social relations that is sometimes called solidarity, social integration, the gregarious instinct, or social security (in the original, not its present debased economic sense). It is the opportunity for comradeship, for mutual support in personal attitudes. The need for communion is the basis of informal organization that is essential to the operation of every formal organization.[27]

Although Barnard's comments are somewhat wider than trust, he picks up the theme that common purpose may often foster an aura of mutuality and shared insight. Importantly, though, several authors emphasize that trust cannot be demanded but must be earned: it can be given but not requested.

To talk of trust seems generally to imply warmth and positive feelings of association: that is, a high trust relationship is a 'good' or cohesive one. People like Goffman point out that trust may constitute a 'kind of intimacy without warmth'[28] and caution against making an assumption of warmth about trust. An alternative illustration is an almost begrudging idea of trust: 'Well, we'll just have to trust him ...'.

This does begin to help tie trust down to context and content. Behaviour which may earn trust in one context may not be that which earns trust in another. Thus, trust is non-transferable to other people and situations but has, in effect, to be learned and earned each time.

This leads to the idea of familiarity, which seems to be an essential basis for developing trust (as well as distrust). Through developing a familiarity with people and situations, responses in a sense do become more predictable, hence building up an understanding of the boundaries to trust. This is more than merely to suggest that to trust is to make an inference from past experience. Rather, to trust requires going beyond this kind of informational input, to make some current evaluation of the risk of, in effect, defining the future.

As we have seen, many see trusting behaviour as associated with ideas of risk taking and uncertainty. To trust implies an expectation of future behaviour of others, which in turn suggests that one is taking a risk on anticipated events. This, in turn, both reduces and increases vulnerability: by showing trust in others, one reduces one's own vulnerability, assuming that this trust is well-founded, but such is the nature of this assumption, that one may also be increasing vulnerability. Likewise, to show trust may help to reduce complexity or alleviate uncertainty in future events, but may simultaneously increase complexity and uncertainty, should such trust prove to be misplaced.

Clearly, there is a temporal quality to the idea of trust. On the basis of past experience, one learns the conditions under which to show trust in anticipation of future events. This also implies some learning process, by which one builds up familiarity and understanding of people and situations, leading to a degree of predictability about others' future actions and reactions.

Many of our contributors claim to have strong feelings of trust in their colleagues and imply this to be reciprocated. Yet there are distinct qualitative differences in the way each describes trust and what this means in each individual context. How one then arrives at some definition or operational definition of trust seems an impossible, if not artificial, challenge. The examples we have selected to introduce and illustrate the notion derive from three different companies (although virtually every company mentioned trust): Beazer, Avon Rubber and Glynwed. Each offers illustrations of relationships based on trust, some better articulated than others. At Avon Rubber, the trust in Mitchard seemed to mean that 'we would do anything for him'. At Glynwed our respondents seemed to talk of trust arising as the result of experience or working together.[29] Likewise, Beazer contributors claimed to trust each other and Brian Beazer in particular. Yet, the way in which they described their trust was more like 'faith', almost in the religious sense. They had faith in Brian Beazer and had faith that they were doing the right things rather than in the sense of cohesion, familiarity and joint commitment implied by Avon and Glynwed. We are not attempting to point out that one form of trust is better than another; what we are trying to say is that in each distinct organization, individual accounts of trusting seem to illustrate similar qualities or understandings: the differences, if such, are more *between* each organization.

And Valuing and Believing – Again

In the previous chapter we devoted quite a bit of space to discussing the issues of values and beliefs, arguing that they influenced (perhaps even determined) the way that executives read situations and the form of action that they took. At that point our focus was upon the individual rather than the team. It is clearly a matter of importance to considerations of team interaction. If members are resolutely incompatible one could anticipate a different outcome to their deliberations than if they were to be resolutely compatible.

In chapter 1 we noted Barnard's comments upon team composition: compatibility was a good thing but, 'excessive compatibility or harmony is deleterious, resulting in "single track minds" and excessively crystallized attitudes'.[30] Our respondents did not talk explicitly of values, but from what many of them did say we inferred that in many cases values were held in common. Most, virtually all, embraced rationality as a value, although a great many, as we have indicated in a previous chapter, also operated on and valued intuitive responses. Most showed evidence of valuing materialism, most had a marked sense of duty, some put a premium on novelty and some on power; and many had a strong orientation to valuing people. There appeared to be few differences *within* teams, a circumstance which, if manifested in actual interaction, no doubt both shapes and creates shared visions and smooth interaction.

Theoretically, of course, as Barnard indicates, homogeneity of values can lead to poor performance if, as we have argued, values influence the way one thinks. Everyone thinking the same way, everyone coming up with the same response would preclude adaptatic .[31] Our respondents expressed themselves somewhat more graphically, but essentially pointed to the same conclusions:

You can only develop this type of management ... if the chemistry is there ... It doesn't necessarily need to be total, but there's got to be sufficient empathy, whatever the word is, with a sufficient sized group of people that somebody can then feel part of ... This chemistry – it doesn't necessarily mean you love 'em or that you have the same ideas and habits and so forth ...

Everybody has their say ... It's one thing not to be listened to and have the decision go against you. It's quite another to have your view acknowledged and understood ... At least nobody can say that your own view hasn't been regarded with a good deal of concern and respect.

Well, if there is a simple answer, it's working together with a common purpose and making sure it works. That doesn't say there aren't any disagreements but then you iron them out and sort them out and you get on the right course and away you go.

First of all, you've met Gareth Davies, you will have met Terry O'Neill, you'll meet Des Gripton and you've met me, and you will find that we are four different people, all with their own different views and their own different styles, but it works because the chemistry is right and that is the important thing: that you get the right chemistry.[32]

Such a conclusion, of course, brings us back neatly to the points we were making in the previous chapter about response and about culture. The enterprise which retains or encourages a degree of random response is likely to survive longer than one that seeks to determine and control each and every response. And here we link back to what we have written about talk and talking. If beliefs affect images and are expressed in metaphors and if language and imagery are indeed powerful shapers of perception and action, then it may be necessary for senior executives to spend a little time reflecting upon their values and the kind of language they regularly employ. It may even be worthwhile to select and/or promote people who do not 'speak the same language' since all singing from the 'same hymn sheet' may be unproductive in the medium to long run. Some of our respondents were vaguely aware of the dangers of selecting and promoting like-minded individuals:

When we have brought people from outside, we've got some outstanding examples of very able people that we've managed to bring in that have brought a slightly new dimension, different culture, tricks that they have learned elsewhere – there's just a feeling that maybe we've been too inbred.

It's people who have got out of the habit of learning and who in a way feel threatened by change. Not so confident as they used to be about accommodating it, and tend sometimes, even subconsciously to stand in the way of it. And that's been a big problem. As you'd expect in an organization that's got old, it has a lot of long-serving people around. To put people into jobs because of the qualities that they have, which may not be entirely right for today. That's been a factor.[33]

There is, however, something curiously static about much of the literature on beliefs and values, describing a world in which executives apparently do not change their values, in which values are something that one has rather than one in which valuing is something one does. And in this active sense – demonstrating what is valued – inevitably there will be change over time, as behaviour is shaped by response and stimulus of others, different situations and circumstances, and different points in time. Although we have little direct data to support our case, we sensed that some of our respondents had changed their beliefs, were more orientated to power and materialism than they might have been a few years earlier and some more into change (novelty) and competitiveness than they had been:

So not exactly a thirst for knowledge, but a healthy respect for keeping yourself up to date and a cross-functional view, an ability to use analytical methods and back them up with some empirical approaches and achieve results. A willingness and an understanding of how to work in teams, as distinct from an individualist culture. They are all absolutely critically important skills for managers of the future.[34]

Dancers, Artists and Riflemen

Our respondents assert that they learn what they are about in talking to and trusting their colleagues, that they often recognize and develop their own views in the very process of seeking consensus, that talking to others heightens their awareness, sharpens their focus. But they also assert that they are in command, that they do plan and shape the future with clear intent, that they know where it is that they are heading. Our data support this perspective as well. Heroic managers, of course, know what they are doing; they have visions, missions and plans and they implement them. Some of our respondents, some of the time, claimed to operate in this manner. And some of our respondents (in several cases the same respondents), some of the time, noted that they did not know what they were doing until they had done it.[35]

The dance metaphor begins to break down at this point; we can stretch it and talk of improvisation on the one hand and the military two step on the other, but to do so would be to mask the kind of images which underlie these forms of dance. The master image that we have of the handful of executives who, in most cases, constitute the top team remains that of a group of dancers, but dancers who, on occasion, assume the characteristics of those who act with military precision and on other occasions display the traits of artists and improvisers. Our respondents, it would appear, are drawn from the ranks of the artists' rifle brigade. They may be taken to be both artists and riflemen; those who discover the target and those who know how to aim at it. The distinction is one drawn by Vincent Tomas, a philosopher with an interest in aesthetics:[36]

When a rifleman aims at his target, he knows what he wants to do. He wants to hit the bull's eye. Before he shoots, he knows what the target is; he knows that the black circle in the centre of it is the bull's eye; and he knows that hitting the bull's eye consists in causing a bullet to pass through the black circle. He also knows, before he has squeezed the trigger, that if, after he has squeezed it, a hole appears in the black circle, he will have succeeded in doing what he wanted to do; and that if there isn't a hole there, he will have failed.[37]

On occasion we congratulate an executive for having learned the rules and having obeyed them. Some of our respondents, most of the time, could be seen to be rule learners and rule followers. Riflemen. Some of our respondents, some of the time, however, were congratulated because they embodied in what they were doing something the like of which did not exist before. When an artist is congratulated for being creative, it is not because he or she was able to obey the rules that were known before he or she painted the picture, composed the music or wrote the novel, play or poem; no one considers it terribly smart if an artist simply does what has been done before. An artist is congratulated because he or she originates the rules he or she 'implicitly follows while he (she) was painting or writing'. Afterwards, others may achieve similar success by explicitly following the newly minted rules, but in so doing the followers are more like the rifleman than the orginating artist.

Our artist/executives, therefore, may be seen as rule creators and as creators of novel and valuable artefacts; but they know not what they do until they have done it.

Although he seems to himself to be 'aiming' at something, it is not until just before he affixes his signature or seal of approval to his work that he finds out that *this* is the determinate thing he was all along 'aiming' at, and that *this* was the way to bring it into being. Creative activity in art, that is to say, is not a paradigm of purposive activity, that is, of activity engaged in and consciously controlled so as to produce a desired result.[38]

Again, when applied to the doing of leading, this takes us a long way from the standard texts with their emphasis upon it being a matter of knowing where one is going and stepping out strongly in that direction. As can be seen here, in the paradigmatic case, the rifleman/executive is supposed to know what he/she wants and to go after it. Providing he or she behaves appropriately – follows the rules – the desired result will be produced. Generations of managers and consultants have been trained in such beliefs. The artist/ executive, on the other hand, has no *clear* vision, no *clear* goal, no *specified* final result. He or she does not have therefore an idea or image of it (or if they have it is one that constantly shifts) so their activity is not 'controlled,' as in the paradigmatic case, 'by a desire for an envisaged result and beliefs about how to obtain it'.

This is not to argue that artists are without purpose. They, and our doers of leading in their more creative phases, have a sense of being engaged in a directed activity, have a sense of going somewhere even though at the time of developing their ideas they would have been unable to say precisely where they were going. On the other hand, they (both conventional artists – if that is not a contradiction in terms – and our unconventional executives – if that is not a contradiction in terms) *can* say that certain directions are not 'right'. Indeed the painter changes a brush stroke because it is 'wrong', the writer scrubs a passage because it is 'wrong' and the would-be leader eschews a course of action because it, too, is 'wrong'.[39] Leading, like any other art, is not a matter of marching off in just any direction. The creative doing of leading, like the creative writing of music or doing of painting *is* controlled, but it is not predetermined. The element of resistance to particular avenues, or, if taken, the retracing of steps, the exercise of critical judgement, is what sets creative activity apart from mere dreaming.[40]

Creative activity in leading and managing, as in art, is an activity subject to critical control by the leader or manager, although not by virtue of the fact that he or she knows precisely the end result.[41] In effect, he or she controls the direction of that which is being elaborated as it develops. A point precisely and forcibly made by C. J. Ducasse in *The Philosophy of Art:*

> To say that art is ... critically controlled ... does not mean that it need be ... controlled either antecedently to or contemporaneously with the expressive act ... But it does mean that a critical judgement is an intrinsic, essential constituent of the productive activity called art ...[42]

Again we are back to the point that we made earlier: the simultaneity of action and reflection. Critical judgement is bound up with action for our respondents as it is for other artists; they manifest a kind of 'feeling mind' that enables them to shape their actions as they occur. Their creative endeavours are controlled not by virtue of the fact that they can clearly envisage the end results, that they can focus upon the bull's eye, but rather, control consists in making critical judgements about what has so far been done. They are not 'pulled' towards a target so much as 'pushed' by a sense of emergence; something dimly perceived, apprehended rather than comprehended, shaping their effort and controlling the selection of particular courses of action. As artists they shape events, bringing together apparently disparate ideas, discovering purpose as they go along. Stephen Spender, poet, novelist and man of letters, captures something of what we wish to say in his comments upon creativity:

A poet's mind equipped for its work is constantly amalgamating disparate experience. The ordinary man's experience is chaotic, irregular, fragmentary. The latter falls in love, reads Spinoza and these two experiences are not connected with the noise of the typewriter and the smell of cooking. In the mind of the poet these two experiences are always forming new wholes ...[43]

Pity about Spinoza – the point, however, remains: senior executives, on occasion, manifest a poet's capacity to bring things together, to form new wholes from apparently disparate perspectives. In part, the doing of leading is creative.

We do not judge an action or a set of actions to be creative unless we believe it to be original. If we take it that, for example, Gareth Davies and his colleagues at Glynwed are *mechanically* applying ideas that they have utilized previously or have acquired from some other company, if it strikes us that this activity is simple repetition, we will deny that it is creative, however successful it may be in turning the company around. In such circumstances Davies et al., artists, become Davies et al., riflemen. We take it that they know what their bull's eye is, and that they know how to hit it. They are simply repeating themselves. To create, on the other hand, is to innovate. And it follows that in such circumstances the creators, in this case Davies and his colleagues, do not foresee the end result. Rather it emerges from their interaction – a product of their collective endeavour. As T. E. Hulme put it: 'to predict it would be to produce it before it was produced'.[44]

We take the action of Gareth Davies and his colleagues at Glynwed to be creative not only because they were different to anything undertaken previously in that setting, but also because they were adjudged valuable. What he and his colleagues wrought at Glynwed (and what they continue to wright) may be seen to be coherent, may be seen to 'hang together', may be seen to be 'all of a piece', and could be said to have integrity. In other words what has occurred there is not fortuitous, it is the product of a controlled approach to the doing of leading and managing. Just as what happened at Metal Box under the direction of Brian Smith is coherent and is the product of a controlled approach, as is what happened at Reckitts and at Marks and Spencer.[45]

The control, however, is of a different order to that exercised by the same executives when they perform as riflemen. The rifleman knows what the target is and he knows what he ought to do to hit the bull:

He knows what position he ought to assume, how he ought to adjust the sling, where exactly he ought to place his left hand, where he ought to place the butt so that it fits the shoulder and cheek, what the sight picture ought to be, how he ought to exhale a little and then hold his breath when the sight picture is correct, and how he ought to squeeze off the shot without knowing exactly when the explosion will come, so that he won't flinch until after it is too late to spoil his aim.[46]

A great deal of the doing of leading and of managing consists in identifying the target and following the rules in order to hit it smack in the middle. As artists, however, our respondents did not follow such consciously formulated rules. Their control appeared to be more a matter of 'intuition' and 'hunch', 'nose' and 'touch' than by anything else. They appeared to claim to have a feel for doing managing, just as Francis Bacon could be said to have a feel for painting, Gyorgy Ligeti a feel for composing, Seamus Heaney a feel for writing poetry.

As could be anticipated, dear old Chester Barnard saw a similar distinction. As an appendix to *The Functions of the Executive*, he published an essay called 'Mind in Everyday Affairs' in which he drew a distinction between logical (rifleman) and non-logical (artist) types of thinking:

By 'logical processes', I mean conscious thinking which could be expressed in words or by other symbols, that is, reasoning. By 'non-logical processes' I mean those not capable of being expressed in words or as reasoning, which are only made known by a judgement, decision or action.[47]

Like us, he considers the approach of the *logical* rifleman to be a matter of explicit goals, an instance of calculation, a case of following the rules. The *non-logical* processes of the artist, on the other hand, he takes to be difficult to explicate, more to be recognized than described or explained. He has, however, something to say about the sources of non-logical judgement:

The sources of these non-logical processes lie in physiological conditions or factors, or in the physical and social environment, mostly impressed upon us unconsciously or without conscious effort on our part. They also consist of the mass of facts, patterns, concepts, techniques, abstractions, and generally what we call formal knowledge or beliefs, which are impressed upon our minds more or less by conscious effort and study. This second source of non-logical mental processes greatly increases with directed experience, study and education.[48]

It seems to us that this formulation comes close to asserting that non-logical processes are essentially the same as logical processes, only they are obscured by experience and learning. Given an ability to disentangle the various strands or given sufficient directed experience, study and education, non-logical processes would cease to be non-logical. This is essentially the line that Herbert Simon takes which, for him, means asserting that intuition is a rational process whereby the brain evokes past memories and experiences to address the problem at hand.[49] He illustrates his point by reference to the 'intuition' of a chess grandmaster:

How do we account for the judgement or intuition that allows the chess grandmaster usually to find good moves in a few seconds? A good deal of the answer can be derived from an experiment that is easily repeated. First, present a grandmaster and a novice with a position from an actual, but unfamiliar chess game (with about 25 pieces on the board). After five or ten seconds, remove the board and pieces and ask the subjects to reproduce it. The grandmaster will usually reconstruct the whole position correctly, and on average will place 23 or 24 pieces on their correct squares. The novice will only be able to replace, on average, about 6 pieces.

It might seem that we are witnessing remarkable skill in visual imagery and visual memory, but we can easily dismiss that possibility by carrying out a second experiment. The conditions are exactly the same as in the first experiment, except that now the 25 pieces are placed on the board at random. The novice can still replace about 6 pieces and the grandmaster – about 6! The difference between them in the first experiment does not lie in the grandmaster's eyes or imagery, but in his knowledge, acquired by long experience, of the kinds of patterns and clusters of pieces that occur on chessboards in the course of games. For the expert, such a chess board is not an arrangement of 25 pieces but an arrangement of half a dozen familiar patterns, recognizable old friends. On the random board there are no such patterns, only the 25 individual pieces in an unfamiliar arrangement.[50]

Simon's formulation places a great deal of emphasis upon experience and memory. The grandmaster's memory holds more than a set of patterns. As he points out, information about the significance of particular patterns is also stored; seeing the patterns enables him or her to estimate threat or promise:

Recognizing the pattern brings to the grandmaster's mind at once moves that may be appropriate to the situation. It is this recognition that enables the professional to play very strong chess at a rapid rate. Previous learning that has stored the patterns and the information associated with them in memory makes this performance possible. This, then, is the secret of the grand-master's intuition or judgement.[51]

We have quoted at length from Simon in order to illustrate just where it is that we depart from him on this issue of artistic control (it is, perhaps, significant that Simon refers to professionals and experts rather than to artists). Clearly part of the time our respondents are deploying intuition in the manner that Simon outlines. They clearly draw upon their experience to make decisions. Like chess players, they look for patterns and consider the implications of those patterns. In such circumstances, like chess players they know the nature of the game, they know the objective of it and they know the rules. In other words their actions are closer to those of the rifleman than those of the artist. The point about 'non-logical' processes is that they are not rule governed, or, rather, that they go beyond the rules and in so doing rewrite them for those that follow. On occasion our respondents appear to go well beyond evoking patterns stored in their minds. Their collective experience may well provide the basis for their activity but in and of itself it is not sufficient to account for their departures from hitherto received practice. It is not simply a matter of being an expert, of having the kind of mind that stores masses of information about managing, art, music, poetry or whatever. Experience in the sense that we are using it here means that 'having been there' is a necessary condition for recognizing that one is now somewhere else, and that that 'somewhere else' is novel and may be valuable, notwithstanding the 'rules' which declare that one cannot get here from there.[52]

Artists and scientists deploy *imagination*; riflemen (or riflepersons) do not, nor do those who simply call upon patterns laid down long ago and far away. There is a quite splendid passage in Jacob Bronowski's collection of essays which captures the essence of what we mean by the term 'imagination':

The ability to hold absent things in mind gives human beings a freedom inside their environment which no animal has. Animals are environment bound; that is, they react to stimuli in a tightly limited way. They have little choice of response. Much fascinating experimental work shows that an animal which has a strong stimulus in front of it is not able to resist its compulsion. Whether the stimulus is food, or is the affection of a hen for her chicks, the animal is unable to make any response but the obvious one. It rushes straight for the food or the chicks; and if there is some obstacle in the way, the animal is so much dominated by what is in front of its eyes that it cannot remember its way around the obstacle. The animal has no words, no mental images, which allow it to visualize anything but the situation in front of its senses.[53]

In terms of the language used in the previous chapter, animal responses are strictly determined; in Bronowski's examples they are very tightly controlled. Human attempts to shape response are much less successful. Put in the crudest of terms, culture means 'directions for behaviour'. A strong culture attempts to strongly determine the options available to people, it attempts, that is, to curtail or, at least severely reduce, the incidence of random response. It attempts to make chickens of us all. To the extent that it succeeds, behaviour takes a standard form and becomes relatively predictable. In a closed institution, behaviour can be very tightly directed indeed. Let us assume for the sake of illustration that one or other of our respondents had spent his entire working life in such an enterprise; man and boy he had been a Bloggs employee, or whatever. Let us further assume (to render the example even more unlikely) that the enterprise was spectacularly efficient at controlling his responses throughout his working career, that the rules of how to be a good Bloggs man had been passed down to him very, very successfully and that being a Bloggs man, he eventually joins his like-minded colleagues – Bloggs men – at the top table. One can imagine the scene: a group of think-alike, possibly look-alike, men defining and responding to events in the way generations of Bloggs men have responded. The chance of a new perspective being *elaborated* in such a group would be slight. Picture now, if you will, another group of Bloggs managers brought in from various backgrounds with no experience of managing anywhere, let alone in Bloggs' industry, and with no one prepared or skilled enough to direct them. Again one can imagine the scene ; everyone talking at once with no-one comprehending what anyone else has to say, very diverse individuals casting around randomly for common ground. The chance of anything new being *recognized* in such a circumstance would be slight.

The examples are, of course, ridiculous: one represents total order, one comes pretty close to chaos and creativity cannot arise easily in either. Many of our respondents fall somewhere along this continuum and all of them move backwards and forwards between the two ends. Team members are socialized through their experience in the enterprise, have the capacity and sometimes a preference for responding stereotypically to circumstances, but some, perhaps many, retain the capacity to respond randomly, to come up with the unexpected response. They retain the capacity to exercise their imaginative capability; to do what humans can do and animals cannot – come up with images in their heads. Human beings are not trapped by their immediate environments, do not have to respond to that which is in front of them; they can (and do) make and hold images in their minds of how things might be. They can and do string together the noise of the typewriter and the smell of cooking (and Spinoza). Words and images provide everyone with the freedom to play with ideas. As Bronowski points out, they also provide a second freedom:

The second part of the freedom which words and images give us is that they are personal to us. All bees have exactly the same language; when one bee dances, the other bees listen simply by imitating the same dance. The bees have only one vocabulary, with the same words and the same meanings. But human beings, because they manipulate words inside their minds for themselves, change them and develop them and give them their own meanings. No two human beings, not even identical twins, speak quite the same language.[54]

It is this personal manipulation of language, this ability to run idiosyncratic images around in our heads, which distinguishes us from other animals and which may well distinguish between executives. Many of our respondents appear to be able to 'read' circumstances quickly: they can and do sum up complex financial circumstances without effort and often display the same facility when talking about people and organizations. Some, a precious few, appear to 'read' things differently. Their responses are not the expected ones. If a major component of the doing of managing is the ability to recognize cues in a situation and then to *not* do what one has been culturally conditioned to do when these cues are noticed, then some of our respondents appear to display that kind of skill. In effect, they have created or operate within a sub-culture which directs them to challenge their own definitions and their own predispositions to respond. One that is based on believing, valuing and hence rewards *imagining*.

Imagining may be a necessary activity for coming up with a novel response, but alone it can never suffice. Creativity appears to be the result of the artist, scientist or leader *critically interacting* with his/her material. Francis Bacon is an experienced painter but is not constrained or intimidated by what he has done, is not trapped by it; instead he confronts it and attempts to go beyond it. Ligeti does the same in music and Heaney in poetry. Sir David Alliance and his team pick up the cues and may come up with a response deriving from their previous experience, but they do not immediately translate experience into action; instead, they may consider what they have come up with and question whether or not it *is* appropriate to the present circumstance. In other words, they test out the possible action against the situation as they have currently defined it and consider what might happen: what if? what then? what next? Collectively they experiment deploying their imagination. Instantly we are in language problems again. Despite the way we have described it, the process is neither necessarily linear nor conscious; Bacon may change a particular brush stroke as he commits it to the canvas (or he may reflect after seeing the result), his behaviour may be the product of reason or intuition or both. It may be random or closely controlled. Sir David Alliance or one of his colleagues may mentally question a response as he makes it or may consider carefully and deliberately what others might say of what he, himself, is about to say and do. Creativity is always a matter of non-stereotypic response but not always a matter of reason and reflection.[55]

The *touchstone* of creativity, the decision as to whether or not the gamble pays off, is a matter of judgement by those who are best placed to judge. As with much else in life, creativity is a response and its very definition depends upon a response. Do those who are in a position to judge take the action to be novel and valuable? Creativity is a combination of both attributes; an action can be novel without it being valuable. A management team could decide to reorganize its entire manufacturing process in a manner that has hitherto not been attempted by them or anyone else. If, subsequently, no-one took that innovation to be a valuable one, then it could not be termed creative; it would be seen as a gamble that did not pay off. To paraphrase Morse Peckham, creativity is socially validated error and error is socially invalidated attempts at creativity. On the other hand, a reorganization of the system may well be seen to pay off, but is not seen to be particularly novel. A number of competitors have travelled that route, so the change is taken to be valuable but not novel. To be taken to be creative, endeavour must be both novel and valuable.

What is clear is that some of our respondents were adjudged by themselves and by others to have done something out of the ordinary, to have transcended expectations, to have shaped meaning and response within their enterprises in a manner which was taken to be valuable. Glynwed, for example, transcended expectations:

He was indicating the kind of performance which he believed would be acceptable not to him but the the shareholders. The one thing was in the kind of performance that would get Glynwed valid in the City. That is important.

And I was more or less saying those levels of achievement are so far away from where we are at the moment, is it reasonable to get to them? And he was more or less saying, 'Well, if you want to get to Birmingham, you'd better start here. This is where we are. It's a long journey but that is where you want to go.' Now in actual fact the long journey has gone long past where we said we would get to, and I think he and I are surprised, maybe even astonished, at the success that we have achieved for several years.

The creative act breaks out of habituated ways of responding and sees the world in new ways and, in so doing, changes the way that we all see the world; creates, as it were, new rules, new standards:[56]

We've gradually got away from the old style British management practices to new style. There's a lot more communication – a performance orientation, the lot. But at the root of it all is a set of solid methods, techniques, procedures, firmly based in engineering ... so it's not the sort of old style business school razzmatazz, the superficiality ... So keeping up to date, communicating ... allows you to start extracting the next topics that merit attack, while at the same time continuing to look ahead and creating a strategic view which you are firming up as you go through the change process.[57]

A matter of challenging habitual modes of perceiving, shaking up experiences, to arrive at a new and, presumably, temporary whole, a new synthesis.

As we have hinted above, creativity is rare; we have probably stretched the definition to accommodate any of the examples we have adduced above; we have certainly fudged the issue of judgement as we have not sought the considered opinions of critics.[58] Our examples may reflect value but not innovation, innovation but not value. They may simply reflect circumstances in which our respondents did things better; where individuals, each experienced in his own craft, applied his ideas to improving things at the margin, *tinkering* with the organization, the market or whatever. Circumstances in which current meanings and responses are elaborated and refined rather than substantially revised. It is likely that the incidence of the former is heavier than the latter; perhaps some leaders are more likely to tinker than to create. Tinkering is not to be taken lightly, it is a valued and valuable acitivity.[59] Tinkering occurs, as it were, within the frame; creativity, as we have indicated, transcends the frame. Paraphrasing Koestler, we take creativity to be an act of liberation – 'the defeat of habit by originality' – and tinkering to be an act of shaping, of extending habit and habitual ways of doing things.[60] Tinkering is as essential to enterprises as is creativity; it involves fewer creative steps, certainly no jumps. It is a matter of craft rather than art.

And in Conclusion

The term consensus has fallen into disrepute over the past few years (at least in the UK), perhaps it is seen as soft, but many of our respondents described processes of definition and response shaping that seemed to be consensual. Most saw the value of seeking the ideas of their colleagues even if, as was often the case, those they sought opinions from were but a handful of the members of the organization. They appeared to recognize that not only were the ideas of others necessary to sound decision making, not only did they need the experiences and challenges that others had to offer, they also appeared to believe that internalized, committed action – genuine cooperation – could only be realized through talking with each other, shaping something together.

Most of the senior managers we talked to identified strongly with their enterprises, they were proud to belong to Avon, Glynwed or whatever, their values were in line with what they took to be the values of the organization. To be sure, part of their attachment was instrumental – man does not work for pride alone – but extrinsic rewards did not figure large in their reasons for working. They were willing to take initiative and show innovation, willing to help others, vigilant in defending the enterprise from detractors, willing to speak up, willing to dissent *because* they saw Avon, Glynwed or whatever as *their* enterprise, something in which they were bound up personally and emotionally. This commitment we take to be part of the doing of managing and partly the product of heavy and effective conditioning – the imposition of a strong culture – and/or the result of a process by which they shared in shaping many of the responses put forward. Day-to-day action, the following of the *spirit* of agreements rather than the *letter* of commands, we take to be the product of talk accomplished in a setting where hierarchy is not stressed; where rank, title and function do not determine contribution.

We can have a discussion in the Boardroom at which there are quite strongly held views on a particular thing that's being considered. And we come to some agreement which may not be the preferred agreement on the part of the person who is going to execute it. I've never felt that the person who's going to execute it has gone out and more or less disregarded not only the decision but also the flavour of the decision ... I always have confidence that the individual concerned has gone out and he's done his best to interpret whatever was agreed in the way in which it was decided ... We haven't had a nit-picking situation where somebody has said, 'Well, I did the letter of the decision', but has done it in a way which is totally unsympathetic to the flavour of it ... Not many people get into the situation where it is a reality. It is here. And I think it's highly prized by the people who are in the team.[61]

Real authority is created when there is a degree of trust between senior managers, when decisions are arrived at in the knowledge that they will be implemented. Chester Barnard, as always, recognizes the location of real authority: 'The decision as to whether an order has authority or not lies with the persons to whom it is addressed and does not reside in "persons of authority" or those who issue these orders.' A senior manager will follow if he shares the direction in which he/she is being led; otherwise he or she may walk.

We take it that where consensus obtains, those who instigate the process and those who sustain it value individuality and value the capacity of their peers, bosses and colleagues to come up with ideas that may be of benefit to the organizatiuon irrespective of their formal title. All members of the team – and it may be, frequently is, a very small team – have the right to participate in a wide range of decisions. This involves the elaboration and sustaining of a culture, a set of more or less articulated beliefs and practices that underpin the unarticulated perspective such that organizing is a restless, evolutionary process, a process in the constant state of becoming. Little is fixed and no one person knows all of the questions, let alone all of the answers. Cooperating is something which has to be achieved on a daily basis if the system is to cohere. An egalitarian spirit, a team spirit, informs the consensus-seeking process and formal decision is, more often than not, a matter of shared agreement. To be sure, the formal leader may reserve some final veto or right of decision to himself/herself. John West puts the point forcefully: 'The authority of the chief executive is indivisible. Only he gets the blame, you can't share it with a committee, so it is the Chief Executive in Committee that decides, after you've listened to all the arguments.' The formal leader may also act as the catalyst for ideas; he or she may initially stimulate discussion, may be the most attentive listener in what follows and may be the person to articulate the emerging agreement, but these activities may be carried out by anyone or everyone in the team. It is not a situation that is cosy, where everyone has to agree with everyone else; far from it, it is a situation in which the expression of differences is encouraged and the reconciliation of positions wherever possible the *raison d'être* of the team.

Some of our respondents take it that seeking consensus encourages innovation and creativity. They imply that the select band of brothers (no sisters in our sample) at the top of the organization can and do champion ideas aggressively, can be and often are persistent in putting forward initially unpopular analyses. By providing a forum in which each is attentive to the ideas and experiences of others, they can and do risk offending each other *in order that* a response, a course of action, can be shaped and affirmed by them all.

And yet again we run the risk of tipping over into categorizations: this or that enterprise operates on charisma, this or that on lead-free consensus. Aspects of both appeared to interpenetrate the companies with which we were concerned. To an extent shaping response in them, 'setting the agenda' as some would call it, appeared to be a matter of charisma, some responded to their formal leaders with a degree of faith, respect, even awe. To an extent it was also a matter of individualized consideration, of treating each other as independent, of supporting each other's integrity; and a matter of facilitating innovative and even creative thinking, even to the extent of inviting challenge to the ideas of all – including those of the formal leader.[62] The categories appear not to be mutually exclusive (although most of the literature holds that they are). Our respondents at one and the same time (or certainly at the same interview) could and did attribute causality to their formal leaders *and* to themselves; could and did demonstrate faith, respect, even awe, without this appearing to be disabling or a demonstration of dependence; and could and did talk of challenge and innovation, consensus decision making in the presence of and with the facilitation of a strong, charismatic formal leader. None the less, time and again in going through the data a passage from Barnard insinuated itself into our minds. Writing about what he termed 'the informal executive', he declared that its functions were:

The communication of intangible facts, opinions, suggestions, suspicions, that cannot pass through formal channels without raising issues calling for decisions, without dissipating dignity and objective authority, and without overloading executive positions; also to minimize excessive cliques of political types arising from too great divergence of interests and views; to promote self-discipline of the group; and to make possible the development of important personal influences in the organization.[63]

It seemed to us that many of our respondents worked together in just this fashion; implicitly they recognized the fragility of their cooperation at the same time as they acknowledged its strength. They could and did put great pressure upon each other, but many also appeared to know when to back off, when not to force a decision.

A number of our respondents saw the process of leading and following as a matter of striking a balance (probably temporary) between involvement in the team and the ultimate accountability of the Chief Executive Officer. In this, what they have to say resonates with the findings of Louis Barnes and Martin Kriger who claim that effective organizational leadership requires both hierarchical and network leadership. The theory of leading that they put forward has much in common with our own:

Our theory of organizational leadership involved: (1) many potential 'leaders' in changing role relationships who (2) moved from the often vague concepts of purpose and vision into (3) struggles with perceived certainty and uncertainty, and (4) reached patched-together decision actions in (5) a spiraling process involving higher and lower, newer and older producers, actors and audience. This concept of organizational leadership included *both* formal hierarchy and informal or quasi-formal networks.[64]

Their conclusion that potentially mutually exclusive notions such as 'exclusive hierarchies' and 'networks' are at once part of the same leadership is very close to our own, particularly in the emphasis they put upon response (whether or not they are aware that this is what they are doing is quite another matter): 'They [exclusive hierarchies and networks] are properties of our interactions with leadership. Depending upon our choice of behaviour, we can cause leadership to manifest either hierarchies or network properties.'[65]

We, of course, would push just a little harder: leading and following is not a matter of either this or that, it is a matter of *both* individual direction and team interaction. A matter of the Chief Executive in Committee to be sure, but a Chief prepared to devolve some of his/her power and authority, prepared to trust his/her colleagues, prepared to talk and listen, prepared to imagine and improvise, prepared, that is, to join the dance and, on occasion, to direct it.

4
The Doing of Organizing Writ Large

Plus ça change, plus c'est la même chose

Change, and particularly changing oneself, is a difficult and often painful business – while not to change is to atrophy and perhaps wither away by inches. Or as my Uncle Sid might say, 'There's nowt so permanent as change.'

He was not a clever man but a wise one. He was a self-centred bachelor, who avoided complications and did little to harm anyone. His standards were Edwardian but he knew how the world changed: how to be one step ahead of change, so as not to change himself.[2]

(And our money's on Uncle Sid.)

The central theme of this chapter is 'change'. Indeed, we might even have called this chapter 'The Doing of Changing'. There are, however, drawbacks to an exclusive focus on change. What the three quotations at the head of this chapter describe in their different ways is the essential paradox of change: that is, persistence. The term paradox unfortunately is often taken to mean opposite forces, or thesis and antithesis which are ultimately resolved in synthesis. In contrast to this 'either/or' or 'resolution-based' approach to change, Watzlawick et al. offer an interesting analysis of persistence *and* change:

The tendency has been either to view persistence and invariance as a 'natural' or 'spontaneous' state, to be taken for granted and needing no explanation, and change as the problem to be explained, or to take the inverse position.[3]

In terms of organizational explanations, change is usually the subject to be accounted for and provides more colourful lively stories than does persistence.[4] But as they go on to add:

... the very fact that either position can be adopted so readily suggests that they are complementary – that what is problematic is not absolute and somehow inherent in the nature of things, but depends on the particular case and point of view involved.[5]

This notion of complementarity in effect poses 'and/and' as a challenge to more traditional 'either/or' ways of thinking. They develop this into their notion of 'frame-breaking' or 'the gentle art of reframing' as an approach to change:

To reframe, then, means to change the conceptual and/or emotional setting or viewpoint in relation to which a situation is experienced and to place it in another frame which fits the 'facts' of the same concrete situation equally well or even better, and thereby changes its entire meaning ... What turns out to be changed as a result of reframing is the meaning attributed to the situation, and therefore its consequences, but not its concrete facts.[6]

Thus they distinguish between first-order change, that which occurs within a given system such that the system itself remains unchanged, and second-order change, which is in effect a change of change which does bring about change to the system. The analogy they use to illustrate these distinctions is of a person having a nightmare: he can do many things in his dream – run, hide, fight – but changing these behaviours will not terminate the nightmare; second-order change in this case would be to change from dream to waking, bringing about a change to a different state.

We have already noted this and/and quality to our material and have sought to avoid the popular conception of organizational paradoxes.[7] Persistence *and* change undoubtedly characterize our data, even where one might have initially attended only 'change'. For example, at Reckitt and Colman, the 1980s have been a period of significant change(s), selling off parts of the organization, restructuring others and buying in yet more. Even so, the common theme to all this has been persistence as they strengthened their development of consumer and pharmaceutical markets, the business they have always been in.

To talk of change tends to imply a particular focus to the exclusion of other viewpoints and sets a powerful frame for interpretation. *The*

Oxford English Dictionary defines change to mean 'to pass from one form or phase to another'. By contrast, what we have described throughout this book is the seamless quality to our data and the unending process of doing organizing. Rather than clear transitions from one form to another, our data seem to illustrate the doing of organizing as a continuous process with occasional punctuation by events which are attributed greater significance and given more detailed explanation than others.[8] It is these which may be taken to signal phases in the organizations' biographies, but importantly they are not the only phases that could be noted.[9] Our analysis is of the stories of change as they were recounted to us.[10] In no sense have we got *all* the phases or *all* the details of any particular story nor have we got *all* the different versions. What we do have are the stories of a number of executives in each organisation, most of whom told similar stories, that is tales around the same themes.[11]

Hence, we cannot fail to be anything but partial in our analysis since it is based on material from a particular group of senior executives. We can only use what they were aware of and gave expression to us. However, they are a particularly powerful group of organizational members and quite clearly their stories and their explanations should themselves be seen as social actions as they provide frameworks for meaning and response which feed back into the system such that where these are widely accepted and judged appropriate explanations, they are commonly shared and take their place in the 'structuration' of organization.[12]

We keep emphasizing the process nature of our analysis which embodies a temporal quality: rather like telling a joke, the timing of the process is crucial. The notion of organizing as explaining has an integral quality which keeps that time dimension alive. The notion of 'change' by contrast does not. Change implies cut-off points for comparison – taking a snapshot from ten years ago and comparing it with one taken today. The interesting aspect of this analogy is that at the time we might have felt that this photograph was quite good, that we looked quite 'appropriate', but on reflection ten years later, we might think that we look dated or uncharacteristic or seek some other explanation for the way we looked then (well, it was a passport photograph ...). That is to say, explanations of a snapshot view change through time. So what might be seen as the starting point of a change period now, might be given more or less significance when reflecting on the period a couple of years from now.[13]

Hence, the stories and explanations our contributors have given us are not immutable but they rightly belong in the immediate present.[14]

Change

None the less, there is a vast array of written material, expressing a multitude of vocabularies and theories around what may be termed phase models of organizational change. For example, there are 'life-cycle' models reviewed by Quinn and Cameron which predict stages in the life cycle through which organizations mature.[15] They prescribe a logical sequential progression of developmental stages, together with different criteria for evaluating effectiveness at each stage. Ironically there is also something of a time dimension to these models. They were proposed during the 60s and 70s and if they seem too static to model contemporary organizations adequately, then perhaps that is merely a reflection of change itself. That is, current authors tend to agree that 'environments' – social, political, organizational, internal and external – are characterized by uncertainty and turbulence which is perceived to far outstrip the organizational experience of the 60s and 70s. Thus the rational approach to planned and predictable strategic change which may well have characterized organizations in the 70s, and certainly gave rise to 'life-cycle' models, does not seem to reflect organizational life as currently enacted.

Quinn and Cameron, as we have implied, were not alone in their support for phase models of organizational change. In the preface to their book on organizational transitions, Beckhard and Harris note that while organization development and change was an 'abstract matter of concern' in most organizations a decade ago, it is 'now everyday management practice'.[16] However, as they develop their conceptualization of organizational transition, it is clearly taken to mean the process by which an organization develops from one state to another. While they do not clarify the beginning and end of such change states, it seems that for them organizational change is about specific identifiable interventions which can be isolated, defined and discretely contained.

It may be stating the obvious to say that any major organizational change involves three distinct conditions: *the future state*, where the leadership wants the organization to get to; *the present state*, where the organization currently is; and *the transition state*, the set of conditions and activities that the organization must go through to move from the present to the future.[17]

It is, indeed, stating that which was obvious throughout the past decade. This kind of approach rekindles the idea of the marksman, trying to hit his target. Effectiveness is measured by the margin of error between his bullet mark and the bull's eye. The analogy is implicit to a large part of the change effectiveness literature. And it does not resonate either with what we have found or with what one might intuitively expect. For instance, as we write, Eastern Europe and the Soviet Union are in the midst of radical change (so radical that even to call it radical change sounds too mundane). Many commentators hold the roots of this 'revolution' to stem from President Gorbachev's attempts to introduce *glasnost* and *perestroika* (openness and restructuring) into Soviet systems of organizing. It seems ludicrous to imagine that Gorbachev, either in the early days of introducing *glasnost* and *perestroika* or even now, dealing with potential Lithuanian 'independence', could have a clear picture of his target or bull's eye. Undoubtedly he has ideas of what he would like to achieve:[18] notions of opening up the system and restructuring it, perhaps some idea of core values which he hold dear in any 'future state'. But this is a long way off from a fixed definition of that 'future state'.

Indeed, sticking with the example, where might you try to locate this 'future state' or cut-off point against which to evaluate change effectiveness? Should it be the changes in systems of political governance which enable free elections to be held? Or perhaps when the Soviet economy is fully open and integrated into world markets and 'the global economy'? Or perhaps when all Soviet citizens have the freedom and disposable income to travel to other parts of the world? Or maybe when the various ethnic regions of the Soviet Union are restructured into some 'federated' system? Which of these cut-off points describes the end of the 'restructuring' change process or the achievement of some targeted 'future state'? In essence, much of the change literature diverts attention from the significant issues by punctuating change processes with arbitrary and fixed marks, based on a rationality and scientific logic which is not found in the accounts or stories or explanations of organizational change of those who manage organizations.

Quinn's model of logical incrementalism attempts to bring together aspects of the more rational approach to change with the more uncertain and unanticipated conditions facing contemporary, large mature organizations.[19] He proposes:

When sophisticated large organizations make significant changes in strategy, the approaches they use frequently bear little resemblance to the rational analytic systems so often touted in the planning literature. Such systems are rarely the source of overall corporate strategies. Instead, the processes used

to generate major strategies are typically fragmented and evolutionary with
high degree of intuitive content. Although one usually finds embedded ir
these fragments some very refined pieces of formal analysis, overall strategies
tend to emerge as a series of conscious internal decisions blend and interact
with changing external events to slowly mutate key managers' broad consensus about what patterns of action make sense for the future.[20]

This is not to propose a piecemeal process of small incremental
changes. As Kanter points out:

Even when attributed to a single dramatic event or a single dramatic decision,
major changes in large organizations are more likely to represent the
accumulation of accomplishments and tendencies built up slowly over time
and implemented continuously.[21]

The role of pulling together and integrating decisions into cohesive
patterns, reassessing the total organization, is the crucial part played
by 'effective executives':

Successful managers who operate logically and proactively in an incremental
mode build the seeds of understanding, identity and commitment into the
very processes which create their strategies.[22]

Hence, incrementalism does not simply mean the cumulative
process of small, reactive changes. Even major change programmes
'rarely end up as initially envisioned', managers must proactively
manage the change process incrementally, 'reshaping their broad
early visions, step by step'.[23]

Quinn and Kanter are expressing ideas which we can recognize
from our data. The following remarks from Brian Beazer sum up the
comments of a number of respondents:

We have a five year plan and it is updated from time to time. I have to confess
that I rarely ever look at it because I think it is a waste of time … I'm not sure
what is going to happen tomorrow, leave alone five years down the
road … Now if that (Koppers acquisition) goes through, we will spend a fair
amount of money on it and therefore will not be buying another opportunity
that arises in Hong Kong because the money isn't there. But if that fails and
something arises in Hong Kong, we can do it. Now maybe we can do both if
we sacrifice something else. It's a question of choice and it's when the
opportunity arises.

Many of our respondents illustrate the integrative idea of fragments of rigorous analysis blending with more intuitive 'judgement'

and 'feel'. For example, Sir David Alliance is acknowledged to have a 'commercial nose', an intuitive feel for buying and selling and an implicit sense of timing, but his team also comprises skilled and thorough analysts. The 'mutating of key managers' broad consensus' is also found in our data – for instance, Terry O'Neill at Glynwed, who remained sceptical to begin with but is now a 'fervent' supporter of Gareth Davies' plans for lowest cost production/bilingual managing, etc. As Gareth Davies put it:

When you start (change) … you (have) a number of sceptics and the greatest sceptics in the end become the best converts.

Kanter's point is more difficult to dissect. Not that we disagree with her sentiments. Rather we would suggest that the attributions made depend on timing and who is making them. That is, whether or not change was brought about by a single event or an accumulation of accomplishments is irrelevant to the extent that the meaning of either interpretation lies in response. What does matter is the explanation which is adjudged appropriate at that time and evidenced in the responses generated. One has only to refer back to the quotation from Brian Beazer to find an example of this. 'It's a question of choice and it's *when* the opportunity arises'.

And Quinn's discussion of 'effective executives' helps to highlight the importance of 'explanation as organization', building 'the seeds of understanding, identity and commitment into the very processes which create their strategies'. Indeed, both these comments draw attention to the process of structuration: 'the dynamic process whereby structures come into being … an active constituting process, accomplished by and consisting in, the doings of active subjects'.[24] Perhaps the most comprehensive illustration is that of Reckitt and Colman – where everything seemed to interrelate and interdepend, like a healthy 'mind and body'.[25]

And thus it is that we are talking about the doing of organizing writ large or in bold type. The themes are similar – of organizations as explanations, attempts to control shared meaning by channelling response and of executives as artists, scientists, craftsmen and wrighters. Only they are given greater emphasis, bolder type when described in the context of changing. We undoubtedly have evidence of major change programmes which 'rarely end up as initially envisioned' but our data describe this situation rather more pragmatically and continuously. At no point does anyone express the view either that they know exactly where they are going or that they have simply achieved what they 'set out' to achieve. The 'doing of organizing' doesn't work like that. But they do all have ideas and aspirations for their organizations' future against which and in terms of which potential changes can be described, shaped, evaluated and developed. Indeed, a vision is an explanation set in the future, an embodiment of ambitions and aspirations.

Ideology

The literature which describes the concept of vision and the process of envisioning is rather disappointing. For a subject so vital and imaginative, the models and theories are surprisingly dull. It is perhaps a case, once again, of our language being inadequate, too linear, to describe the complexity of social life, in the imaginative leap from present to future. The following illustration from Robbins and Duncan helps to make this point and highlights just how difficult, if not impossible, it is to describe envisioning in any way close to human experience. They define vision as:

... the shared, aspired future state for the organization which identifies the organization's values, sets priorities for goals and objectives, and sets the guidelines by which these goals and objectives will be pursued.

From this, they argue, it follows that:

... envisioning, or the process by which the CEO and top management create and utilize visions, for the future to initiate change is the key to the initiation and implementation of a major reorientation for an organization.[26]

They go on to identify two phases of the envisioning process, individual sensemaking and vision creation, in which:

... top decision makers interpret and make sense of environmental and organizational contingencies and translate those characteristics into a strategic vision which is specific and makes sense for that particular organization.[27]

The first *phase* is all about triggering the need for action, interpreting the contingencies and recognizing the need for change in the form of a new organizational vision.[28] The second *phase* includes formulating an initial vision, communicating it 'to top management and the rest of the organization', and developing a negotiated vision. From this emerges the 'ultimate vision', based on commitment from and consensus of organizational members.

While our respondents might claim to have no ultimate theories to guide their actions, they certainly have ideas and aspirations. Indeed, we might be tempted to say that they have visions, only not in the sense described above. That is, each had *some* personal or individual idea about the future and also shared a collective view about potential aims and possible achievements, even though individually these ambitions might not be identical in their potential realization. In this sense, it was a blend of communication and/with commitment, of shaped and random response and/with values and belief. It is tempting to conceptualize these ideas into some notion of ideology, both personal and organizational, although we must stress that this ideology can be revised and modified according to time and place. Sederberg notes:

Ideologies are commonly associated with groups advocating significant change, because they must justify something new, whereas the defenders of the established order can usually depend upon the tacit, and essentially automatic, support of much of the population.[29]

We detected in some of our commentaries a hint of 'ideology', in the sense of 'visionary speculation' about what they might be able to achieve. Rather than the prescribed serial triggering, interpreting, recognizing and communicating, of some specific strategic vision, our respondents describe a more vital notion of remaining sensitive to possibility; like good pragmatists, continually asking 'what if' kinds of questions.[30]

Bringing these ideas together in illustrations of organizational changes, we find it more helpful to talk of ideologies, shaped by values and beliefs which in effect provide the framework which guides thinking, acting and, what others might call, envisioning. We wish to make very clear that we are not about to debate the issues of political ideologies and the inevitable conflicts which, for political scientists, are expressed in 'ideological struggles'. Nor are we claiming that our respondents are in any way blinded by some grand ideological commitment. Indeed, we are not using the term ideology as might political scientists and if we could find another term for it we would. But the notion of ideology is the best way we can find to capture the sense of some set of core values and beliefs which guide the actions of our respondents and the choices they make about *future* action.[31]

Organizational theorists seem to have borrowed and used such concepts as values, beliefs and ideologies in quite haphazard fashion.

Some talk of organizational values, others of personal values,[32] and the concept of ideology, although not so widely used, tends to be defined almost as a forerunner to organizational culture. We can see the logic in relating ideology to culture but wish to take a step back from it. Organization culture is highly 'feelable',[33] but emerges, as we suggested earlier, in directions for behaviour. It has an immediacy which is felt and enacted in the daily practice of managing and organizing. Ideology, we suggest, is not so palpable but rather has a more subtle influence on guiding future actions and responses. This is rooted in the values and beliefs currently preferred and embodied in the dominant definition of organizational reality.[34] As a set of ideas, ideology has a powerful influence on shaping 'ways of thinking' and 'visionary speculation' as people deal with the future. Hence ideology guides (perception of) the choices and decisions and imaginary ventures made about the yet unknown, whereas culture guides thinking and acting in the here and now.

Karl Weick has pointed out that the common adage of 'I'll believe it when I see it' should be 'turned on its ear so that it approximates more closely the ways in which people actually act: "I'll see it when I believe it." Beliefs are cause maps that people impose on the world after which they "see" what they have already imposed .·. Believing does control seeing, but ... the seeing in turn conditions further beliefs, which in turn constrain seeing, and so on.'[35]

We are using the term ideology to describe this kind of belief system, which has a strong pragmatist thread to it, interrelating belief and action (together with implied risk). If you place this in the framework we have of meaning in response and structuration, then you see the emergent 'ing' nature of this process. As we have already suggested in chapter 3, our respondents are imagining people: they 'see' a range of possibilities and their belief systems enable them to use experience and imagination to challenge rather than to constrain what they might see. That is, ideology implies some notion of future action: either in the sense of testing out and developing through action your ideological beliefs or of converting others to share these with you. And this we find to be much more compelling than the notion of vision or envisioning. Essentially, there is no single answer to 'what if ...?'. Rather, the answers keep moving, keeping pace with change/action. It is truly an iterative process of going to and fro, between key people to evaluate potential response to ideas (not just your own) and to assess 'what else might ...?' depending on the answer to 'what if ...?', guided by and shaping an ideology.

To recall how Brian Smith put it:

If I tell you what happened, I hope you don't think that it is because I am a
guy who is sufficiently well organized and logical to have it all spelt out on a
programme in advance. It's done by listening, feeling and tuning.

Vision implies some fixed sense of what might be achieved: it
suggests a goal or a target or at least some intention or aspiration.
Different visions suggest different targets or aspirations and again we
have the image of the marksman, following a set of rules and
procedures aiming for his target: that 'pull' process which is evaluated in terms of degrees of error or 'miss' from the target. Ideology
on the other hand, implies nothing of this: rather, it provides a push
to action and a way of thinking which will undoubtedly shape some
sense of 'visionary speculation', embracing values and beliefs. But
rather than a set of different visions for different situations and
circumstances, an ideology allows you to deal with any number of
situations. So where one might conceive of a vision as some future
state and envisioning as the deductive process of working out how
best to achieve that, ideology, as we are using it, is a rather more
pragmatic and inductive notion, building up from current circumstances, shaping one's actions and responses to situations in the
process of enacting an ideology. Undoubtedly this is not random, nor
is it a one-way process: ideology is a powerful push which influences
and is influenced *by* thinking and acting in dealing with events. But it
does mean that it is a continuous process: there is no clear endpoint,
unlike achieving a vision. And it is an open and interactive concept,
rather than being framed by a logic which describes how to achieve a
vision.

Sir Owen Green captures these ideas and makes a crucial point in
the context of large diversified enterprises:

I like to think we're a very catholic group, in the sense that you can have
many faiths, just so long as the interpretation of the faith is such that it can be
compared – which is vital.

He also helps to give a clue as to the role of the centre: that is, to
provide a broad framework of ideology which embraces many
different interpretations. The centre does not and probably could not
dictate to all members exactly how to interpret the common ideology.
And part of the strength of the corporate centre seems to stem from
the fact that, within any of our organizations, there was a sufficiently
broad range of interpretations to ensure diversity and difference,
adapting to each subsidiary or divisional priorities. Within each
enterprise, however, there was a common ideology, a core belief

system and sense of what was valued by the organization providing the glue which binds them all together and it is the role of the corporate centre to communicate this faithfully [sic] to all members.[36]

Ideological Conversion

As we discussed in chapter 2, the structuring of organization is as much part of the communication process as are the things people say and do and don't say and don't do. That is, they together communicate and shape what the enterprise values, a sense of beliefs through channelling response. Hence to change in any significant sense means to depart from (at lease some of) these 'structures and communications' – a new direction in this communication process. Some change, however slight, from the established patterns needs to be communicated by every means possible to shape new meanings and channel new responses. And this way, we argue, the communication process takes on greater emphasis as, in terms of our notion of ideology, senior managers engage in a process of 'converting' others.Thus, while the everyday patterns and routines communicate the established order (that is, infusing steadily through reiteration and reinforcement of current messages), in the case of change, the power of communication must be stepped up to convert people: that is, to persuade others of an ideology and engage their commitment. Indeed, if you have faith and the ability to communicate, then it is possible to 'convert' others.[37] In Barnard's terms, this is 'conviction':

The creative function as a whole is the essence of leadership. It is the highest test of executive responsibility because it requires for successful accomplishment that element of 'conviction' that means identification of personal codes and organization codes in the view of the leader. This is the coalescence that carries 'conviction' to the personnel of organization, to that informal organization underlying all formal organization that senses nothing more quickly than insincerity.[38]

Where Barnard places this vast responsibility on the shoulders of 'the leader', we emphasize that it is the responsibility of the leadership, – the Executive team, sharing with their Chief Executive/ Chairman – each blending personal and organizational codes. Like all good preachers, much time is spent trying to persuade others 'to see it in order to believe it': and without belief, we suggest, action and risk cannot be integrated in any coherent sense.

There are many different ways of approaching the ideological conversion business and our data illustrate quite a few, typically as ever, in the context of 'other stories': for example, about the enormous commitment of time and energy in talking to people to bring about change:

Last Friday night, we completed a tour of every business unit and major function, the Chairman and Chief Executive and I, plus the relevant portfolio director ... we visited every business team ... where really we were saying, 'Come on ... what are you doing to make things move? What are you doing to involve your employees and let them have fun in creating change?'... It's a lot of talking and exhorting in a way.

Or about prompting change in their divisions while still allowing divisional autonomy and responsibility:

It's not an imposition on anyone, it's more a persuasive philosophy rather than a very highly disciplined series of orders that give rise to these changes.

Or about leading the process of major change:

Now how did we do it, really? I suppose if the truth were told, by being a missionary. By going to every individual who holds responsibility and telling him what his part is in doing it. We have told hundreds of people this ...[39]

There is something of the religious conversion in this process of preaching a faith, an ideology, a set of values and ideas of what might be possible. And it is all about talk and words.

As the quotations above suggest, in some cases there may be a more subtle deliberate flavour to this process, whereby the Chief Executive might ask a question, or point something out to someone – provide the initial prompting – and then ultimately this other person becomes the champion or initiator within the enterprise.[40] As John West puts it: 'The ideal thing is to get people to propose things and to fight for them that you would rather like to see proposed and fought for yourself.'

Sir Owen Green provides another illustration of a similar process:

You've got to have stimulation but I think it's a good thing for people to have a feeling about where they are. Part of setting scenes, when you are changing – developing a new policy again, to me, should never be a surprise. Very difficult to get it over anyway, if you were suddenly bringing down a tablet from the mountain. Then you've got to sell it very hard in an organization like ours. The way to do it – you don't have to bring it down suddenly, but you start to talk about things, share extracts from views and news, etc. in front of people, and introduce it in conversation, and steadily, like water dripping ... Then you produce the proposal and most people will claim it for their own anyway. You can get a lot of things done that you could probably get done anyway but they get done because everybody feels that they have participated, they own it.

Inevitably what each chooses to be receptive to depends partly on experience and imagination. In Sir Owen Green's case, his long experience of success, based on financial rigour and management accountability, means that he probably evaluates these aspects 'without even thinking'. In reviewing the business plans of a BTR company he explains:

the sort of thing that you usually find written down in 15 pages is in our minds ... We can look at plans and we can ... see ... whether they are symmetrical or whether there is something out of kilter.

So perhaps even implicitly for him, these things must be in order before beginning to make other changes.[41] He goes on to talk about managing the relationship between centre and subsidiary, where the companies are given autonomy and responsibility for their development:

We will influence. Again, the profit plan is a scene when you can very quickly review things, but part of management right through the year is ... a continuing dialogue with managers and general managers... A lot of our strategies and a lot of our tactics are developed through dialogue, through, if I say 'casual', I mean not really 'planned' (dialogue) ... So I think you can get a long way through discussion on very level terms with people .. My practice has always been to walk into the person's office and ... if he's not busy, sit down and have a cup of tea and a chat and talk about what's been happening and what's going to happen. Perhaps I've been to a meeting somewhere, with some influential people, and what we've talked about – not that we believe too much in relating to too many of these clubs. But one finds that messages get through in that way in a relatively unstructured way, but it's structured in the sense that we provide for that sort of exchange.

Gareth Davies at Glynwed is an accountant by training and background and for him financial data are an important basis from which to develop. Obviously, however, he goes far beyond the figures and emphasizes how he has sought to ensure his managers *'understand'* what the ratios do for their business and what their business does for the ratios'. On a more 'macro' level, under his 'executorship' the Group has moved from 'this sort of Midland metal basher to being described as a fast growing engineering Group'. In order to do so, some difficult decisions have been taken which have perhaps contradicted conventional wisdom at the time:

It was difficult for people to believe that steel was going to come into this country in any quantity but we felt that this was likely to be the case ... And we therefore decided we would resize the Group to take into account all those factors, following a Group philosophy that we should always be the lowest cost producer in any market which we supplied.

Again, faith, belief, values and conviction. As he goes on to explain, the workforce was cut by 40 per cent and inevitably some companies were contracted or closed.

Don't let the market contract it for us. Let's force the contraction *if we believe* that it's going to contract.

In the process of reorganization, new relationships have been forged and the organization runs on what he describes as 'controlled autonomy', where companies have autonomy within 'fairly tight financial parameters'.

Within Glynwed, change is encouraged from the companies – they are charged with growing their businesses and as those who know most about their business, they are expected to come up with ideas about products, markets, production, distribution, etc. However, some of these suggestions do emanate from the top. Gareth Davies described how he had spotted a particular product idea which required two different companies to work together, when they would not otherwise interrelate. He himself prompted the initial contact and made it organizationally possible for them to establish this link-up:[42]

They actually picked that one up – didn't do anything with it for about 18 months but they picked it up.

Gareth Davies illustrates the sense of continuity as one thing unfolds into another. Talking about a recent acquisition, he explained that they were particularly interested in one aspect of the newly acquired distribution system, 'but they are also distributors of sheet and rod which takes us off into another strategy which we will develop'. Once again, one gets the feeling that there is a sense of possibility and immanence about this process.

Terry O'Neill has already been noted for his comments on the 'missionary zeal' with which they set about 'converting' their managers. But, he also notes the change in change itself: that is, the change in expectations about what is possible and achievable for and by the Group:

I think probably the most important thing that I have learned in the last ten years is that we didn't really know where the winning post was and we still don't know. Now if you say it (our pace of change) is astronomical and I say, yes it is astronomical if you start with your feet on the ground ... but I don't know that it is *that* astronomical now ... It's only remarkable compared with what we used to have.

Again, there is that *crucial* time dimension to the doing of organizing – writ large or small. We have already noted the ability to 'simplify the past through explanation' – that is, highlight a particular pattern of meanings by which to make sense of present action and to guide the range of future response. Their unique biographies of experience in this way help to guide and shape their own 'visionary speculations'.

Imagination and experience can act as constraints for some people, restricting their range of response to what is mutually or culturally expected. In others, imagination and experience together pose challenges to that constraint – to make new connections, generate different frames and try out new steps.[43] For instance, faced with crisis in an organization which was rubber technology based with a long history in tyre manufacture, it must have taken some considerable imagination for executives at Avon Rubber to propose moving away from tyre production. Some would say that they reframed the problem to the level of second-order change, although we feel sure that if asked what they felt they had done, their responses would be more in terms of risk and gamble, both organizational and personal. Indeed, in the way the story was recounted, there was more a sense of evangelical faith and belief as the support gradually grew for this second-order change and gradually the idea 'made more sense'.

These examples are quite typical of our data and are packed with themes for the organizational analyst: for instance, anticipating market changes, simple group objective, proaction, financial control and management responsibility, strategic leadership, communication, change and so on. But even the very act of naming these organizational themes somehow puts a distance between action and analysis as to focus on one such theme implies to 'not focus' on others and begins to take apart that which exists as a whole.[44]

However, what is common to these explanations are three elements of Pragmatism – belief, action and their associated risk. Indeed, to highlight these does not reduce the explanations. The notion of belief or conviction goes beyond that of vision to describe a continuing and developing faith rather than the implied individual or particular state envisioned. Faith or belief is evidenced through action and response. And in this way, so one demonstrates one's values: that is, by enacting what it is one values which underpins belief rather than the prescription to 'set organizational values' through describing a vision.[45]

Curiously, the individual envisioner's role is rarely mentioned in the envisioning process. It is somehow objectified or at best left implicit that the envisioner will not allow personal motivations to 'intrude'. Clearly this is nonsense and we argue that there is a good deal of the personal invested in envisioning. Indeed, we have already had a taste of it, as Tony Mitchard feels his spine 'steeling' as 1,000 workers respond by apparently accepting his vision of what might be Avon's future. Likewise, the business press is littered with tales of personal crisis and Board room coups where chief executives have failed to persuade others to share their vision. And organizations have been known to fail because of a leader 'blinded' by personal conviction which is not shared by anyone either within or without the organization.

Indeed, conviction seems to lie at the heart of it. If you are to persuade others that in answer to a 'what if' question, it is possible to imagine this or that particular organizational opportunity, then there is an element of 'pigs might fly' to it. Persuasion and communication are important parts of the process and there are similarities to religious conversion. Gareth Davies notes that his managers were initially sceptical about his ideas but that he managed to persuade them and they are now the best converts.

However, even Gareth Davies was at pains to 'depersonalize' his account, attributing successful change to a 'team effort'. But how do such ideas become the collective vision or at least sufficiently supported to become the priority for the enterprise? For instance, in BTR's case, the team of three had been together for nearly 20 years such that in effect, they could no doubt speak for each other and be able to anticipate what response a particular visionary speculation might prompt in the other two. Similarly Sir David Alliance and John Ashton were particularly close, yet not so close as to exclude other more recent newcomers. And at Reckitt and Colman, the team was bigger and more diverse with a mixture of newcomers and old hands – yet they described a particularly consensual view of future organizational aspirations.[46] Indeed, when asked about change under his forthcoming 'Chief Executiveship', John St Lawrence said that at most he would anticipate a change in style since as a director he had contributed to policy over the last few years and was a party to the decisions taken by the 'Chief Executive in Committee'.

In this way, though, one begins to see the problems inherent in attempts to focus simply on and to define change. Is it to be defined at an overall global level, in terms of organizational mission, or more specifically, in terms of strategic direction, or more pragmatically in terms of practice and tactics? Alternatively, perhaps a definition of change should ideally embody all these levels. But should it be expressed in terms of change state or process? Should the definition be taken as that described at the outset or is there sufficient flexibility for review and reappraisal in the light of contingencies? And so on.

Trying to answer some of these questions we note that undoubtedly there is a distinction to be drawn between change states and processes. Yet from our point of view they are both part of the doing of organizing: although one is a snapshot and the other a (black and white?) video, they are both attempts to describe action and attribute significance to selected particular organizational actions and each feeds back into the process and shapes subsequent response and change. As March notes:

Theories of change in organizations are primarily different ways of describing theories of action in organizations, not different theories. Most changes in organizations reflect simple responses to demographic, economic, social and political forces.[47]

However, rather than attribute such 'change action' to 'simple responses' we wish to emphasize that in doing organizing our contributors are in effect 'doing acting' – that is, both responding to and creating action.

At this point, we refer back to chapter 2 and the 'Doing of Organizing' where we proposed that the culture of an organization helps to direct much of what takes place and provides the context against which action will be evaluated and judgements of appropriateness made. It is thus important to have a common understanding of expected response. However, what this framework does not allow you to do is to predict change in the abstract. That is, perhaps through intimate knowledge of the organization one might be able to anticipate potential changes: but this does not allow you to predict change in the sense that most organizational change theories attempt to do. But this in effect highlights the ultimate irony of the subject: if you can predict change, then it loses its essential 'uncertainty' and instead becomes part of 'predictable' organizational routines.[48]

And Vandalism ...

Sederberg uses the term 'cultural vandalism' to describe 'significant innovation' in the context of leadership. In effect, what he is describing is the ability 'to generate a range of potential behaviours and ... the ability to break away from previously established pro-clivities and select a divergent response from among the potential alternatives'.[49]

We agree with his outcome of cultural vandalism but we do not go so far as asserting the necessity of conscious or deliberate choice between potential alternatives. Our data do not always illustrate such clear decision making. Rather, we find more pragmatic notions of belief, action and risk which may lead to a choice between alternatives or, with hindsight, might be reconstructed to imply that alternatives must have been discarded.[50] And the test of 'truth' of such actions is their practical consequences.

Our respondents probably do not think of themselves as vandals but, in effect, change demands the destruction of some 'directions for behaviour' and the construction of some new ones. At Metal Box, on opening the bird cage doors, Brian Smith in effect was destroying the previous directions under which managers had been tightly constrained by cost-cutting and introspection and giving new instructions which said, you have independence and responsibility – see where it takes you. The emphasis on cultural change here is that a simple instruction such as 'you have independence, now fly' is not sufficient: the whole doing of organizing has to be reworked in order to reinforce and reiterate such changes in message.

We must stress that there is no evaluative implication in these comments: indeed, cost-cutting had been an important cultural direction *at the time*. Without it, Brian Smith would have been heading up a very different Metal Box. But having led a sustained period of substantial cost-cutting, his predecessor, we are told, felt that the nature of change required subsequently to grow the business was best led by someone not associated with this inevitably introspective period. A new perspective was required. Indeed, Brian Smith had had a similar experience following a major cost-cutting programme in a previous role he had in ICI:

It's very difficult if you've once had an ethos of clamp back, cut back and retrenchment, to suddenly say, 'Right, I've lifted my head. Now all of you lift your heads and do it'. It's easier for an outside agency to come in and ask a whole lot of new questions, without constraint.

His colleague, Geoff Armstrong sums up some of these ideas for us:

It's a series of principled strategic questions rather than making the best decision for yourself. I think the days of the decisive decision maker at the top of an organization, taking all the important decisions, are gone. Nobody's going to be that clever any more. And it's very much a process of process management that is required of top managers now. So that you create the framework, the process, by which others are enabled to work effectively. It isn't doing their jobs for them.

These ideas of questioning and enabling bring us back to our master metaphor of senior managers as artists/craftsmen – wrighters. In this instance, they may be taken to adopt the role of the theatre director, not someone who appears on the stage, but someone whose advice and response shapes the performance of those who do. The good theatre director nudges and prompts his/her actors, he or she sets the frame within which they perform and gives them 'notes' (feedback) on their enactments. Some of the flavour of this collective improvisation is caught in the following comments:

So there's no-one who can know the details of everything in a group such as this or any group. What you should know is the important issues. Somebody then has to define what are important issues and that's going to vary in every company in accordance with size, in accordance with its activities.

We (four directors) have a coordinating role and hopefully an influential role. You don't just produce figures, you help people interpret them and say, 'What the hell can we do with them?' For example, my drive at the moment is ... And then that I hope will initiate management action.[51]

On getting change into the system:

And last September we flew, trained and bussed 8,000 of our UK staff into a theatre for 12 performances in the course of a week. Listened to an exhortation from me to do better or whatever. If it had been in my job description, I wouldn't have taken the job, with lasers and dry ice and all the rest of it ... I don't know whether the thing was successful or not. Ask me in ten years time. The way of measuring the success of a thing like that is your bottom line, market share and all the other things. These things don't respond in six months.[52]

So we have our teams asking questions, talking, proselytizing, and persuading in the doing of organizing/process of enacting organizations. There is a lot of nudging and prompting to this process and it is continuous – demanding enormous amounts of time, energy and commitment from team members. It is about belief, action and risk, as in the best Pragmatist tradition – they have to make up their minds and act.

... and Propagation

But to what ends? If we say it is not helpful to characterize this as 'change' and we find in our data little primacy given to planning and formal evaluation of strategic alternatives,[53] then what is it they are about and where are they going?[54] We haven't mentioned Barnard for a while as he says practically nothing about 'organizational change' in terms which relate to contemporary understanding of the concept. What he does talk about, though, is organizational purposes and changing purposes and he also makes reference to a rather elusive notion of efficiency, all of which is based on an assumption of growth. He notes 'the innate propensity of organizations to expand. The maintenance of incentives, particularly those relating to prestige, pride of association, and community satisfaction calls for growth, enlargement, extension.'[55]

And although he never quite spells out exactly what kinds of things constitute 'growth', it is an idea we find our respondents talk about more readily than some abstract or universal conception of change:

The greatest motivation of all, I think, is growth. The new experience. The new challenge. The changing scene for people. Particularly people who are in areas of influence ... a manufacturing manager, Managing Director of the smaller companies, growth positively excites them ...

They are charged with growing their business ... and all I want are managers who can grow businesses.[56]

This is not to claim some simple goal of aggrandizement. The doing of organizing is much more subtle and ultimately paradoxical. Many at the time we spoke with them were engaged in a process, such as Avon Rubber, of reducing in order to 'grow'. The change literature talks about restructuring, reforming, transforming, as different kinds of change processes. We suggest that to re-frame these in terms of growth, they are essentially all the same. And we take as our definition of growth a situational one which is based on the 'background of prior products'; that is, the tradition in which they are growing. So for example, both Avon Rubber and Metal Box illustrate 're-structuring' on very different scales, given that they are in size terms a minnow and a whale. And the nature of restructuring was quite different in each case with different objectives and foci, but common to each was a sense of growth.

Each organization has a history and a 'background of prior products' relative to which each is engaged in growth. In our data, these backgrounds emerge as the 'punctuation marks' in their stories: that is, the critical factors which are signified in their explanations as being what they see to be key to their development. Inevitably this can only be evaluated in a qualitative sense although they may each be able to indicate some quantative markers. Indeed, each organization had its own criteria against which to evaluate growth although we are hesitant to put it in such terms. That is, we are not claiming a set of measures, comparable across all our contributing organizations by which to obtain some objective evaluation of growth. However, each organization was comprised of different parts and the parts have to be able to talk to each other and generally speak the same financial language which enables the centre to make comparisons. And in each organization certain indicators were given greater significance than others.[57]

Inevitably, though, such criteria are part of the communication process by which the Executive team nudges and shapes the nature of growth. By setting performance criteria for subsidiaries and leaving them to decide how to meet them; or by acquiring businesses and integrating them into the organization; or by selling off businesses or reducing in size other parts of the organization; or by refocusing their businesses through restructuring to signal priority investment areas; or by encouraging new systems of work or reward or whatever. By all of these and no doubt more, the Executive team signals and communicates what it takes to be the primary purposes of the enterprise. And as contributors were at pains to point out, while it is important for them to know what is going on, 'it really is impossible in this organization to interfere with other people's businesses, provided they perform'.[58] Rather, it is a process of enabling the different parts of their organizations to 'grow' and to perform effectively. In a sense, it is a case of 'pushing back the limitations' rather than defining the limitations to be achieved (in the sense of adding up the constituent parts to arrive at some total 'vision').[59]

Barnard actually has quite a lot to say about purposes: 'common purpose' is one of his three key elements of organization, together with 'communication' and 'willingness to serve'.[60] These are the necessary and sufficient conditions of organization. The notion of purpose though, he argues, 'is axiomatic, implicit in the words "system", "coordination", "cooperation". It is something that is clearly evident in many observed systems of cooperation, although it is often not formulated in words, and sometimes cannot be so formulated. In such cases what is observed is the direction or effect of the activities, from which purpose may be inferred'.[61]

He is often criticized for his conception of organizations as systems of *cooperative* effort.[62] We suggest that this is a little harsh since there is nothing idealistic in his notion. In his discussion of purpose, he goes on to point out that organizational purpose and individual motive are only very rarely identical (with the exceptions of family, patriotic and religious organizations). 'Individual motive is necessarily an internal, personal, subjective thing; common purpose is necessarily an external, impersonal, objective thing, even though the individual interpretation of it is subjective'.[63] Hence he does not seem to be claiming cooperation without conflict or difference.

However, Barnard is not entirely consistent in his development of the concept and we would tread more carefully in distinguishing between individual and common purpose because it is a crucial point, largely glossed over in contemporary literature. We agree with his first point about individual motive but differ in our understanding of common purpose. On the basis of our evidence, we agree that it is often something not formulated in words but suggest that it *becomes* 'an external, impersonal, objective thing' through the cumulative actions of individuals. In the process of nudging, shaping and prompting organizational members, so the Executive team communicates a sense of purpose which becomes 'objectified' and part of the organization 'structuring'.[64]

As Barnard goes on to note: 'once established, organizations change their unifying purposes. They tend to perpetuate themselves; and in the effort to survive may change the reasons for existence'.[65] Indeed, one is tempted to argue that his is a very pragmatic notion of change.[66] His logic, though, becomes slightly confused when talking about the objective environment of decision:

It may seem strange perhaps that purpose should be included in the objective environment, since purpose of all things seems personal, subjective, internal, the expression of desire. This is true; but *at the moment of a new decision*, an existing purpose is an objective fact, and it is so treated at that moment in so far as it is a factor in new decision ... But no matter how arrived at, when decision is in point, *the purpose is fact already determined* [emphasis added]; its making is a matter of history; it may be as objective as another man's emotions may be to an observer.[67]

Perhaps he is suggesting that it is the individual's *interpretation* of purpose which makes it *seem* subjective: if this is the case, though, he is neither as clear nor as forceful in asserting the 'objectiveness' of purpose as he was earlier. However, his final point helps to crystallize the way in which individual becomes common purpose and in transition takes on the quality of objective structure, encompassed in decision – 'when decision is in point, the purpose is fact already determined'.[68]

Formulating purpose is one of the three key executive functions according to Barnard and he goes on to explain:

It is more apparent here than with other executive functions that it is an entire executive organization that formulates, redefines, breaks into details, and decides on the innumerable simultaneous and progressive actions that are the stream of syntheses constituting purpose or action. No single executive can under any conditions accomplish this function alone, but only that part of it which relates to his position in the executive organization.[69]

The 'stream of syntheses'. What a wonderful phrase. John Ashton helps to identify the dilemma facing those in search of a more tangible sense of this stream:

One can oversimplify and perhaps over-formalize something and say, 'very clearly here is sort of ... ' and start drawing family trees. and 'here is the Group generation of ideas', 'here is where it is implemented', 'this is the policy producers', 'this is the policy implementation part of the thing', 'this is where the action takes place', 'and here is the profit responsibility', and so on. I suppose that does exist but not in such a clear cut way as perhaps you are hoping. It works. It is people being used to working together and knowing what's in each other's minds and what their philosophies are and then getting down to it. And, as I say, very much the inter-action of people.

It works. And as Barnard goes on to conclude: 'The function of formulating grand purposes and providing for their redefinition is one which needs sensitive systems of communication, experience in interpretation, imagination, and delegation of responsibility'.[70] We believe this is recognizable to all our contributors.

However, this does also help to highlight a very interesting point which we found evidenced in the stories we were told. That is, it is easier to manage a failure than it is to manage a success. In essence, the organization facing 'failure' already has part of the communication process played out for it. For Tony Mitchard, persuading his employees to accept his definition of appropriate action was much aided by the fact that the signs were 'obvious', the organization was publicly reporting poor performance figures, there was evidence of declining markets in tyre production and increasing cheap competition, there were many members of the organization already aware that Avon had for some time faced a difficult situation which needed 'radical' action. His persuasive attempts picked up on a message already being relayed around the system.

However, to persuade an organization which by all accounts is 'doing well', or returning acceptable performance figures and apparently doing good business to accept a change in purpose means the communication systems need to be much more 'sensitive' in Barnard's terms and even more persuasive. Sir Brian Corby made this point:

It has, I think, been much more difficult in the case of the Prudential where the staff on the whole are doing perfectly well but the market share happens to be declining because the market is growing really very fast. Now it's much more difficult to persuade people like that to make radical changes in their working methods. In this sense, I see management of an ongoing company that's performing reasonably well as being very much a matter of persuading people to change way before there is any necessity to change.

And Brian Smith perhaps sums it up best for us:

These are the great management changes that are going on because the environment's changed and the speed and rate of reaction has changed and you've got to train people to respond and to share this challenge with you. And it's an awesome task, I think. But if you don't do it, then you will just lag behind and become obsolete, so there's never any doubt that it has to be done. The hardest thing to do, in a funny way, is to make real change when the business appears to be in good shape. If a business is in a crisis, or heading for disaster, then the human race reacts to that and there is a common purpose that's easy to identify ... When you've gone through that phase, and you're going from competence to excellence, and you know damn well that today's excellence will be tomorrow's competence, and that it's a never-ending game, that is when it is harder to get people to have a common purpose to accept change and work together.

And perhaps this is what the 'truly' successful executive team is all about: being sufficiently in control of their enterprise, communicating and generating responses to common purpose to shape and nudge in the right direction before others define direction of shaping and nudging for them.

5
'And Now for Something Completely the Same'

What's the special condition that exists in the company? I honestly don't see anything that isn't reproducible. I have to accept that the ... corporate environment of this company has been important. And I suppose the corporate environment is influenced by people – it isn't something you can pick out of a book ... We're on to chemistry again. So unless you have the sort of people that we have had and have, I suppose you couldn't reproduce it. But short of that, I can think of nothing that isn't reproducible.

Sir Owen Green, BTR

It would appear that all that is needed for success is the right sort of corporate environment which, in turn, is dependent upon the right type and mix of people – the chemistry. The allusion to chemistry is slightly misleading in that chemical reactions are relatively easy to predict and reproduce; organizations are less easy to predict and much less easy to reproduce. We do not know the elements in the same way as elements are known in chemistry and we certainly are in no position to make definitive statements about particular combinations of actors. Indeed, the drift of our argument throughout this book has been and is that actors and actions are unique.[1]

And so we continue to avoid prescriptions, categorizations and component parts but in this chapter, we will have more to say on executive process. We have tried throughout to keep an eye on 'doing', the active, developing and temporal qualities of our material which the linearity of language and analysis easily obscures. So we have sought regularly to remind ourselves that there is a sense of wholeness to our material and that the themes of the previous four chapters are punctuation marks of our choosing. We happen to think they are the most appropriate punctuation marks and they enable us to develop our understanding of executive process: the interweaving of the doing of managing, of organizing, of leading and of organizing writ large does keep our subject alive and restless. However, such is the *integral* quality of this material that we have a number of ideas which might have appeared in any one of the preceding four chapters (and indeed, some have already been touched on briefly). These include Pragmatism and paradox, whole–part relationships and story-telling, learning and creativity. And in re-viewing some of our material, this chapter will address these themes. We will also comment on what, by comparison, seem rather more fragmented and somewhat hackneyed notions of competence, performance and effectiveness. This perhaps sounds like a conceptual rattlebag, but we see no harm in a little commotion.

Pragmatists

It all starts from understanding how you make a profit. It's as simple as that.

Once again, Sir Owen Green has it in a nutshell and from the comments of our other contributors, we believe they would agree with his comments; they are, after all, running some very large, highly profitable organizations. But there is rather more to it than that, as even Sir Owen went on to admit. Underlying the preceding four chapters is a very powerful sense of continuity and of energy. They variously describe themselves as 'doers', – 'a coat's-off organization', to give a couple of examples.[2] Very much immersed in the action of their organization, although not so immersed they become submerged. That is, none is so determined to be 'hands-on' that it is 'hands-in'. All eschew interfering in what their companies actually do in terms of day-to-day operations. Rather, 'executive work is not that *of* the organization, but the specialized work of *maintaining* the organization in operation'.[3] And some go as far as explicitly casting themselves in the role of 'serving the units' within their organizations.

I won't have people who I have to tell what to do nowadays. I will only employ people who will tell me what we should do ... He's got to create an impetus, the Managing Director and his colleagues. He's got to come and say where he wants to be in five years time and how he is going to get there. And we try to help him get there. I am here to serve them ... Some businesses, I might talk to them every week, maybe twice a week ... some businesses maybe every three months. It depends on the business ... If it is a business that the Managing Director thinks and I believe that I can help, then I'm in touch ... Sometimes just to motivate the man, sometimes to hold his hand and give him a bit of encouragement, sometimes guide him where to sell, sometimes to go with him to sell, or go with him and buy, or sit with him and interview people. It depends. It depends on what is his need.[4]

From their commentaries, we identified what we could best describe as the doing of managing. The present participle contains a note of urgency, a sense of immanence in that while this may be the process of managing today, it has developed out of past practices and will evolve into future ones: the present is merely that messy hinterland in between. However, 'process' is rather bland and universal as an organizing theme and too easily leads to the fragmented approach of identifying kinds of process (decision making process, strategic planning process, and so on). Undoubtedly the notion of process is very useful and has been used throughout to describe that progressive quality by which events develop and unfold.[5] But it lacks the energy and immediacy which seem to underpin our data and is overburdened with a chronology and linearity, describing 'stages in the process'. The events described to us were complex and inchoate, they were real and immediate, having to be dealt with and managed both short and long term, having to be initiated and driven in some cases, having to be identified and passed on in others. As we began to look closely at the idea that meaning lies in the response to events, we were struck by the ability common to all to make it 'sound so simple': their descriptions, analyses, commentaries and expectations of hugely complex situations were pared to bare essentials – responding in a way which could simply be described as pragmatic. Obvious though it may sound, our respondents were practical and matter-of-fact about doing things, about reading and wrighting: reading situations and sensing possibility, wrighting situations and making the 'best' out of limited resources, creating opportunities where others might not imagine them to exist – pragmatic.

Pragmatism is generally associated with American philosophical thought at the turn of the nineteenth and twentieth centuries, and in particular with the writings of Peirce, Dewey, James and Mead. Although we have some knowledge of their work, neither of us is steeped in the philosophical debates, the history and traditions out of which pragmatism arose and developed. Hence we are reluctant to embark on a detailed discursion on the subject which can inevitably only be superficial – as no doubt those better versed in the subject will be able to point out. However, some mention of pragmatic philosophy seems important because without prior intent, our analysis seems to be underwritten by some very pragmatic notions. That is, we did not set out to conduct an analysis of our material guided by pragmatic philosophy: rather, it seems that our analysis has developed a collection of themes for which we find support and voice in pragmatic philosophy.

Without even embarking on the academic literature of pragmatism, a simple dictionary definition draws attention to some of these themes:

The philosophical doctrine that the only test of the truth of human cognitions or philosophical principles is their practical results, i.e. their workableness. It does not admit 'absolute' truth, as all truths change their trueness as their practical utility increases or decreases.[6]

The three key notions embodied in this definition have been evidenced time and again through this book: 'that the only test of truth is their practical results, their workableness'; 'that the ability to judge potential workableness is crucial'; and 'that practical utility may increase/decrease and so bring about a revision or change in the perceived workableness/truth of ideas'. We gave an illustration earlier on in chapter 2 of Tony Mitchard persuading a large union meeting to share his belief in a future which would mean redundancies. We recycle it here as it illustrates all three of these points. There was no absolute sense of truth in what he was saying – he was not describing the *only* possible future – simply, the practical results of his explanation, its workableness demonstrated it to be true. It was based on his ability to judge potential workableness although even he explains he was not entirely convinced he was making the 'right' decisions, but that his convictions grew as events unfolded. Through the iterative process of reading and wrighting similar responses from different groups of people, so the potential workableness of ideas gathers strength. And the issue of practical utility changing so bringing about the revision of perceived workableness of ideas is again illustrated in this case: where what might have been perceived as a tentative solution at the start of the process gradually strengthens in 'perceived workability' as other parts of the 'structuring' develop in support and it receives positive responses which also have the effect of fading out potential alternatives.

In essence, Pragmatists were insisting upon an intimate connection between thought and action, and pragmatism is sometimes described as a philosophy of experience. It seems that the main criticism of pragmatism centred on the theory of truth, which Rorty summarizes: '"truth" is just the name of a property which all true statements share'.[7] This radical standpoint in effect questions philosophy back to Plato and the millennia of philosophical debate over the 'nature of truth or goodness or rationality' and so on. Rorty goes on to describe how this does not mean that Pragmatists propose a 'new, non-Platonic set of answers to Platonic questions ... rather that they do not think we should ask those questions any more'.[8] That is, rather than distinguishing between different kinds of truths ('truth-by-correspondence-with-reality' and 'truth-as-what-it-is-good-to-believe'), Pragmatists were arguing that there is no need to consider what 'makes' a sentence true. Indeed, they argued, one should ask what would it be like to believe that? – that is, relating thought and action – asking 'what if ...?' kinds of questions.[9]

Tempting though it is, it would be misleading (and rather opportunistic) to simply cull from pragmatism those ideas which help further our case.[10] Pragmatic philosophy itself has a time and a place in philosophical debate and should be seen against the background of, for example, traditional empiricism, logical positivism and rationalism, against which it stood out as being radically different. However, we point to it as a body of thought, a philosophy, which argues a set of principles or reasoning which elaborates some of the kinds of ideas we have tried to develop in advancing our understanding of the doing of managing.

Going back to our data, the preceding four chapters contain many illustrations of Pragmatist principles. In working at what is the 'best' course of action or in a general direction in which they wish to steer events, there is a strong, albeit rather blurry, notion of trying to imagine or envision what it *might* be like. None claims to have a singular or absolute view of where they are going. None argues that they know how they will end up when and if they get there. But there is an idea that this is the general direction they would like to go in and these are some of the things which might happen or might have to be tackled in the process of heading that way. And theirs is a 'vocabulary of practice' rather than of theory: about 'doing' rather than about abstract conceptualization. We recall the quotation from Brian Smith in chapter 4: 'If I tell you what happened, I hope you don't think that it is because I am a guy who is sufficiently well organized and logical to have it all spelt out on a programme in advance. It's done by listening, feeling and tuning.'

So in pragmatist philosophy we find the core idea that 'truth' must be sought in the relevant effects or consequences of action, which we argue underpins our central theme that the meaning of any action lies in response. With no concept of absolute truth, it is hardly surprising that Pragmatists are criticized for being 'subjectivist', 'relativist' and 'anti-philosophical'. But to give a flavour of what draws our attention to pragmatist philosophy, we give a long quotation from J. E. Smith which summarizes some key principles and echoes much of what we find in our material.

It is the belief that thought is always in *transit* which defines the open-ended quality of pragmatism, and bestows upon it that tentativeness which has often disturbed its critics. For Peirce, no less than for James and Dewey, tentativeness belongs essentially to all inquiry, and cannot, in principle, be overcome. One has simply to live with it, and accept the risk which tentativeness entails both in belief and action. The demand of action, and the need to respond to what a situation 'calls for', to be sure, cuts short the tentativeness of thought or inquiry in transit because resolute action requires firm belief; this fact, however, only serves to point up both the importance and the precariousness of the 'practical' from the pragmatic standpoint. We are constantly forced to believe and to act – *here* and *now* – against the background of a knowledge which is not final; it will do us no good to pretend the case is otherwise. Action does not require us to convert a tentative knowledge into an absolute certainty, but it does require us to 'make up our minds' as to what is relevant and what we must believe if we are to act at all. It was the belief of the pragmatists that the inescapable demands of the situation will help to select from our store of theoretical knowledge what is *relevant* for dealing with that situation; the background of inquiry and of thought in transit, however, endures. Practice intervenes and forces us to judge, to decide and to act against this background, but the demands of practice do not alter the character of inquiry. It is simply that belief and action are always accompanied by risk.[11]

The idea that thought is always in transit beautifully sums up what we have been implying when using words such as process and immanence. This will surface again later when we talk of learning and experience. Certainly none of our respondents is complacent or arrogant enough to claim to have the *only* solution or even the *right* one: dealing with tentativeness is part of life for them, and they are well aware of the risk this entails in both belief and actions. There is no shortage of 'deciders' amongst them. Indeed, we argue that their abilities as managers are inferred from their actions, hence they are well practised in 'making up their minds'.[12]

The idea that such action is based on knowledge which is not final – tentative knowledge rather than absolute certainty – is particularly important. It is often assumed that 'unshakeable facts' are the stock-in-trade of senior managers.[13] Not so. None of our contributors claimed full knowledge and indeed, perhaps with one exception, did not even try to make it appear as if all decisions were based on 'full knowledge'. There is a body of literature which analyses ambiguity and indeed, managing ambiguity is a current buzz-phrase used to imply a key senior executive skill.[14] From this pragmatic viewpoint, however, we can step one pace back from the approach which sees some situations or facts as clear and others as ambiguous and describes a theory of managing in these terms. For the Pragmatist, it is not a question of distinguishing between clarity and ambiguity of information but more a case of asking 'what would it be like to believe this information (be it clear or ambiguous)?'.

This pragmatist philosophy which integrates risk entailed in both belief and action provides a very elegant answer to dealing with something which particularly troubled us in our analysis: namely, paradox.[15] Indeed, at one point we almost contemplated trying to develop a theory of paradox as our organizing framework. However, it is a little like the political perspective on organizations – once you begin to notice political themes or in this case, examples of paradox, you see them everywhere.[16] But we have much evidence of situations in which respondents are both controlling and not controlling, of centralizing and decentralizing, of empowering and strengthening central power, of developing persistence and change. We described this in chapter 4 as an 'and/and' quality which is the essence of paradox. However, our respondents were less keen to accept these examples as being paradoxical. For them, it was more simply a case of 'That's the way it is'. So in pragmatist terms, rather than seeing something as contradictory, complex and ultimately stressful, they choose to focus on what for them is relevant in that situation; for example, they held that individual managers should be at one and the same time responsible, accountable, powerful, free, monitored and controlled. A position shot through with apparent contradictions, but one that *worked*.

Story-Telling

Although these ideas will surface again in this chapter, we have to pick up the point about 'selecting from our store of theoretical knowledge what is relevant for dealing with this situation'. It is a particularly important idea which we arrived at by a different route. One thing which struck us early on in our analysis was the ability of each respondent to tell stories. Indeed, searching for metaphors or analogies we were rather taken with the idea of 'organization as explanation': that is, 'organizations may be treated as *if* they are explanations or, more precisely, explanatory structures'.[17] The 'stories' or explanations we were being given in effect were/are the organization about which we were talking: that is, they gave voice to the shared meanings, evidenced by mutually expected responses, enacted in the doing of managing and organizing in each enterprise. Put another way around, 'organizations incarnate explanations'.[18]

As we worked on this theme, though, our concern with process drew our attention away from the explanation itself to the process of explaining. From here, it was but a short step to the analogy of story-telling which seemed to suggest some interesting parallels and insights into our material. As Italo Calvino rather eloquently puts it:

The tale is not beautiful if nothing is added. Folktales remain merely dumb until you realize you are required to complete them yourself, to fill in your own particulars.[19]

We like the notion of story-telling because it is something which has both a sense of art and craft to it. There is real artistry and imagination in creating and telling a story and real craftsmanship in shaping and fashioning it with time and telling. It is a variation on the theme of organization as explanation but it is particularly helpful in locating contributors *in* their explanations and in the *process* of explaining. Indeed, this must be the case: our respondents are the tale and their tales are a mirror in which they (and we) can see their particular story.[20] What we have collected and discussed here is a particular telling of each tale, at a particular time. In this sense, the tale is the theme on which they improvise, bringing it to life anew with each telling.

Indeed, this is partly Polanyi's point when he notes that to speak of human knowledge is 'a troublesome prospect':

For the task seems to be without end: as soon as we have completed one such study, our very subject matter would have been extended by this very achievement. We should have now to study the study that we have just completed, since it, too, would be a work of man. And so we should have to go on reflecting over again on our last reflections, in an endless and futile endeavour to comprise completely the works of man.[21]

This is very much the case we have here. In telling their stories, each contributor has indeed added some more to the stock of knowledge and so added a little more to the process of shaping and 'structuring' their organizations, controlling and restricting our response to it and their own.

Professional story-tellers tell stories which are notoriously difficult to analyse. They seem to be half 'real', half fiction – based on elements of local culture, local 'characters', but at the same time adding to that culture and those characterizations, becoming 'larger than life'. And the stories change and develop and reflect changes and developments in the context in which they are rooted. In a recent interview Jim Eldon,[22] a professional story-teller, described how he continually modifies and embellishes his stories, adding a bit here and taking out a bit there, according to time and situation and whatever seems to work to give a good 'feel' to the story. However, what he cannot do (or more accurately, will not do) is to dissect the story to describe where the different parts have come from and what part they play in the development of the whole story. To do this, he claims, would destroy the story because he could no longer believe it.[23]

Over time, the story grows and matures and becomes a good story (i.e. people respond to it). It has a wholeness which can be added to and modified but it cannot be deliberately re-fashioned from component parts. It is perhaps the case that the component parts do not necessarily bear close examination, gaining their meaning in the context of the whole: a meaning which they do not have when divorced from the whole tale. For instance, most folk tales have a hero, a villain, some other characters and some events which describe good battling against evil, but merely to know the parts does not determine how they will configure in a particular tale.

There are no doubt many ways of making this point, as the notion of part–whole relationships has a long history in philosophical thought. But perhaps the simplest analysis for our purposes is offered by Polanyi when he talks about a hierarchy of boundary conditions in which 'the principles of each level operate under the control of the next-higher level'.[24] So, he argues, the voice you produce is shaped into words by vocabulary, and vocabulary is shaped into sentences according to grammatical rules: 'each level relies for its operations on all the levels below it'.[25] But to describe a higher level in terms of any lower levels does not determine its presence. That is, to have voice and vocabulary does not determine the presence of sentences shaped by grammatical rules. He illustrates the point by describing the process of reading a text written in a foreign language. If you do not understand the language, you can see the letters which form the text without being aware of their meaning. But you cannot read the text without seeing the letters that convey its meaning. Thus he distinguishes between focal and subsidiary awareness, concluding that once the subsidiary becomes known as the focal, it changes the nature of our knowing it and we lose our conception of the whole, instead focusing on the part. In this way, it is possible to move our focus from whole to particular, but the reverse is not the case. That is, in shifting attention to the words, they lose their linguistic meaning; something which is only regained in terms of the 'whole' of linguistic structure and understanding, rather than simply moving back from particular word to text.

This is a rather elaborate but none the less important point. Not only did we note that our contributors were generally good story-tellers, but we also found they shared the ability to move from 'wholes' to particulars in talking about their enterprises, but not from particulars to wholes. That is, in making their assessments of organizational patterns, decisions and the like, they described an ability to make sense of the whole organization while bearing on particulars. It was not an additive process of summing particulars into some integrative whole. A knowledge of the particular plans of the subsidiaries of, for example, Lucas does not necessarily predetermine actual knowledge of Lucas Industries plc. And the same point can be made for all our organizations. Their subsidiaries could converge into any number of different organizational configurations, not necessarily the ones currently enacted by their corporate 'wholes'.

I regard myself as having to stay aloof ... and take the broad view ... I always say that if – let's say I'm at Carpets Division – I am working for Carpets then at that moment. All right, perhaps in a Group context, but nevertheless I'm working for them. I say, 'When I'm here I'm working on your problem'.[26]

Like story-tellers, our respondents are about persuading people to share their belief in their tale. Part of the art of telling stories is to draw one's audience along and to 'capture their imagination': that is, to make them 'believe' (or alternatively, to suspend disbelief) in the story. The same can be said of our organizational story-tellers: they are seeking to capture the imagination of both organizational members and other key 'outsiders' to persuade them to believe the tale. As with everything else, this is known only by response and they spend large amounts of time deliberately talking to people across the breadth of their organizations and beyond, to City analysts, bankers, brokers, consultants, and many others who might in some way be considered to have some influence or value, real or potential, in shaping their futures: in effect, keeping in touch with and shaping current meaning and response.[27 28]

The story-teller also needs to be able to believe his story and there seems little doubt of such faith amongst our respondents. In chapter 2 we spoke of valuing and believing which, in chapter 4, we developed into the notion of ideologies and ideological conversion expressed in and through their stories. The relationship between belief and action is also at the heart of pragmatist philosophy. Indeed, they shared a passionate belief in their enterprises, although none so blindly that they could be called complacent. Again, the idea of whole–part awareness helps to understand this sense of belief and believability. Perhaps not individually, but collectively they generally seemed to have a sense of 'wholeness' extending beyond their organizational boundaries, locating their own enterprises as particulars in an even bigger whole.

Sederberg argues that those who work at this level in organizations are 'more likely to suffer losses of meaning than those at lower levels ... organizational leaders must respond – determine some meaning – for that is the burden of their positions and why they receive generally high compensation. Often such responses must be made in the absence of sufficient information or, even worse, upon the basis of contradictory information'.[29] We take the point he is making but do not entirely agree with the line of argument which gets him there. In our analysis, we too are attributing to organizational leaders the responsibility for determining some meaning in giving their responses. However, we take a more pragmatist view and do not go so far as saying that this may be hampered by insufficient or contradictory information. Rather, we suggest that it is for each individual and team to make whatever use it chooses of whatever information, cues and ideas it will. Indeed, we would argue that it is here where the real distinction lies: that is, in judging what is 'sufficient' information or making use of 'contradictory information' to reach an appropriate decision or determine some appropriate meaning. Pragmatists would describe this in terms of the 'tentative knowledge' which requires us to make up our minds as to what is relevant and what we must believe if we are to act at all.

A Couple of Pages ...

Time and again, it was stressed in our accounts that brevity is a virtue. It was not that they sought *all* possible available information to inform their decisions: rather, they sought the briefest highlights of the *relevant* information, openly acknowledging that this entails someone to make a judgement of what is considered 'relevant', which as Brian Beazer suggested (quoted earlier in chapter 4), depends on circumstances. Discussing the quality and quantity of information underpinning decisions and relationships at Board level (with particular reference to acquisitions), he noted:

Oh, I tell them (the Board) immediately I know anything in this business that is important to them. They'll know that day. They won't wait until the next day, they'll know that day … So you see, that lot of paper there (acquisition drafts) cost $3 million to produce. It's all available. It's all given to them. I think that, more sensibly than inundating them with that, a couple of pages explaining what it's all about and a good telephone conversation is what is required. That's what we generally do.

And these sentiments were echoed by most of the other respondents. Norman Ireland, sometime Finance Director of BTR, gave a very interesting analysis of information use at BTR. It is an organization which, certainly to most outsiders, is seen as being strictly financially controlled by a tight financial information system.[30] However, as he explains:

… if you like to describe that as tight financial control, OK, but I don't. I'm saying it's the monitoring aspect (i.e. *use* of financial information) which was the important one and keeping up behind people on the monitoring. Because the controls themselves were very simplistic.

He later went on to add some interesting points about information, financial and otherwise – particularly interesting when one considers that BTR had a turnover of around £5 billion per annum at this time. He described their style as:

… informal formalization … I wouldn't like to feel that anybody ever thought that BTR was a formal company. We probably very rarely use DCF calculations. We didn't use sophisticated management techniques in management accounting or management controls. They were simplistic and they were direct. But they could tell you the answer just as easily … the management controls were very simplistic, easy to read, not only by financially trained minds but also the others … a mass of figures is a waste of time and I wish the profession would teach accountants to write rather than add up. I'm dead serious. Because if you can be descriptive and highlight in a very simplistic way where the problem is, and what the problem is, then the other guy can understand it … you should be able to put your case in two pages. You can have as many appendices for somebody else to read as you want to, but your case should be stressed in a very brief form so that people can get to the matter. We were handling numbers of decisions so, again, you had to summarize. You had to have your back-up papers, you had to do the work, but the guy who was reading it was working on the trust basis, he just wants to have a summary.

With many similar views expressed in our data, we have to stress that it is not the quantity of information that is important (assuming it might ever be possible to set finite bounds to potential information needed for a decision); rather, it is the quality which is crucial. Individually, one may still have to forage far and wide (knowing bigger wholes) in the process of 'doing one's homework' but to make some judgement or decision collectively, it is a 'couple of pages' which count. What was described to us was a more informal organization based on the implicit trust each had to have if only in order to operate: that is, a sense of trusting another's breadth of understanding in judging what constitutes the most crucial couple of pages for making a decision.[31] So even were one to try to make a case for some set of 'objective' criteria for gathering information necessary for some key decision, on the basis of our evidence, we would have to refute this. Glaring at us from each of these illustrations is the quite open acknowledgement that *people* deal with information – they interpret and evaluate it in terms of its usefulness for purposes, they shape it and edit it and make judgements about it. And ultimately, other members of the team trust their judgement to do that in a way which serves the common purpose.

Pushing Back The Limitations

At this point, it is tempting to stop and say that a number one skill of senior managers is judgement, however vague and woolly that might sound. Certainly, most respondents made some reference to judgement:[32] although none was able to describe of what it might consist, each felt able to recognize it if they saw it.

You haven't necessarily got to go round the field with a label on the back saying you're the team captain. If people don't recognize you for what you are, then there's something wrong.[33]

In a sense, we are back to Polanyi's point of things 'about which we can know more than we can tell' which is why it is almost impossible to describe something of the qualities demonstrated in senior managing without building a wall around the subject. However, we think we have found an alternative.

In the process of telling their stories, each respondent related what he took to be important to the doing of managing. Judgement certainly rated quite highly, but so also did the abilities to communicate, to persuade, to influence but not to interfere, to perform, to ask questions, to trust, to embrace difference, to challenge, to time – to name a few from amongst the many. Each of these was described in the context of some story – some illustrative example of when or how it might have been demonstrated or recognized rather than some abstract conceptualization of what each might be taken to be. In a sense, these describe what Polanyi calls 'rules of art'.

Rules of art can be useful but they do not determine the practice of an art: they are maxims which can serve as a guide to an art only if they can be integrated into the practical knowledge of the art. They cannot replace this knowledge.[34]

That is, they serve as a guide to an art only if they can be integrated into its practice. Indeed, this is how these people themselves have learnt and are learning and encouraging others in their organizations to learn. Integrating into practical knowledge of the art, though, means that these rules change and are modified with time and context. For this reason, we have attempted to avoid categorizing people and situations as exemplary of more or less of a particular concept. And indeed, in this sense we have invited readers to question some of the more traditional ways of thinking, reasoning, writing and ultimately knowing about executive process, managing and organizing. Yet again, though, there is a fundamental irony in this struggle and it is described most succinctly by Chester Barnard:

Unfortunately, not only the processes of education but habitual behaviour and customary understandings persistently obscure the extent to which we live and act in a world of unknowns and unknowables. Textbooks are written about what is known, not about what is unknown ... the propaganda in science puts all its emphasis on the known, and only rarely does a scientist in general popular discussion emphasize the unknown.[35]

Clearly if all textbooks simply regurgitated only the 'known' there could be no advance in understanding and knowledge of any subject: we hope that our text sheds a little more light on some of the 'unknowns' of managing. However, his point is quite perceptive and the notion of 'unknowables' needs to be regularly signalled to prevent the common assumption of the world-taken-for-granted and affliction of myopia. We noted in many of our accounts an underlying logic and rationale to their explanations which after a time and with some exploration often evaporated or at least waned. Indeed, it seemed that in giving expression to reflective explanation, trying to describe a complex situation to others, there was an implicit need for a logic of causes and effects, of stimulus and response, even though that logic may only be a *post hoc* invention. And we suggest this simplified explanation of past events is an important part of the learning process – distilling and making sense of the complexity. The point we wish to signal here, though, is that such is the evolving and organic/systemic nature of organizational action, there will always be 'unknowables', as well as much about which 'we can know more than we can tell'. And if our work helps cast doubt on some of the prescribed solutions, the ready-made frameworks and operational models so much in consultancy vogue, then we will have made a useful contribution.

Indeed, we ourselves have had to readdress ideas with which we embarked on this work.[36] At the beginning of our project, we had a general understanding of the concept of competence, although in the course of our research our doubts have grown apace such that the only thing we can say with certainty is that the concept of managerial competence, as currently conceived in the literature, is lumpish and lifeless.[37] Indeed, 'management competence' looks set to challenge 'leadership' as being one of the most written about yet least understood subjects in organizational literature. In making this observation, though, there is a lesson to be learnt. Mintzberg notes that such is the regularity with which authors and reviewers decry the state of leadership research, 'that this has become the establishment view'.[38] The field of competence seems to be heading for a similar destiny and, in some senses, for similar reasons. Leadership research has long been criticized for its tendency to over-attribute to the individual:[39] as we made clear in chapter 3, it is not just leaders who lead groups who achieve goals, as those who are led must also play their part in achieving. However, it is much easier to explain group achievements in terms of an individual hero than it is to offer an inevitably more diffuse and ambiguous explanation of collective, purposive action.[40]

Much the same can be said of competence literature. It is a burgeoning field and the word 'competence' is currently much in vogue, which helps to add to the confusion. Where such themes might once have been described as managerial skills, traits, abilities, leadership qualities or characteristics, or even styles, they are now more often described as managerial competenc(i)es.[41] Like leadership research, these accounts attempt to dissect some notion of competence in component parts, resulting in lists of competencies which successful managers 'should have'. Many such studies begin by stressing the climate of economic, social, political and organizational uncertainty which is taken to be characteristic of modern times and which means a need for different competencies from managers. Morgan provides a typical example from the introduction to his book:

The ability to combine technical, human and conceptual skills to create efficiency often provided a basis for success. During the 1970s and 1980s this has begun to change. While these skills and abilities are still relevant, increased environmental turbulence has created an atmosphere of change and uncertainty that calls for new abilities.[42]

In the light of our data, we have to ask is this really the case? Is it that there have been changes of such power and magnitude that we need to add a whole new set of managerial competencies? Or is the problem more in the way we conceptualize the subject? Undoubtedly, there has been much social change in the last decade but one can always make an argument for life not being the same as it used to be.[43]

I think every generation of management feels their generation has seen more change than any other generation before. However, there are certain comparatively brief periods in the history of a big group like Lucas that are relatively stable compared with others, but in the longer perspective there have been changes before, there are big changes now and there will be big changes in the future, and when there aren't, you are on your way out.[44]

Competence and effectiveness, we are arguing, are judged through their expression in performance.

The only authority that's worth having and the only authority that works is that of competence. You've got to respect somebody because you know they can do that ... they feel confident in what this person is telling them because they regard them as competent. So the authority of competence for me is very strong. I don't care about epaulettes and titles within organizations. People think I'm very democratic. The fact is that I believe competence is the factor that really persuades people to do things ... You can see it in companies – identify the leader. I think the chemistry is something to do with competence – I'm back to body language. How the hell do you tell competence? I think it's something that people assess in other people, in talking to them and listening to them and studying their performance.[45]

Performance takes place in a particular place at a particular time with a history and future as well as an immediate present – a continuity of action. Like other artistic pieces, executive performance is judged in terms of the tradition from which it comes. And the idea that any such performance can be broken down into component parts, being illustrative of this or that competence, exposes the central nonsense of the conceptualization. But the question 'what makes a good manager?' is so much part of common parlance that it is difficult to deny its associated implication of some assembly process to management development – so much financial ability added to a bit of marketing and some strategic leadership together with some interpersonal skills and a hint of ...[46] But we suggest that where we seem to be missing the point is by thinking about a list of skills or competencies, such that change signals the need to add a new one to the list. From our material and analysis, we wish to propose an alternative approach: in answer to the question 'what maketh the man(ager)?', we argue it is 'his *limitations*'.[47]

Wagging More than a Finger

William James makes the point forcefully that each human being is a mass of unrealized potential and unused resources.

Most people live, whether physically, intellectually or morally, in a very restricted circle of their potential being. They *make use* of a very small portion of their possible consciousness, of their soul's resources in general, much like a man who, out of his whole bodily organism, should get into the habit of using and moving only his little finger. Great emergencies and crises show us how much greater our vital resources are than we had supposed.[48]

That is, there is much which remains unknown about and to people – those aspects which lie beyond the current 'limitations', having not (yet) been expressed and realized in performance. But you will only ever 'know' what they are when you extend the boundaries and push back the limits, through 'experience'.

Although perhaps best known as an eminent psychologist, James' writings also laid some of the foundations to Pragmatist philosophy. And reiterating some of those ideas here helps to break away from too literal an interpretation of 'pushing back the limitations'. It is easy to picture this idea as being something along the lines of body building – exercising this or that muscle so that it eventually copes with the marathon rather than the 60 yard dash. That is, although the limitations are being expanded, the definitions are still 'known' and in a sense, there is some absolute quality to this particular dimension of muscle development or whatever. What James was arguing, though, was that an individual develops by making adjustments when 'some new idea comes up which he can graft upon the ancient stock (of old opinions) with a minimum of disturbance to the latter, some idea that mediates between the stock and the new experience and runs them into one another most felicitously and expediently'.[49]

ours is a *whole* notion of 'limitation', not one composed out of particulars, and it merely describes what is currently known: truth tested through practical consequences.

Surfacing every now and then throughout this book have been issues of learning and experience, although perhaps not boldly spelt out. But we have talked about learning mutually expected responses, experiencing cultural directions as well as testing out randomness and vandalism. In addition, we mention senior executive experience and learning which is demonstrated and attributed such qualities as 'commercial nose', 'feeling', 'tuning', 'smell 'em', and so on. We cannot dissect these qualities or say that a spell of doing this or that job of managing provides the experience on which such qualities are based. However, most respondents were quite clear that they had achieved positions of some responsibility and challenge early in their careers, and that they had continued and still continue to learn – in the broadest possible sense. Although these are all highly exper-ienced and respected practitioners of managing, they still claim to be 'learning the business' and are receptive to difference. What they seem to be suggesting is a process whereby something catches their attention or interest – something in their current experience chal-lenges past understanding and experience and exposes it to be inadequate. Alternatively it is sometimes described in more reflective mode.[50]

And in our obsession with survival, we probably (a) didn't devise the right kind of strategies to go forward as quickly as we should have done, and secondly, I think that even when we were doing so, we didn't communicate it well enough to our employees and to our investors. Now, we're doing it a lot better now but ... this doesn't sound like a success story, does it! ... People recognized that the kind of things I was suggesting were sensible but they were none the less painful, not very pleasant to close factories that you yourself have opened, and it's not very pleasant to make people redundant, it's not very pleasant to have decisions that you made some years ago overturned. And while people welcomed the prospect of surviving, none the less they didn't like it very much and perhaps that was a piece of style that I personally would have to learn if I were reliving this situation, of how to do that without appearing so severe and bleak and such an irritant. On the other hand, one had to get it done. I believe it could have been done with somewhat more finesse ... [with] hindsight.

This is very much the 'vocabulary of practice', the voice of the Pragmatist and the actions which they took, although painful and unpleasant, were deemed to be highly effective and essential at *that* time. On reflection, Stuart describes how through the experience, he is questioning some past assumptions, ideas, asking 'what if' kinds of questions, and just logging that there might be refinements they could make if they ever had to do it again. It is almost impossible, though, to describe this process in any way which does justice to the actual human experience. It is largely unconscious and it is also continuous, just occasionally brought to the surface through reflection.

Trying to push these ideas further, Bruner has some interesting comments about what he calls 'sense of potency – what we think is possible for us':

Perhaps the chief vehicle in the relation between man's subjective sense of himself and his sense of the world of nature is the idea of fate. Fate is that which is beyond one's control; it is an outer limit. The inverse of fate is the sense of potency – what we think is possible for us. That is to say, our view of fate shapes our sense of potency and vice versa. Fate is the residuum that is left after one has run through the census of what is humanly possible. Each discovery of a way of proceeding, of a way of discovering, forestalling or effecting is, then, an incursion into fate that in effect rolls back what we take fate to be.[51]

From these ideas, the result is not so much a case of adding something else to a badly or even undefined jigsaw. Rather, it seems more a case of 'liberating' some *unrealized* potential or potency. Sir Owen Green encapsulates the point when talking about the excitement and challenge of new experience, particularly for people in areas of influence: 'It's like being between the age of 12 and the age of 20 – the things that happen then are never to be repeated in terms of the sheer tingling excitement' – the period of pushing back the limitations of adolescence. But we would add, in as much as some adolescents feel threatened and insecure, remaining essentially unreceptive to the challenge and uncertainty of new experience and learning opportunity, so likewise some managers reach a similarly unimaginative conclusion – conclusive in the sense that the 'limitations' are to be pushed no further.

These ideas turn much of the competence debate on its head but there are a number of points we must elaborate to give them a more coherent shape. First of all, we must be clear that, true to our emphasis on process and temporality, we are talking about effective performance as being, if you like, the artistic product from which we make inferences about the creative ability of the performer and creative process.[52] For those seeking a more prescriptive answer, we develop our reasoning thus: if effective managerial performance could be conceptualized as some separate or independent thing or event, then it might be considered to have separate or independent causes. In our analysis, effective managerial performance cannot be conceptualized in this way. Rather, it is known as 'part' of a bigger 'whole' which shapes its meaning and response. Hence from our standpoint, the search for such 'causes' is meaningless. And the idea that this is prefigured by possession of some set of attributes or competencies reduces management development to something akin to collecting I-Spy badges.

But this is not to say that such abilities are irrelevant. That would be patent nonsense. Our respondents talk of all manner of qualities of 'good' managers – the things they look for in others – both individually and as team members.

We've always believed that you will find people of energy and competence in any business. We're not looking for geniuses, anyway. But what you want is energy and persistence and ability to manage.

Our only real criterion in this group for promotion is the ability to be able to perform. We frankly don't care whether a chap went to Eton or the local comprehensive. I'm not very impressed with paper qualifications. What impresses me is how long has a person had in their previous job. That to me is a very important issue ... I'm interested in results, not the academic qualifications. You just can't lay down rules for success, and therefore on our experience we have all sorts of people with all sorts of qualifications at all levels of management. Some of our brightest people have no professional qualifications at all. Some of our brightest people are highly qualified. If you look at our board of directors, I have no professional qualifications of any description. Most of the others are engineers or accountants.
There is a lot talked about needing brilliant, brilliant people to run your businesses. In our industry, at least, we don't need those very, very brilliant ones. Ordinary people, properly motivated, can and do make money.

They need to have acquired a sound understanding of the consumer goods business. They need judgement. I think they need integrity, courage to take unpleasant decisions and tackle some of the management and people issues that inevitably arise in any organization. Those are the sort of characteristics we would be looking for. They need an ability to manage people, good human relations skills are clearly very important in this day and age.[53]

But even assuming one could define and measure some of these, at any level of, say, 'persistence', there could be more or less effectiveness: for instance, dogged persistence is sometimes effective and sometimes it is not – sometimes it is more effective to leave something alone and wait for a more opportune moment to pursue it rather than persevere doggedly.[54] So for us, there is no sense in even beginning to talk of abilities in this way for it clouds one's understanding.

But the idea of pushing back the limitations does have appeal as it fits much better the fluid and developing nature of our material. As organizational circumstances change, so effective performing and audience responses change and so the 'limitations' get pushed back or redefined. As Brian Smith summed it up: 'today's excellence is tomorrow's competence'. It is, however, a difficult point to make because on one level, the idea of pushing back the limitations sounds like advocacy for complete anarchy: 'give them total freedom to realize their full potential' or some Utopian ideal. Of course, it doesn't work like that. From a managerial point of view, it is quite possible that, on opening the bird cage doors, you find that the birds can't or at least won't attempt to fly: 'habitual behaviour and customary understandings'[55] make the security of the cage walls more inviting because if you have never tried flapping your wings before, how could you know about flying? The crucial link is the process of learning and experiencing.

Again we find ourselves picking through difficult terrain: we want to talk about learning from experience, but we do not want to dissect or dissemble what seems to us to be a continuing, integrating whole process of developing. Theorists talk about developmental experiences, about turning points and about mentors[56] as being 'critical incidents' from which people learn key lessons. But rather like the problem we discovered with Critical Incident Technique at the outset of our study, they provide an artificial or *post hoc* imposed chronology which fragments what is otherwise a whole complexity of experiencing. With CIT, there is a need to 'get a full report of a specific past occurrence, with a beginning, a middle, and an end ...'[57] and the same tends to be the case with recounting 'turning points'. They are described as discrete events from which a 'particular' lesson is learned.[58] Such a discrete quality or independence is something which is added with hindsight. One cannot 'know' the value of 'experiential events' at the time: it is only with hindsight in the overall complexity or 'whole' which makes up personal development that they are attributed 'particular' significance. (And the 'lesson' may also be revised from subsequent experience.)

This is in part what makes it such a difficult subject. Csikszentmihalyi and his colleagues have spent many years studying what he calls 'flow experience',[59] developing a research technique called the Experience Sampling Method (ESM). Using electronic pagers, a transmitter is programmed to send signals to pagers at random times of the day and the respondent completes a questionnaire whenever the pager signals. 'Combined with a booklet of self-report forms, the pager ... makes it possible for the investigator to prompt respondents to give a high-resolution description of their mental states as these are happening'.[60] We argue this is not 'as they are happening' but 'as they have happened'. And we would add that their significance can only be evaluated with hindsight. That is, it is only from the vantage point of, in these terms, the 'next experience' that one might be able to re-view past experience and attribute some 'lesson' or developmental quality to the experience. For instance, Terry O'Neill remarked: 'He (Gareth Davies) started passing on these performance criteria for the units at an important conference – it turned out to be important but it wasn't seen to be any different to any other conference at the time.' And this makes the fundamental point that, as George Kelly put it, 'it is the *learning* which constitutes the experience'.[61] Because, to recycle Aldous Huxley's succinct expression: 'Experience is not what happens to a man, it is what a man does with what happens to him.'[62]

In these terms, we have a number of individuals whose limitations are expressed in a number of individual ways. In some cases they may have shared similar collective experience but the impact and quality of learning from this will be incorporated and configured in quite individual ways. These ideas relate to the curious paradox which underlies our work which is that while we seek to identify common themes or patterns which are shared by managers/executives, what actually distinguishes good executorship or managerial performance is its uniqueness – its *difference*. We argue that such performance is not a case of a manager having a superior level of ability in a particular skill or technique, but that his/her limitations expressed through performance are judged by others to be superior in that situation. In a sense, this refers back to the notion of creative ability. That is, it is from the performance that observers infer some qualities about the performer and process which led to that performance. And that what is attributed to be successful or effective depends on context and 'prior products'. So for instance, while Brian Smith appears to have been very effective and creative during his Chairmanship of MB Group, some might argue that he is drawing heavily on his previous experience at ICI where Sir John Harvey-Jones had apparently been advocating the frigates approach for some time. However, this is not to belittle the value of Brian Smith's contribution both in terms of changing MB Group as well as developing the MB Executive teams and others in Metal Box. Rather, the illustration is of the process of learning from experience and the attributions of novelty or creativity in different contexts. In each of our organizations, we find cases of executives learning from others and people deliberately brought in for what they might be able to contribute to the experience of others. Indeed, a crucial point is that respondents tell us how important it is to have a high-quality discerning audience. That is, they seemed to welcome the critical eye of other experienced executives. Learning is a two-way process – interactive – and so for each member, there is something to be gained from working with the others. They are both performers and audience to others' performances and like all good audiences, have a part to play in shaping performance.[63]

Interdependence is stressed time and again such that to change one member of a team *does* impact on others, even where there is no apparent redrawing of formal responsibilities. For example, Reckitt and Colman provided an illustration of an almost classic matrix design, where responsibilities assigned to each member changed and overlapped – so geographic responsibility overlapped with product responsibility, but regional or product definitions could be redefined according to identified needs.

A strong sense of continuity and change to this overall team meant that each move or addition or change of responsibility seemed designed to groom a person individually for the next development and collectively to expand the boundaries. So when bringing Owen Parmenter into the team from his position in Australia, although there was no apparent change in terms of formal definitions of responsibility of team members, it did have a collective impact in that he set about asking questions *across* the matrix, not guided by product or regional responsibilities.

In several cases, we also have illustrations of whole teams engaging in more formal learning, when facing a situation for which they felt a fresh approach was required or simply to provide some kind of challenge against which they might test their previous (experience and) assumptions. For example, John West at Reckitt and Colman explained very casually that they took themselves away for one or two courses, when they formed the Executive team. At Lucas, they found some new ways of structuring required new ways of thinking and managing in order to be successful and so devised formal courses accordingly.[64]

An important idea which comes out of some of these examples is the clear sense of interdependence amongst executive team members. They are not necessarily interchangeable or even substitutable for each other. They really are *necessarily inter-dependent:* balancing dependence and independence. And as we noted earlier, they know each others' strengths and weaknesses and play to this knowledge rather than 'using' it in any negative or political way.

I think it's important that if they can be complementary to each other in terms of strengths and weaknesses, that's a big help. Each is good at something the other one isn't good at and vice versa. You want technologists and selectors and commercial executives not just to work as a team but to cover for each other's shortcomings so that between them, they can ask all the right questions and deliver all the right answers. And frequently, of course, people clash.

Yes, it was very much a team. I know I keep using analogies like football and mountain climbing and all that, I suppose I am a team player and my role is captain. I am the supreme optimist. I translate his philosophy into the reality here. Mine is a very voluble, visible style. I don't have any great academic merits but I do have the driving force. I believe it is management's role to lead and to deliver by example. I believe it is a team effort in all these things. Like playing a football match with one player – just talk about the Chief Executive – the best goalkeeper in the world is never going to win the game, because nobody is scoring goals. And I believe it is all about teamwork. And whilst one person triggers it off, it's a pyramid, a structure, or a team, to carry it through. That's my belief.

The key thing is you get people to play the ball rather than the man. You have to have a total belief in a common objective and the culture with it. And if you do that, then people will work towards that rather than working towards each other.[65]

In this sense, the team effect is to expand the range of (individual and) collective 'limitation' and as team members change, so the boundaries become redefined.[66] And one of the most fascinating points about this is that very largely, it was the same people achieving substantially improved results or effects, with perhaps one change in team membership; or alternatively when talking about subsidiaries, there might be no change in team membership, but different guidance from the senior executive team. So at Coats Viyella, where they have considerable experience of mergers, they talk about giving 'greater degrees of freedom' through the merger process:

It is much easier to generate goodwill and good working relationships and therefore have the wherewithal for doing things together if you are taking chains off, rather than trying to say this is the best way to run the land ... What one is doing is – same people, but what one is doing is perhaps influencing greater degrees of freedom in terms of decision making, decentralization, a slightly more entrepreneurial, enterprising culture, to use the word.

Sir Owen Green calls this the catalyst approach:

What (an acquisition) has to do is to start performing according to our particular style, marching to our drum beat, fitting in with our rhythm. It doesn't have to do any more than fitting it. So yes, I suppose we haven't bought anything that we haven't been able to persuade them to improve. And that to me is the most fulfilling part of the business – to see people, almost the same people, doing much better by the catalyst approach than by anything else. I think it's marvellous. Not financial jiggery-pokery or balance sheet engineering, just people doing better.

In a sense, the preceding discussion shows how easy it is to get side-tracked. That is, while advocating that we only know about managing and organizing through performance, we have allowed ourselves to reflect on and infer qualities to individuals, teams and the process of managing. Indeed, it is extremely difficult to break out of ways of thinking which are so deeply ingrained in management theory. However, this does mean that in answer to the question, what is 'it' that we are talking about? – what are these 'limitations'? – we have to remind ourselves that they are qualities of performance, personal properties known/publicly expressed only in, through and by performance and attributed meaning in response to performance. Hence the elusive character of such an idea and hence the impossibility of defining any compositional arrangement of performance characteristics.

Performance ...

Volumes have been written about performance and effectiveness, most of which we find hard to relate to our data. To be clear, much of the debate has for us the quality of Socrates' question to Meno, 'what is goodness?'. If you do not know what it is, how are you going to look for it? But if you know already what it is, then why ask the question? Unfortunately, most of the literature of performance and effectiveness does not have the imagination and stimulation of a Platonic dialogue but the paradox underlying Socrates' question raises what we take to be a central issue: which lies in the distinction between knowing how to do something and being able to say how it is done. What our respondents seem to be saying is that they know how to perform successfully or that they recognize effective organizing, but we add, that each time they do it or recognize it, they are in effect challenging or expanding or justifying that prior knowledge of other performances or examples of organizing.

Cameron points out that there is much confusion and conflict around evaluations of effectiveness. In his view, part of the problem stems from lack of distinction between outcomes and effects of strategic actions, from arbitrary selection of effectiveness criteria and from basic confusion: 'A survey of the literature finds structure, decision processes, culture, congruence, job design, innovation, sensitivity to constituencies, and environmental responsiveness as synonymous with effectiveness. Seldom is a rationale or justification given for selecting the particular criteria set. One problem is that *determinants* of effectiveness often get confused with *indicators* of effectiveness.[67]

He argues that organizational effectiveness is inherently paradoxical: 'simultaneous, equally compelling, contradictory attributes exist which create both balance and dynamism. Loose coupling and tight coupling exist in both independence and dependence in effective organizations'.[68] But to maintain such a stance would require us to depersonalize our material and attempt some 'organizational' analysis which we find impossible to divorce from the people who provide our data. Cameron very correctly questions the domain of activity to be assessed, at what level, from whose perspective and for what purpose, with what data and time frame, and against what judgemental referents – all of which influence the evaluation of effectiveness. Clearly, our research was not focused on making a formal analysis of effectiveness, hence we cannot answer these questions. But judgements of performance and effectiveness are implicit in *any* observation of action and clearly guide our respondents' thinking and acting: they take a critical eye to their own performance, to that of their colleagues both individually and as a team, to that of other organizational members as well as to the collective sense of organizational performance and effectiveness. Again, there is an interrelating of whole–part awareness, of an almost unconscious or at least often only semi-conscious critical evaluation, in the sense of learning and experiencing, which on occasions can be brought centre stage and held up for close scrutiny.

For these reasons we argue it is quite unhelpful to our work to pursue definitions of effectiveness and performance, as to do so immediately draws one into distinguishing parts from wholes, imposing arbitrary punctuation marks on the developing process, and ultimately trying to make attributions between individual and collective action. In our analysis, individual and collective action integrate in the doing of managing and organizing, hence are 'known' in performance. One can hypothesize that, say, the actions of one individual in one context might be considered to be highly effective, but that the same actions by the same individual in another context might be considered ineffective. We stress this is hypothesis. In order to accommodate all these contextual, temporal and relational qualities to such a judgement renders the concept of effectiveness quite unhelpful. Which is why we prefer the line of our respondents who generally make such evaluations continuously and implicitly, simply in observing, performing and most of all, learning (testing current experience against past experience) about the doing of managing and organizing. And that where 'particulars' are formally evaluated in the context of a whole, the criteria for evaluation will depend on the meanings embodied in response to that 'particular' situation. And in this sense, as Lombardo and McCall put it, 'effectiveness is a function of who defines it'. So depending on organizational context, different criteria will be important, depending on culture and shared appreciative systems, different values and ideologies will guide the process.

So, for example, the operating results of a company in effect relate to past performance and the quality of decisions made a couple of years ago. These may be helpful in making formal evaluations of past effectiveness and inevitably are the data used for public scrutiny. But in terms of the doing of managing and organizing, it is the more immediate imprecise evaluations embodied in listening, feeling, tuning, which guide current evaluation and awareness.

Any one can take actions. It's achievement that you measure on. There is an illusion that dashing around is working. It's whether you actually do things [that is important].[69]

We have to note that Barnard was especially concise on the subject of effectiveness:

Thus the executive process, even when narrowed to the aspect of effectiveness of organization and the technologies of organization activity, is one of integration of the whole, of finding the effective balance between the local and the broad considerations, between the general and the specific requirements ... Control from the view of the effectiveness of the whole organization is never unimportant and is something of critical importance; but it is in connection with efficiency which in the last analysis embraces effectiveness, that the viewpoint of the whole is necessarily dominant.[70]

He goes on:

Since the details cannot be summed up into a whole and the results of cooperation cannot be known except by the event, the final efficiency of organization is dependent upon two quite different factors: (a) the efficiency of detail; and (b) the creative economy of the whole.[71]

The efficiency of detail is much about non-money values. 'Any merchant or politician knows that smiles have values, and that sometimes the presence or absence of smiles may be the strategic factor between success or failure, but no one can measure their effects.'[72] Of the second factor, he notes, it is:

essentially non-technical in character. What is required is the sense of things as a whole, the persistent subordination of parts to the total, the discrimination from the broadest standpoint of the strategic factors from among all types of factors – other executive functions, technology, persuasion, incentives, communication, distributive efficiency. Since there can be no common measure for the translation of the physical, biological, economic, social, personal and spiritual utilities involved, the determination of the strategic factors of creative cooperation is a matter of sense, of feeling, of proportions, of the significant relationship of heterogeneous details to a whole.

This general executive process is not intellectual in its important aspect; it is aesthetic and moral. Thus its exercise involves the sense of fitness, of the appropriate, and that capacity which is known as responsibility – the final expression of the achievement of cooperation.[73]

And In Conclusion

It is this sense of fitness, of appropriateness which we have argued throughout underpins the doing of managing and organizing. We also stress that it is in this sense that we choose to talk about 'pushing back the limitations'. That is, it is not an absolute sense of limitation nor is it simply praise for the 'unlimited' (if it were possible to conceive of such a notion): a team full of Branaghs would be disastrous. Collectively their 'limitations' would be insufficient to deal with the range required of our executive teams.[74] Complementarity and contrast are crucial in order that their breadth and range is *different*: that they can contrast each other and conflict with each other. As we noted before in chapter 2, however, it is conflict against a background of trust. Although Barnard's terminology is perhaps more appropriate to the 1930s, this essentially accords with his notion of the moral aspect of executive process. He develops this moral aspect into a quite detailed analysis of both personal moral codes and organizational morals, again in terms of codes of conduct. He also talks of the executive responsibility for creating morals for others. In this sense, we find much which relates to what in contemporary language is called culture, for which we used the crude shorthand of 'directions for behaviour'. And while we would not go so far as to say their intention is to create morals for others, their whole doing of managing and organizing is about symbolism: they signal their own personal intent and commitment in what they say and do and, in so doing, communicate to others a sense of what is valued in the enterprise. So, for instance, visiting factories and following up previous contacts and conversations, going to social events run by subsidiaries, sending out copies of 'interesting books', and many other examples of behaviour far and away from the classic planning, decision making and implementing functions – all symbolize what is valued and what is appropriate.

The code of conduct amongst the executive team, developed around the strength and integration of both individual and collective purpose, is such that the expression of differences are not taken as personal conflicts. We have illustrations of almost the reverse situation – where to avoid raising a difficult issue (or to raise it first with 'others') might well be taken personally.

We often disagree about things, but we don't disguise the fact. I will occasionally drop into someone's office and say, 'Look, I'm in some difficulty because I don't actually like very much what you are doing for various reasons'. Now it's up to him to say whether he thinks he can satisfy my objections. He wouldn't resent that. What he would resent would be if I went to the Chief Executive and said, 'I don't like this very much. Couldn't we sort of more or less between us scotch it?' And the other director would quite reasonably, as I see it, say that I had been rather deceitful about it. And my colleagues are the same. They'll come and tell me if they don't much like what I am proposing to do. And I wouldn't say, 'I'm the Chairman of the Board. What the hell has it got to do with you?' I would say, 'Thanks for telling me'.[75]

And we have many similar illustrations, reporting 'flaming rows' after which they may perhaps go for a drink together, or 'heated debates' which seem to be expected almost as part of the process of achieving common purpose rather than creating personal divisions. The themes of trust, believing and valuing, and ideologies developed earlier in this book are all evidenced here. There is a belief about what is appropriate, demonstrating what is valued, which integrates into an ideology which in its expression requires the demonstration of trust, itself an admission of vulnerability. But taking action, the doing of managing, embraces the Pragmatist themes of belief, action and risk, if you are to believe something, it requires conviction and personal commitment, hence being persuaded by others to share their belief which is perhaps not the same as yours is not done without emotion. As John West put it, 'people skill is still the big trick ... [you've] got to develop a bit of passion – you know, lose your rag and get angry a bit and care a bit more than the average'.

At Metal Box, introducing a system at executive team level of identifying five key task areas over and above the individual's normal operational role was done in a way which deliberately created diversity in order to generate some difference. Rather than collectively debate what these task areas might be, each individual wrote down five key things they were trying to achieve, as also did the Chairman, both for himself and his team members, 'and then put them together. We did that quite deliberately because the danger if you talk first is that you'll talk each other into a consensus view very quickly, whereas if you write them down separately and then put them together, then the reality of what each individual really thinks is there.' It is perhaps a very small example but it continues to reinforce the message of what is appropriate to their doing of managing and organizing.

If it is possible to criticize Barnard at all, it would be for never fully developing what he meant by the aesthetic quality of executive process to the same depth that he debated its moral quality. Instead, it surfaces throughout his work in terms of 'sensing' and 'feeling' and one must infer from his analysis that this is the most important quality of executive process. Indeed, he concludes the appendix to his book:

The inconsistencies of method and purpose and the misunderstandings between large groups which increasing specialization engenders need the corrective of the feeling mind that senses the end result, the net balance, the interest of the all and of the spirit that perceiving the concrete parts encompasses also the intangibles of the whole.[76]

The idea of the 'feeling mind that senses the end result' sums up rather neatly the kind of quality which is common to our respondents but could never find expression in any analysis of management competencies. But this aesthetic quality has pointed our analysis in many directions. We have explored ideas of creativity and imagination and attempted in chapter 3 to describe something of the creative process by which they innovate and create difference or 'novelty'. Creativity has also surfaced again in this chapter, referring to creative product, process and performer. And we think it provides some valuable insights into what we have described in and by our data.

Evaluations of creativity are based on the creative product – the picture or the poem, seen against a background of 'prior products'. As Briskman points out, it is from this product that we infer that the performer must be a creative person who engaged in some creative process to produce the product. It is a retrospective analysis – rather as we find in our data. Only when a decision has been taken and action initiated can people make some evaluation of the quality of that decision. As John West put it: 'Somebody has to say, "Right, this is what we are going to do". Everybody then thinks this a great decision, but there are risks involved and the ability to have a shunt at it and take risks is something you have to do in this job'.

Again there are echoes of the pragmatic, even in the creative process – about belief, action and risk. Artists certainly take risks in the choices they make throughout the creative process. But it is this which makes the process of creating more exciting and stimulating than the achievement of the final product. It does seem to be a case of 'better to travel hopefully than to arrive'. To give a familiar example from Einstein:

In the light of knowledge attained, the happy achievement seems almost a matter of course, and any intelligent student can grasp it without too much trouble. But the years of anxious searching in the dark, with their intense longing, their alternation of confidence and exhaustion, and the final emergence into the light – only those who have themselves experienced it can understand that.[77]

We are not so gross as to draw comparisons with Einstein himself, but the process of 'anxious searching in the dark' draws attention to Barnard's aesthetic quality of executive process. That is, the stimulation of sensing and feeling, the excitement and enjoyment of the 'doing' rather than the reflected glory of the 'done', the achievement of the product. And again, we have to say this echoes what our respondents tell us. They enjoy what they do. They find it exciting and stimulating as well as sometimes perhaps frustrating and even frightening in its challenge. Brian Smith talked about the things people do in their private lives – from amateur dramatics and playing tennis onwards. From his understanding, people find it frightening and stressful but extremely stimulating and good fun:

And you want to harness that in business because it can be just as much fun if you get these things rolling. Particularly in factories and tight-knit units, you can get that sort of excitement running. A team working together is the ultimate ethos people enjoy and that gets you back to where we started. What is it that unites a team? Common purpose and a belief that you're winning.

We take this to be part of Barnard's aesthetic quality of executive process. But it does not end there. As the artist feels compelled to explore different expressions through new works, so too do our executives. This is in part what gives the subject its restless and relentless quality – there seems to be no end to it because the 'achievements' simply are punctuation marks in the continuing process of achieving.

However, this does not in our analysis constitute an argument for the endless pursuit of novelty and creativity simply for the sake of novelty and creativity. Again, we draw on the Pragmatist idea that in seeking truth which lies in the practical consequences of action, so one may be challenging or expanding or even simply justifying knowledge, meanings and sense of fitness. Either way, the creator is learning from the interaction with his/her own prior products and as members of executive teams, so also are they learning from the creative process and products of other individuals as well as their collective sense of purpose.

No work of art has been created with such finality that you need contribute nothing to it. You must recreate the work for yourself – it cannot be presented to you ready-made. You cannot look at a picture and find it beautiful by a merely passive act of seeing. The internal relations that make it beautiful to you have to be discovered and in some way have to be put in by you. The artist provides a skeleton; he provides guiding lines; he provides enough to engage your interest and to touch you emotionally. But there is no picture and no poem unless you yourself enter it and fill it out.[78]

Notes

Preface

1 Daft and Weick, 'Towards a model of organizations as interpretation systems' (1984, p. 285).
2 The 'upper echelons' perspective is that which was proposed by Hambrick and Mason (1984). According to this view, the organization is a reflection of its top managers. The logic of the view relies on early work by theorists of the Carnegie school, who argued that complex decisions were the result of behavioural rather than economic factors. The work of the school can best be seen in a recent publication, *The Executive Effect: Concepts and Methods for Studying Top Managers*, edited by Donald C. Hambrick (1988).
3 Clearly we will disappoint those seeking a more traditional statement of method and methodology. From approaches to 18 large organizations perceived to be managing successfully (and we willingly acknowledge it was no more formal than that), our final choice was determined by those who were willing to talk to us.
4 Weick (1977), 'Repunctuating the problem'.

Chapter 1

1 All italicized words should be read as if they had been marked *forte*. Those already irritated by our heroic overuse of musical terminology will be pleased to learn that it fades rather rapidly over the next few paragraphs.
2 The comment is, of course, tendentious. Not every one, perhaps not even many, can be fitted neatly into one or other of these bands. The point is not a major one to us and we would be happy to concede it. We took it from Gareth Morgan and Linda Smircich (1980) and it simply serves to get us off and running.
3 Morgan and Smircich (1980), 'The case for qualitative research'.
4 Gareth Morgan (1980), alone this time, 'Paradigms, metaphors, and puzzle solving in organization theory'.

5 Karl Weick (1981) remarks: 'Context-free arguments are irrelevant when applied to actors who are never free of contexts.'

6 Chester Barnard, *The Functions of the Executive* (1938, p. 21). We are strongly influenced by what Barnard has to say. His text is one of the very few that addresses issues of senior executive behaviour and although not the easiest of reads is well worth the effort. At times our own work becomes a kind of three way conversation between our respondents, ourselves and the shade of Chester Barnard.

7 Unlike Barnard, however, we do not rule out such activity. Getting out and selling, or being prepared to tackle a problem on the line, may well be not only practical but also highly symbolic activities signalling to all and sundry what kind of an executive you wish to be taken to be.

8 Barnard (1938, p. 217).

9 Barnard (1938, p. 235).

10 In an earlier version of this text we followed Barnard's categorization of executive functions into communication, securing essential services and the formulation of purpose (traces of this are readily apparent after several rewrites). We found ourselves, however, increasingly hostile towards all standard forms of categorization since they appeared to lead, willy nilly, to lists. We developed a distaste for the kind of book that promulgates the five rules of success, the three forms of enterprise, the seven types of ambiguity (although that is a good book) or whatever and we do not wish to fall into the trap of providing quick guides to the doing of managing. None the less, we feel the need to provide some headings, to furnish the reader with some rudimentary organizing of our material and that is what we have – some 'imperfect beginnings' which we would wish to see abandoned even as we bring them into being.

11 Barnard (1938) holds that the need for a system of communication creates the first task for the would-be coordinator and that this need is the harbinger of executive organization. He or she who would attempt to coordinate the activities of others must have people and positions. People, primarily, are the *means* of communication, positions or offices the *systems* of communication.

> The center of communication is the organization service of a person at a place. Persons without positions cannot function as executives, they mean nothing but potentiality. Conversely positions vacant are as defunct as dead nerve centers. This is why executives, when functioning strictly as executives, are unable to appraise men in the abstract, in an organization vacuum as it were. Men are neither good nor bad, but only good or bad in that position. This is why they not infrequently "change the organization", the arrangement of positions, if men suitable to fill them are not available. (p.218)

12 Quotes taken from transcripts of Hanson, Metal Box, Beazer.

13 Quotes from Beazer, Metal Box, Hanson, Marks and Spencer.

14 Following loyalty, Barnard takes general abilities to be important to the holder of an executive position: 'general alertness, comprehensiveness of interest, flexibility, faculty of adjustment, poise, courage, etc.'(pp.221–222). It is the 'etc.' that is the give-away. Barnard does not know, any more than the rest of us know, what these general abilities are; effective senior executives, presumably, are those with 'feel' and 'judgement', those with some sense of 'appropriateness', some notion of 'balance' (all terms he uses elsewhere). But these qualities, if such they are, like 'poise', 'courage' and the rest are recognized rather than described. Notwithstanding the vagueness of the desired characteristics, Barnard takes them to be 'innate' and 'developed through general experience'.

15 Quote from Metal Box.

16 Barnard sees the essence of the executive process as a matter of facilitating the 'synthesis in concrete action of contradictory forces, to reconcile conflicting forces, instincts, interests, conditions, positions and ideals'. In other words he posits a circumstance in which individuals differ about what is to be done, fight their corners but eventually are reconciled to a particular set of actions. Compatibility most certainly does not imply conformity:

> It seems to me to be often the case that excessive compatibility or harmony is deleterious, resulting in "single track minds" and excessively crystallized attitudes and in the destruction of personal responsibility. (Barnard, 1938, p. 225)

17 Quotes from Metal Box, Avon.

18 In Barnard's view, informal executives promote the sharing of ideas, suggestions, suspicions, thus affording opportunity for personal influence and minimizing the likelihood of destructive political activity. It is clear that he sees informal executive relations as the means through which major differences are identified and resolved in a strictly non-hierarchical, non formal manner:

> The functions of informal executive organizations are the communication of intangible facts, opinions, suggestions, suspicions, that cannot pass through formal channels without raising issues calling for decisions, without dissipating dignity and objective authority, and without overloading executive positions; also to minimize excessive cliques of political types arising from too great divergence of interests and views; to promote self-discipline of the group; and to make possible the development of important personal influences in the organization. (Barnard, 1938, p. 225)

Our respondents, if anything, rate teamwork higher than does Barnard.

19 Quotes from Avon, Coats Viyella.

20 A point neatly encapsulated in the following quote from McDonald (1972): 'If the power center at the top is in chaos, what hope has the rest of the corporation for constructive action? Business cannot go on as usual. Limp, anxious and vulnerable, the organization is unable to react effectively to new threats. As the contagion spreads, even distant departments are soon infected with pettiness, personal rivalries linked to different leaders, and arbitrary rulings of little logic or importance.'

21 Barnard (1938, p. 225).

22 Developing on the work of Morse Peckham, Peter Sederberg makes this point. Although neither could be taken to be in the mainstream of writing about organizations, their work has been of particular interest to us. Peter Sederberg is a political philosopher and Morse Peckham more difficult to classify but, if anything, a philosopher interested in aesthetics (or someone with skill in literary aesthetics interested in philosophy). Of the two, he has had the most influence upon us, as will be evident throughout the rest of the book. His book, *Explanation and Power: The Control of Human Behaviour (Peckham, 1979)*, is an important and sadly neglected work. Peter Sederberg's *The Politics of Meaning: Power and Explanation in the Construction of Social Reality*,(1984) is more accessible and nearly as stimulating.

23 These were the limits at the time of the study. They have subsequently been raised.

24 Quote from Hanson

25 Quote from Avon.

26 Quotes from Marks and Spencer, Coats Viyella.

27 Chester Barnard (1938, p. 260).

28 Chester Barnard (1938, p. 283).

29 Quote from Marks and Spencer.

30 See Ed Schein (1985), *Organizational Culture and Leadership*.

31 Quote from Beazer.

32 Barnard's consideration of this function is much more direct than ours, concentrating almost entirely upon purposes and objectives as classically conceived. Some followed Barnard into specifying objectives:

Accordingly, the general executive states that 'this is the purpose, this the objective, this the direction, in general terms, in which we wish to move, before next year'. His department heads, or the heads of his main territorial divisions, say to their suborganizations: 'This means for us these things now, then others next month, then others later, to be better defined after experience.' Their subdepartment or division heads say: 'This means for us such and such operations now at these places, such other at those places, something other here, others tomorrow there.' Then district or bureau chiefs in turn become more and more specific, their subchiefs still more so as to place, group, time, until finally purpose is merely jobs, specific groups, definite men, definite times, accomplished results.But meanwhile, back and forth, up and down, the communications pass, reporting obstacles, difficulties, impossibilities, accomplish-ments: redefining, modifying purposes level after level. (1938 p. 232)

This is Barnard at his worst, ascribing value to the kind of tedious nonsense that passes for the doing of managing in many an enterprise. By the time all this passing to and fro of purposes and objectives has gone on, most of those who began it will have retired or the enterprise will have gone into liquidation.

33 Quote from Metal Box.
34 The notion of purposing that we are using relates to Barnard's conception of purpose, as developed by Peter Vaill (1982) 'The purposing of high performing systems'. See also chapter 4, note 62.
35 Polanyi (1967, *The Tacit Dimension*) would no doubt refer to this as 'the tacit dimension'. He develops the concept of 'tacit knowing', which refers to the idea that 'we can know more than we can tell'. He explains this notion by use of the analogy of police identikit methods: with the choice of thousands of pieces of physiognomy, it is possible to build a face, but, he argues, it is still missing 'something', that something by which we could recognize it from a crowd of other faces. His work has provided many fruitful insights and we refer to him again in later chapters.
36 Braybrooke (1964) claimed several years ago that senior managers may be less aware of their stratagems than outside observers. Not only may they be less aware, they may also be less articulate; Braybrooke claims that in their everyday activities they do not have to meet the tests of articulate-ness that academics have to meet. Our observations, however, do not support either of these assertions. Most of our respondents seemed to be aware of what they were about (even if they were unable to frame their activities in academic terms) and they were to a man articulate. As we will point out in a subsequent chapter, each of our respondents lived by his tongue; he talked himself and others into situations and out of them. One final, not entirely facetious point, from where does David Braybrooke call up his evidence to support the notion that academics meet demanding tests of articulateness? In our experience, few would pass the most rudimentary of tests.
37 Barnard (1938, p. 291). Definitions of intuition describe it as some kind of ready apprehension, 'immediate knowledge by contrast with mediate' (*Chambers Dictionary*). So where intellectual knowledge is mediated by inference and reasoning, intuitive knowledge is not. Polanyi's discussion of tacit knowledge is particularly helpful to understanding this elusive idea. He defines tacit knowledge as:

that which dwells in our awareness of particulars while bearing on an entity which the particulars jointly constitute.

Smith pushes the argument a little further in his analysis of the role of aesthetics in science by postulating a two-way flow between facts and intuition. On the one hand, he claims that 'Although atomistic details are insufficient for full understanding, they cannot be ignored.' All the established 'facts' must be considered before imaginative interpretation can be indulged in. On the other hand, 'Nothing is a thing by itself; it takes meaning, indeed, existence only, as it interacts with something else.' He seems to be saying that we apprehend detailed 'facts' by an imaginative leap and once apprehended we interpret them through a further act of intuitive imagination.

Geoffrey Vickers pursuing a similar line to that of Smith, indicates the next and decisive step although he can't quite bring himself to take it:

> My thesis is that the human mind has available to it at least two different modes of knowing and that it uses both in appropriate and inappropriate combinations in its endless efforts to understand the world in which it finds itself. One of these modes is more dependent on analysis, logical reasoning, calculation and explicit description. The other is more dependent on synthesis and the recognition of pattern, context and the multiple relations of figure and ground. The first involves the recognition or creation of form irrespective of the elements which compose it. Both are normal aspects of the neocortical development which distinguishes man from his fellow mammals. Both are needed and both are used in most normal mental operations.
>
> They are often referred to as rationality and intuition. The main difference to which I refer is that a rational process is fully describable, where an intuitive process is not ... The possibility that the brain might be capable of both processes in combination seems not to have been considered.

Arnheim takes the step:

> Intuition is privileged to perceive the overall structure of configurations. Intellectual analysis serves to abstract the character of entities and events from individual contexts and defines them 'as such'. Intuition and intellect do not operate separately but require each other's cooperation in almost every case.

Together these ideas help us to understand the notion of simultaneity which we are pushing so hard. The building of the part–whole understanding is a combination of awareness of overall configurations coupled with more 'as such' analysis which, together, form the basis for action. In our data we find examples of various combinations of knowing. The 'commercial nose' of Sir David Alliance at Coats Viyella was described as critical to perceptions of overall configurations – he displayed a sense of what was and was not possible in terms of, say, potential merger targets. However, this feel was combined with much more rigorous reasoning in terms of 'as such' analysis before action was taken.

A couple of other ideas may be helpful to the discussion, both derive from the work of Louis Pondy and are to do with the notion of 'creativity' and 'performance'. His central point, which to an extent we share, is that rationality and intuition are joined not in some abstract space but only in performance. He cites Rollo May's concept of 'ecstasy' – 'a union of the subjective and the objective, a union of Dionysian passion and vitality with Apollonian form and order'. Ecstasy 'is not to be thought of merely as a Bacchic letting go, it involves the total person, with the subconscious and unconscious acting in unity with the conscious. It is not, thus, irrational; it is, rather, suprarational. It brings intellectual, volitional, and emotional factors into play all together.' What is more, it brings them together in 'lived experience'.

For further discussion see: Polanyi, *The Tacit Dimension* (1967); C. S. Smith, 'Structural hierarchy in science, art and history' (1980) and G. Vickers, 'Rationality and intuition' – both of these papers may be found in J. Wechsler (Ed.), *On Aesthetics in Science*, 1980; Arnheim's work is found in an interesting collection of writings, edited by Elliot Eisner (1985); Lou Pondy, 'Union of rationality and intuition in management action' in Srivastva and Associates (1983).

38 See particularly the work of Danah Zohar, *The Quantum Self* (1990), from whom the present discussion is adapted. Similar ideas are expressed in *The Dancing Wu Li Masters: An overview of the New Physics*, by Gary Zukav (1979). Since neither of us is a physicist (nor is either of the writers mentioned), we are somewhat nervous about the authority with which we make comments. No doubt someone somewhere will correct us.

39 For further comments upon acting thinkingly, etc., see Karl Weick (whom God preserve) (1983), 'Managerial thought in the context of action' which is to be found in *The Executive Mind*, edited by Suresh Srivastva and Associates. In the same book there are other notable papers of direct interest to us by William Torbert, Henry Mintzberg/James Waters, David Kolb and Louis Pondy (already mentioned above).

40 Quote from Lucas.

41 The quotation is from Weick (1983).

42 Donald Schon has written extensively about 'knowing in practice' and 'reflection in action'. By the former he appears to be saying something somewhat similar to us (and Weick). Reflection in action he takes to be different and it 'consists in on the spot surfacing, criticizing, restructuring and testing of intuitive understandings of experienced phenomena; it often takes the form of a reflective conversation with the situation ... When a manager reflects in action, he draws on a stock of organizational knowledge, adapting it to some present instance. And he also functions as an agent of organizational learning, extending or restructuring, in his present inquiry, the stock of knowledge which will be available for future inquiry.' Whilst not denying that such activities may well occur in organizations as in science, our position is that they are rarely as conscious as terms such as criticizing and testing makes them appear. See Donald Schon, *The Reflective Practitioner* (1983).

43 Our respondents insist upon an intimate connection between thinking and acting, denying, as do many philosophers of a pragmatic persuasion, the notion that thought is autonomous and that truth is objective. It is probable that for our respondents 'all thought is for the sake of action' and equally probable that they would, if they thought long and hard about it, conclude that 'truth' is simply a matter of instrumental intelligence. These caricatures of pragmatist philosophy perhaps exaggerate the point, but essentially, thinking actingly is a central tenet of pragmatism. We have more to say on this in chapter 5.

44 Barnard (1938, p. 194).

45 W. Torbert, 'Cultivating timely executive action', in Srivastva and Associates, *The Executive Mind* (1983).

46 John Arden, in his splendid novel, *The Books of Bale* (1988), captures the essence of our point in the following passage, in which Bale tells his daughter about the exploits of one of their ancestors:

> About one hundred years before, or more than that maybe, there was a man Bale, or Ball, or perhaps Bull, the names have shifted. At all events, he was also a John: my father said, an ancestor. A Lollard, which is to say a Protestant after the teaching of Wycliffe ... Not a clergyman, but a soldier, an archer who had fought at Agincourt, and then left the royal service because Monmouth Harry was burning Lollards. A very brave man, my father told me, but even the bravest must conceal the True Word in those days, there were so few of them that held to it anywhere. He went south and east, first to Bohemia, where for a time he found Protestants and joined in their glorious war.
> The baron whom he served was killed in battle and his troop scattered: but not all of it. The residue passed over, under their captain, to a prince-bishop of the popish church, a scarlet cardinal, who used them as his own, very fiercely against the Turk, and – grievous to tell it – against certain honest Christians as well ... And John the archer came to believe that his serving such a gross fat behemoth ... gave cause for the anger of God ... So John the archer bethought him a purpose. He would slay and kill the Cardinal: who was, you see, well guarded against all customary attempts, so it had to be by a fashion that none could look for. And yet for all his puzzling of it, Archer John could find no way. He did not forget his purpose: but he kept it only in the back-closet of his mind: God, he thought, would call him to it, at whatever hour the time was ripe, so let him wait ...
> Now it happened, that after dinner, when the Cardinal must rest his horrible swollen belly in a cool and pleasant place, he would enter a small garden in the very midst of his vast castle. All doors to the garden locked and guarded. No windows overlooked it: except one. And that one, so high in the wall of the great hall, who could think

any man could contrive to attain it? But upon a day John walked to his duty, sentry-go on the uppermost leads. He was alone, and for no clear reason, he did not follow the usual path, up the tower in the south-west courtyard and so across the roof of the chapel: instead he took the turret in the south-east courtyard, and thence turned north along a passageway which was builded in the thick height of the side wall of the great hall. At his elbow, as he walked, he saw a slit of a window, giving light to the passageway from the light within the hall. He turned his head and looked through the window – and what did he see? but over against him, in the opposite wall of the hall, in line but lower, the other little window, a round hole most like a flower with four half-round petals, no more than two foot wide and with neither glass nor shutter. He looked straight through first one opening, across the top space of the hall, and then through the other – all indoors was deep shadow, but there beyond, the Cardinal's Garden: a cusped tiny circle of green and gold, a fire-gleed of afternoon sunlight hardly bearable to his eye.

And there, therein, dead centre, in the heart of his garden, the Cardinal strolling, straight athwart the archer's glance, fanning his huge white face with his hat, alone at his loathsome ease, in a green-gold glade of sin. I say there could not in all Christendom have been two men capable of such a shot, there and then, as the Cardinal moved! Think of it, child, two openings, the nearest hardly wider than the barb of an arrow, and the man in the far garden moving, as I have said! The arrow caught him straight in the folds of his throat: oh dead he was, slain stone dead for the enhancement of God, just like Eglon King of Moab, you recollect? in the Book of Judges. I tell you not this to excite your maiden heart toward manslaughter, nor to stiffen you in your adult days to cry blood vengeance upon your enemies: but to cause you to reflect upon how and why John the archer took that passageway the day he did. He thought it was a whim or fancy: but then afterwards he knew how it must have been a Providence. Only by Providence *a man might act, without plan or second thinking, so long as he hath his purpose, all in a moment he is sent a chance, he either taketh it or is lost for ever.* [The emphasis is ours.] (Quoted with permission from John Arden, *The Books of Bale*, 1988).

47 Quote from Metal Box.
48 Quoted Weick (1979).
49 Polanyi (1967, p. 6).
50 Danah Zohar (1990, pp. 10–11).
51 Polanyi (1967, p. 18).
52 Polanyi (1967, p. 19).
53 Quoted in Briskman (1981).

54 For more on pragmatism, see chapter 5.
55 Quote from Brian Smith of Metal Box.
56 Chester Barnard (1938, p. 322). An interesting feature of this quotation is the dichotomies which Barnard spells out: 'attaining proportion between speed and caution, between broad outlines and fineness of detail ...' etc. It signals a recurring theme and one with which we struggled for some time. Each time we identified one characteristic in our accounts, we could almost invariably come up with examples of its opposite. This is not uncommon within management theorizing and indeed, Quinn and Kimberley (1984) furnish a list even longer than our own. As our analysis developed, however, we decided that the problem in making such distinctions between opposing dimensions was actually one of our own making: conditioned by 'either/or' thinking which requires a choice (by implication, some evaluative choice) between more or less of a particular characteristic. Hence, we went on to develop what we describe as an 'and/and' quality, found in our data, by which respondents talk not of opposing dimensions but of, in effect, 'attaining proportion between this and that', doing one thing *and* the other. Indeed, it is very often only by knowing what something is not that one can gain reference to what it is. In this case, it makes sense that 'attaining proportion between ...' is a key feature of executive process, particularly when one notes that this sense of proportion will change according to time and situation. We will refer to this 'and/and' quality again in later chapters.

Chapter 2

1 See Colin M. Turbayne, *The Myth of Metaphor* (1970, p.214). For further discussion of metaphor see George Lakoff and Mark Johnson, *Metaphors We Live By* (1980), and numerous texts/articles by Gareth Morgan and others.
2 We deal with stories in more detail in chapter 5.
3 As we indicated in the preface, our ideas derive directly from the data we collected and the discussions we conducted. Our subsequent reading has influenced our expression of these ideas and we have found particular support in this section from the work of Morse Peckham (1979) and Peter Sederberg (1984).
4 This discussion draws on the work of Morse Peckham and Peter Sederberg. Their work provides some useful support and confirmation for ideas we have found in our material. We quote directly from them and, on occasions, make reference in the notes. We have adopted this course for stylistic reasons, not in any way to imply that our debt to Peckham and Sederberg is not direct and substantial.
5 Peter Sederberg (1984, p. 131).
6 Who is the management, of course, is at the root of the struggle. Do the scholars run the University or do the administrators? Whose explanation

is to prevail? Nor, of course, is it quite as simple as such statements would imply. There are divisions within the administration just as there are competing explanations put forward by different academics. Pluralism rules OK?

7 In the present circumstances, our enterprise, like many another, has to live with competing explanations.
8 William H. Starbuck and Frances J. Milliken, 'Executives' perceptual filters', in *The Executive Effect: Concepts and Methods for Studying Top Managers*, edited by Donald C. Hambrick (1988, pp. 35–66).
9 Quoted in Starbuck and Milliken (1988, p. 45).
10 Daft and Weick (1984) talk about interpretation, which Starbuck and Milliken call sensemaking. However, for Daft and Weick, scanning, interpretation and learning are the three key stages in their model of organizational interpretation (p. 256). What our data seem to illustrate is a simultaneity, in which these processes distinguished by other writers interrelate as executives go about *reading* their enterprises: that is, notice *and* make sense.
11 Sir Geoffrey Vickers, *The Art of Judgement* (1965, p. 67).
12 We stress the phrase *influenced by* : that is, we are not arguing for some unchanging homogeneity called an executive team. Quite the opposite. Part of their strength lies in their difference and we will expand on this theme in chapter 5. The key point here is that they do share *an* appreciative system.
13 In a delightful book entitled *Pluto's Republic*, Peter Medawar debates 'Two Conceptions of Science': of science as 'an imaginative and exploratory activity' and of science as 'a critical and analytical activity' (1984, p. 31). He then goes on to show how 'what are usually thought of as two alternative and indeed competing accounts of *one* process of thought are in fact accounts of *two* successive and complementary episodes of thought that occur in every advance of scientific understanding' (p. 33). He concludes on an interesting point, questioning the notions of *a* scientific mind or *the* scientific method: 'a scientist, so far from being a man who never knowingly departs from the truth, is always *telling stories* in a sense not so very far removed from that of the nursery euphemism – stories which might be about real life but which must be tested very scrupulously to find out if indeed they are so' (p. 40).
14 These are points made forcefully by Sederberg (1984, pp. 134–5).
15 Simon (1989).
16 More on paradox in chapters 4 and 5.
17 Starbuck and Milliken (1988).
18 This relationship between thought and action and simplifying explanation is explored more fully in chapter 5.
19 This definition derives from the work of Geert Hofstede, *Culture's Consequences: International Differences in Work-Related Values* (1980) and D. Hambrick and G. L. Brandon, 'Executive values' in *The Executive Effect: Concepts and Methods for Studying Top Managers* (1988, pp. 3–35). There is, of course, a great deal of published material that purports to deal with

values, but little of it is of direct relevance to our focus upon senior executives. We take it that values are the fundamental premises that we all use to judge what is important and what we *believe* in. They are intrinsic, deep-seated factors which influence every major decision we make – our moral judgements, our reactions to others, our willingness to make commitments and our support for or rejection of organizational goals. Values may well determine the way things are, what really counts. As Rowe and Mason (1988) put it, values 'form the hidden source of strength, commitment and dedication that goes beyond normal incentives and rewards'.

It is not usual to find values directly addressed in management texts other than those deriving from the humanistic perspective where it is rare for them not to be addressed. Typical of them would be the paper by Tannenbaum and Davis (1969) who are clearly against what they term 'bureaucratic values' and are decidely for humanistic ones: 'Growing evidence strongly suggests that humanistic values not only resonate with an increasing number of people in today's world, but also are highly consistent with the effective functioning of organizations built on the newer organic model.' They fail to cite the nature of this evidence and there is little in our data that would support this kind of assertion. Their analysis suggests a sharp division between what they term old and new values: away from a view of man as essentially bad towards a view of him as essentially good; away from avoidance or negative evaluation of individuals towards confirming them as human beings; away from a view of individuals as fixed towards seeing them as in process; away from resisting and fearing individual differences towards accepting and utilizing them; away from utilizing an individual primarily with reference to his job description towards viewing him as a whole person; away from walling off the expression of feelings toward an individual towards one of being open and direct; away from marksmanship and game playing and towards 'authentic' behaviour; away from using status for maintaining power and personal prestige towards the use of status for organizationally relevant purposes; away from distrusting people towards trusting them; away from avoiding facing others with relevant data towards confronting appropriately; away from avoidance of risk taking towards a willingness to risk; away from a primary emphasis on competition towards a much greater emphasis upon collaboration. Some of these movements, if movements they be, can be discerned in some of our respondents but, as elsewhere, we are disturbed by the desire to sort values into either this or that.

To the best of our knowledge only Quinn (1988) has consistently explored the possibility of coexisting yet competing values:

> However, master managers do not create high performance by using one or other of the philosophies described above [sets of values]; instead they employ both. (p. xvi)

At the heart of his thesis, 'High performing managers work with complexity and contradiction to achieve temporary synthesis and "synergy".'

> The key to becoming a master manager is seeing past one's own blinders and the blinders imposed by the expectations of others ... It involves a certain amount of cognitive complexity and means experimenting with opposing frames of reference. (p. 24)

Quinn argues that in every organization there are at least four general perspectives on what 'good' managers do. At the perceptual level he holds that these perspectives are contradictory and emotionally held 'moral' positions. Good managers develop the ability to see more cues or stimuli than those who are less sophisticated. 'They see these cues as moving flows. They learn to focus on the most important cues and then develop a conscious plan based on a particular set of values. They keep to this plan while observing other cues and, when appropriate, they drop the old plan in favor of another plan. This new plan may reflect a contradictory set of values. That is, these managers have the capacity to see problems from contradictory frames, to entertain and pursue alternative perspectives ...' Yet even this notion of competing values does not adequately reflect what our respondents seem to demonstrate and talk about. And, of course, there are a number of problems with a passage such as this. If values are, as we have argued, deeply held, Quinn's super managers seem to be bereft of them as, apparently, they can and do readily switch values with, apparently, no difficulty, no sense of loss. So much so that one is tempted to regard them as beings entirely without values, mountebanks and charlatans apparently happy one moment to be, for example, completely at home in dealing directly with another human being and the next insidiously exploiting the same human being. The phrase, 'when appropriate' also gives us difficulty. How is one to know when it is appropriate to dispense with one set of values and take up another?

The notion of paradox and contradiction implied in much of Quinn's work, however, is an important and potentially fruitful one. It is a theme picked up by Peters and Waterman (1982) when they note that in what they term 'excellent' companies, managers have an unusual ability to resolve paradox, to translate conflicts and tensions into excitement, high commitment and superior performance. In reviewing the book, Van de Ven (1983) applauds this insight (as do we) and notes a grave inadequacy in the theories generated by researchers. He argues that while the managers of excellent companies seem to have a capacity for dealing with paradox, administrative theory is not designed to account for this. In order to be internally consistent, theorists tend to eliminate contradictions. He holds that there is a need for dynamic theory that can handle both stability and change, that can consider the tensions and conflicts inherent in human systems. (Some of these ideas surface again in chapter

4, note 7.) Among other things, Van de Ven notes, the theory would view people as complex actors in tension-filled social systems, constantly interacting with a 'fast-paced, ever changing array of forces'. The theory would focus upon 'the ethics and value judgements that are implied when leaders and followers raise one another to higher levels of motivation and morality.'

Quinn takes us part of the way when he notes that 'We want our organizations to be adaptable and flexible, but we also want them to be stable and controlled. We want growth, resource acquisition, and external support, but we also want tight information management and formal communication. We want an emphasis on the value of human resources, but we also want an emphasis upon planning and goal setting' (1988, p. 49). The problem with Quinn and with most of us who write in this vein is that we fail to emphasize process: we can have all of these things if we talk not of beliefs but of believing, not of values but of valuing, not of organizations but of organizing, not of perception but of perceiving, not of becoming adapted but of adapting, not of stability but of stabilizing. We can never have any of these 'things', we can only experience them in process as 'ings'.

20 We made no attempt to measure values. No doubt a careful analysis of the texts would reveal more about the values of this particular group of individuals. What we have included here is representative rather than exhaustive.

21 Quotes from BTR, Reckitt and Colman.

22 All these quotes are from one company: Reckitt and Colman – a none too subtle way of reinforcing the point we made earlier about appreciative systems. Other companies also had things to say about innovation.

23 Quotes from Avon, Beazer, BTR.

24 Quotes from Avon, Beazer, Marks and Spencer, Coats Viyella.

25 Quotes from Coats Viyella, Reckitt and Colman, Metal Box, BTR.

26 Refer to Hambrick and Brandon (1988) for examples.

27 Barnard (1938, p. 259).

28 In support of this point, Hage and Dewar (1973) found that the values of the top groups of professionals in health and welfare organizations were better predictors of subsequent innovations than were the values of the executive directors alone. However it could be argued that managing professionals is quite a different bag of worms to managing other kinds of executives. One could anticipate that professionals would hold strong professional beliefs that may conflict with the beliefs of someone seeking to contain and direct their energies. The reference is cited in Hambrick and Brandon (1988).

29 Quotes from Metal Box, Beazer, Marks and Spencer, Coats Viyella, Reckitt and Colman, BTR.

30 Quotes from BTR, Reckitt and Colman, Hanson.

31 Lawrence B. Mohr, *Explaining Organizational Behaviour*, (1982, pp. 107–111).

32 Peter Sederberg has a section on values and ideology which we pick up on in chapter 4.

33 Giddens' theory of 'structuration' is at the heart of these ideas: the process by which interaction informs structures which in turn constrain interaction and interpretation. We expand in greater depth on his work in chapter 4, note 25. It is a theory which, at least implicitly, underpins much of the work of interpretative theorists and we suggest a paper by Weick and Browning (1986) as an excellent example. Their focus is communication and in particular, distinguishing between argumentation and narration as different forms of organizational communication. They propose that 'argumentation' is based on a rational perspective, requiring skilled advocates who are competent in their subject, to reason and resolve through analysis and argument. In contrast, the narrative style is more persuasive, non-formal and non-expert, requiring people to 'judge probability and fidelity' (p. 242). This paradigm is less thoroughly researched in the literature, but they suggest it embraces story-telling, gossip and coherence. Although we develop the notion of story-telling in chapter 5, we start from a different point to Weick and Browning, and our analysis does not share their micro-level focus. That is, we are not trying to distinguish between two different kinds of communication paradigm but instead, simply take 'organization as explanation'. Given the nature of our data, our focus is more wholistic and relates to the broader concerns of 'doing organizing' as expressed by senior executives.

However, in summing up the implications of their work, they provide a useful summary which in effect, expresses Giddens' theory of structuration in terms of organizational theorizing:

> Conversation itself has real consequences that endure. Face-to-face conversation builds, reaffirms and can change the pattern of the organization. Managers should not take conversation for granted, because what they say and to whom they say it creates the working structure for the organization. (p. 255)

34 At the start of James Hanson's career as a businessman, in Yorkshire.

35 These limits have since been raised.

36 We have more to say on stories and myths in chapter 5.

37 The comparison between the laboratory and a theatrical performance is Peckham's. The addition of a commercial/industrial enterprise and some of the points made are ours.

38 Other tests refer to this aspect of managing as socialization or, occasionally, as conditioning. Hanson was clear that in his enterprise it was 'doctrination'.

39 The term 'presenting himself' should not be taken to imply that Tony Mitchard, any more than any one of us, was consciously adopting a persona or cynically playing a role.

40 It is for these reasons that watching a play on TV at home is a quite different activity. No amount of careful TV production effort can control the alternative sources of stimulation and randomness of response generated in a domestic environment.

41 A number of such conferences are now 'staged' professionally, particularly those which are designed to launch a new product or a new initiative. Employees are wined and dined (or beered and sandwiched, depending upon their status) and carefully groomed, well-rehearsed executives put across the message to the accompaniment of videos, music, light shows or whatever. In addition, our respondents described increasing use of such events to bring people together, to listen and talk to each other, to develop common purpose: or as one executive put it, 'to whip on the troops'.

42 Quote from Tony Mitchard of Avon Rubber.

43 See Mangham and Overington (1987, p. 120).

44 The principle of cultural redundancy is developed by Peckham (1979, pp. 166–9, and 182–4).

45 Quotes from Marks and Spencer, Metal Box, Prudential.

46 Another more everyday example may help illustrate the point, adapted from Peckham (1979, pp. 167–8). He talks about major intersections, we have extended the example to include roundabouts.
Recently drivers in the United Kingdom have had to negotiate many more roundabouts than hitherto. Previously many intersections were controlled by lights and those roundabouts that existed were such that it was clear which driver had priority. In the past few years, many lights have been removed to speed the flow of traffic and priority to the right has become the desired response. The incidence of collisions at intersections has risen. Under the old system drivers were reminded to stop, or at least slow down, before proceeding cautiously. They were reminded by signals at the road side which told them an intersection was coming up, they were reminded by painted signs on the road itself, by heavy lines across the road and by the lights – red for danger. Now they may or may not be warned that a roundabout is ahead, often by little more than a small blue sign depicting three arrows forming a circle, there may be lines on the road implying that a reduction in speed is advisable, but the key piece of information – 'priority to the right' – is left to memory.
Lights and stop signs reiterate the key message 'Stop'. They do not rely upon the driver remembering that intersections require caution: they assert it. Roundabouts are much less successful in bringing about desired response because not only is the message itself – 'priority to the right' – absent from the situation but, even for those who can remember it, who goes first is a matter of judgement. Three cars approaching simultaneously may either each stop or each proceed; each driver is convinced either that someone else has the priority or that he/she has it. Failing to stop at lights or at a major junction is an offence which, if observed by random policing, will result in a fine and/or deprivation of one's licence to drive. Screwing up the priority at a roundabout appears

not to be a punishable offence. Lights and stop signs are relatively successful in bringing about the desired response, roundabouts much less so. It appears that learned behaviour can be maintained and made reliable only by constant reiteration of instructions for behaviour. If the highway authorities want drivers to give way to the right, they will need to find ways of reminding people that that is the desired response at the point where that response is desired. If managers want to effectively channel response they too must constantly reiterate their message and be prepared to enforce it.

47 This phrase is taken from Sederberg (1984). See also chapter 4.
48 We have more to say about cultural vandalism – change – in chapter 4.
49 The notion of being condemned to innovate is Peckham's.
50 Peckham again.
51. Morse Peckham makes some similar points but, again, our conclusions derive directly from our data and our discussions.
52 Bruner (1964) develops an interesting idea of the relationship between what we take fate to be and our own sense of potency – the latter making incursions on the former and, in effect, rolling back whatever it is we take fate to be. These ideas are discussed more fully in chapter 5.
53 We have more to say about pragmatism in chapter 5.

Chapter 3

1 This is rarely discussed in the literature, although there are exceptions. The most notable exception is Jill Graham whose work we pick up on in note 3, below.
2 In a paper entitled 'The romance of leadership', Meindl et al. (1985) expose our romanticized conception of leadership:

> The argument being advanced here is that the concept of leadership is a perception that plays a part in the way people attempt to make sense out of organizationally relevant phenomena. Moreover, in this sense-making process, leadership has assumed a romanticized, larger-than-life role ... leadership is perhaps best construed as an explanatory category that can be used to explain and account for organizational activities and outcomes. (p. 79)

They go on to demonstrate, through surveying a wide range of both academic and business publications, that leaders can be blamed for the fate of their industries, let alone that of their organizations. From this they conclude that their analysis provides:

> reasonably coherent and compelling evidence for the premise that a romanticized conception of leadership is an important part of the

social reality that is brought to bear in our informal analysis of organizations – and perhaps in our more formal theories as well. Ironically, though, a heroic vision of what leaders and leadership are all about virtually guarantees that a satisfying understanding will remain beyond the grasp of our best scientific efforts, particularly since the thrust of scientific inquiry is to do away with mysteries. (p. 100)

3 It is tempting at this point in the chapter to indulge in some attempt to say precisely what we mean by *leading* and *following*. Indeed, in an earlier draft we succumbed and spent some considerable time and energy in categorizing behaviour which we took to be *directing* and *obeying* and in distinguishing these activities from *leading* and *following*. Obeying we took to occur in circumstances where individuals had comparatively little freedom of choice; directing, therefore, we took to be coercive, leading more a matter of choice. Indeed, we took it that it was impossible to speak of leading *unless* following was problematic. Without free choice for putative followers, the notion of leading would disappear, to be replaced by the idea of directing or supervising. We were quite taken with the idea, but a more wholistic review of our data suggested that the distinction was too pat, too precise to be of use to us. Relations between senior managers do not appear to be a matter of either directing or leading, obeying or following, but a seamless blending together of them all; a particular activity, action, piece of dialogue or exchange between several members of an organization may be seen as an instance of directing and/or leading; a particular response or series of responses an instance of obeying and/or following. Indeed, it may be categorized in one way at a particular point in time and as something else at another point. The points about directing and leading, obeying and following, derive from Jill W. Graham, 'Transformational leadership: fostering follower autonomy, not automatic followership' (1988) – a title which hardly trips off the tongue, but a challenging article to be found in J. G. Hunt et al. *Emerging Leadership Vistas* (1988).
4 Barnard (1938, p. 230).
5 For some this appeared to be a major factor in the securing of commitment to the enterprise. It is, perhaps, worth noting that much of the recent movement towards incentive payments, in Great Britain at least, has occurred within an environment that takes money to be the measure of the person. People have been led to believe that they *ought* to want material things, have been led to rate themselves and others in terms of their earning and spending power. It appeared to us that some of our managers saw the need for pay rises more as a matter of keeping in line with their peers than of simply providing for a higher standard of living, important though that may be to them.
6 Quote from BTR.
7 Quotes from Avon, Marks and Spencer, Glynwed.
8 R. J. House, an article intriguingly titled 'A 1976 theory of charismatic

leadership', in J. G. Hunt and L. L. Larson (Eds) *Leadership; The Cutting Edge* (1977).

9 Quote from Glynwed.

10 Quote from Glynwed.

11 H. W. Simons, 'The carrot and stick as handmaidens of persuasion in conflict situations', in G. Miller and H. W. Simons (Eds) *Perspectives on Communication in Social Conflict* (1974).

12 Quote from Glynwed. Barnard as so often also has something to say on the matter of autocratic management:

> The necessity for avoiding formal issues, that is, for avoiding the issuance of numerous formal orders except on routine matters and except in emergencies, is important. I know of major executives who issue an order or judgement settling an important issue rather seldom, although they are functioning all the time. The obvious desire of politicians to avoid important issues (and to impose them on their opponents) is based upon a thorough sense of organization. Neither authority nor cooperative disposition (largely the same things) will stand much overt division on formal issues in the present stage of human development. Hence most laws, executive orders, decisions, etc. are in effect formal notice that all is well – there is agreement, authority is not questioned. (1938 pp. 225–6)

13 Quotes from Reckitt and Colman, Lucas Industries, BTR, Hanson, Metal Box.

14 Barnard, (1938, p. 225). We have more to say on 'difference' in chapter 5.

15 Barnard (1938, p. 17).

16 Yet another interesting paradox – the idea that teamwork both *creates* and *reconciles* difference.

17 See *The Androgynous Manager* by A. G. Sargent (1981). The use of this term within the text, of course, is deliberately provocative, but what other term adequately encapsulates the opposite of 'macho' management, a style which we all know and love. Very few would like to be called androgynous managers – none the less, Sargent's work is worth a read even if the title has to be obscured if reading it at work.

18 Anthony Powell (1951, *Dance to the Music of Time* : 1. A Question of Upbringing p. 6).

19 'The basic sense-making device used within the organization is assumed to be talking to discover thinking. How can I know what I think until I see what I say? The action of talking is the occasion for defining the articulating cognitions.' (Weick, 1969, p. 165).

20 Alice M. Sapienza 'Image making as a strategic function', in Lee Thayer (Ed.). *Organization-Communication: Emerging Perspectives* (1987).

21 Quotes from Beazer, Avon, Glynwed.

22 G. Simmel,from K. H. Wolff, *The Sociology of Georg Simmel* (1950, p. 318).
23 Niklas Luhmann, *Trust and Power*, (1979, p. 24).
24 Luhmann (1979, p. 24).
25 Luhmann (1979, p. 10).
26 Deutsch (1962). This definition is that which was modified by Zand (1972).
27 Barnard (1938, p. 148).
28 Erving Goffman, *The Presentation of Self in Everyday Life* (1959).
29 *Effecting Organizational Change* by I. L. Mangham (1988) has a relatively lengthy discussion of the development of trust within groups. It would be tedious to repeat it here, but it is certainly worth a read by those who are smart enough to recognize that the development of trust is a difficult and often fragile process.
30 Barnard (1938, p. 225).
31 Hambrick and Brandon (1988), after discussing the issue of executive values come up with an obvious but none the less interesting conclusion:

   1. As long as the organization's strategy is stable and generally suits conditions in the environment ... homogeneity of values will yield decisions and a very efficient process for arriving at those decisions. An efficient decision process is fast and consumes relatively few organizational resources.
   2. When the environment is disruptive and discontinuous, heterogeneity of values will yield the most effective decisions. The team will not be particularly efficient; for example dissensus and 'political loops' will abound. However, eventual decision quality will surpass what could be achieved by a homogeneous team.
   3. Since environmental disruptions can occur at any time and without warning, an organization maximizes its chance of long-term survival by having at least some diversity of values within its top management team. (p. 26)

32 Quotes from BTR, Reckitt and Colman, Avon, Glynwed.
33 Quotes from Reckitt and Colman, Lucas.
34 Quote from Lucas.
35 That is to say, in the terms that we introduced earlier, they did not know what they had read until they had wrighten what they wrought.
36 Vincent Tomas, 'Creativity in art' (1958).
37 Tomas (1958, p. 1).
38 Tomas (1958, p. 2).
39 We hesitate to use the word 'wrong' because it tends to imply some absolute sense by which right and wrong are evaluated. In the creative sense, what is being evaluated is whether or not the brush stroke or the passage 'works' – a matter of 'feel' or 'sense' that, in the unfolding process of creating, it is appropriate. We suggest it is the same for the would-be leader, testing out what feels to be the right course of action while at the same time remaining open to being converted or persuaded of some alternative.

40 Tomas (1958, p. 3), refers back to Coleridge and the idealists to make this
point: 'Coleridge and the idealists were correct, therefore, in so far as they
distinguished creative activity from the exercise of passive imagination, or
fancy. Essential to the former, while absent from the latter, are critical
judgement and fastidiousness.'

41 There is another crucial parallel with the creative process which organizational analysts tend to overlook and which is extremely difficult to
describe. That is, at some point an artist must call a halt to a piece of work
and take up something else. The descriptive problem is that this does not
necessarily mean a picture is 'complete' nor does it mean a sequential
process of first one thing and then another, as often ideas run simultaneously – the next painting may already be emerging in the mind's eye in
the process of 'doing' the previous one. However, the difficulty is located
in our attention to artistic product, the 'tangible particulars', rather than
the creative process, the 'whole'. In his book entitled *Art as Experience*,
John Dewey (1934) argued:

> It has been repeatedly intimated (in this book) that there is a
> difference between the art product (statue, painting or whatever) and
> the *work* of art. The first is physical and potential; the latter is active and
> experienced. It is what the product does, its working ... When the
> structure of the object is such that its force interacts happily (but not
> easily) with the energies that issue from the experience itself; when
> their mutual affinities and antagonisms work together to bring about a
> substance that develops cumulatively and surely (but not too steadily)
> towards a fulfilling of impulsions and tensions, then indeed there is a
> work of art. (pp. 632–3)

On this basis, Dewey goes on to talk about 'the organization of energies'
which may be embodied in an artistic product. In his view, the 'work of art'
embraces the creative process of making as well as the object of creation:

> We have *an* experience when the material experienced runs its
> course to fulfillment. Then and then only is it integrated within and
> demarcated in the general stream of experience from other experiences.
> A piece of work is finished in a way that is satisfactory; a problem
> receives its solution; a game is played through; a situation, whether
> that of eating a meal, playing a game of chess, carrying on a conversa-
> tion, writing a book, or taking part in a political campaign, is so
> rounded out that its close is a consummation and not a cessation. Such
> an experience is a whole and carries with it its own individualizing
> quality and self-sufficiency. It is *an* experience ... In an experience,
> flow is from something to something. As one part leads into another
> and as one part carries on what went before, each gains distinctness in
> itself. The enduring whole is diversified by successive phases that are
> emphases of its varied colours. Because of continuous merging there
> are no holes, mechanical injunctions and dead centers when we have

an experience. There are pauses, places of rest, but they punctuate and define the quality of movement. They sum up what has been undergone and prevent its dissipation and idle evaporation. Continued acceleration is breathless and prevents parts from gaining distinction. In a work of art, different acts, episodes, occurrences melt and fuse into unity, and yet do not disappear and lose their own character as they do so. (pp. 596–7)

It is this quality of movement, with occasional pauses and places of rest, which best describes the process by which 'the work of art' finds expression in art objects. As Dewey put it: 'A "conclusion" is no separate and independent thing: it is the consummation of a movement' (p. 599). And, we would add, the movement continues to other consummations.

42 C. J. Ducasse, *The Philosophy of Art* (1929), cited in Tomas (1958, p. 11).
43 Spender (1951).
44 'Speculations' in *The Problems of Aesthetics* edited by Eliseo Vivas and Murray Krieger (1953). Cited in Tomas (1958, p. 4).
45 Our data on Marks and Spencer are thin – one interview.
46 Tomas (1958, p. 1).
47 Barnard (1938, p. 302).
48 Barnard (1938, p. 302).
49 Herbert Simon, 'What is intuition', in *Intuition in Organizations*, edited by Weston H. Agor (1989). The article is very similar to another that he wrote on creativity in organizations. He appears to make little or no distinction between the two processes.
50 Simon (1989, p. 29).
51 Simon (1989, p. 30).
52 We have more to say on experience and learning in chapter 5.
53 Jacob Bronowski, *The Visionary Eye: Essays in the Arts, Literature and Science* (1978, p. 10).
54 Bronowski (1978, p. 12).
55 The ability of a company's senior managers to absorb what is going on in the business community and to act on that information with appropriate moves is central to the process of leading. Many of the appropriate moves are a consequence of experience, products of the collective previous doings, as it were, but an over-reliance on these, a propensity for unquestioning activation of them could lead to the demise of the enterprise. Adaptation depends upon creativity and creativity on challenge to accepted ideas. One way of challenging current practice may be through the process of planning. A handful of our respondents used planning in this fashion. A good planning process (our emphasis is upon the process, not the plans) is one in which members of the management team share and change their mental models of their company, their markets and their competitors. This occurs through talk, through interaction: new models are an outcome of discussion. The adoption of new models may be accelerated by the use of particular approaches to planning, by the deliberate use of planning as a catalyst and may, indeed,

result from a process that few would recognize as planning. What is important, whatever the label, is the process whereby that which is taken to be known is challenged. See, in particular, 'Planning as learning' by Arie P. De Geus (1988).

56 The linkage of creativity to response implies, of course, that judgements may be revised. Our data suggest that they are on a regular basis. Coats Viyella has been a 'goody' and a 'baddy', up and down over the past year or so. ConsGold, where we interviewed the CEO, was praised for its creative defence against takeover by Minorco and within weeks was acquired by Hanson (another of our respondents).

57 Quote from Lucas.

58 Our choice of companies, as we explained in the Preface, was dictated in part by their willingness to talk to us at all. Given the exploratory nature of this study, we have not pushed to secure the comments of analysts. This may be a line of research that we would wish to pursue in the future.

59 Zaleznik (1988) calls it *bricolage*, which appears a bit over the top, even for him.

60 Koestler (1981).

61 Quote from Reckitt and Colman.

62 The paper by Bruce J. Avolio and Bernard M. Bass, 'Transformational leadership, charisma and beyond' (1988), provides an interesting commentary on current thinking. The complete collection, *Emerging Leadership Vistas*, edited by Hunt et al. (1988) is well worth a look.

63 Barnard (1938, p. 226).

64 Louis B. Barnes and Mark P. Kriger, 'The hidden side of organizational leadership' (1986).

65 Barnes and Kriger (1986, p. 24).

Chapter 4

1 Frederick Harrison in programme of Hull Truck Theatre company, May 1988.

2 Bruce Chatwin, *In Patagonia* (1979).

3 Watzlawick et al. (1974, p. 2).

4 'Persistence' in organizations is about stability and continuity, the habituated routines which form the 'taken-for-granted' of organizing. It is only when some fragmentation occurs, some deviation from the 'old order', that it becomes possible actually to identify what the 'old order' was. As Weick (1985) puts it: 'People learn how they have always done things when someone tells them to do things differently' (p. 386).

5 Watzlawick et al. (1974, p. 2).

6 Watzlawick et al. (1974, p. 95).

7 Time and again our material illustrates this 'and/and' quality. As analysts, we have had to struggle with our own inclination to impose order by more

simple 'either/or' conceptualizing. For instance, many spoke in one breath about encouraging autonomy and responsibility of subsidiaries and then, in the next, described the tightening of controls by the centre. How can you increase autonomy and responsibility at the same time as increasing control? Likewise, we have descriptions of the need to have clearly defined responsibilities on the one hand, and on the other, examples of considerable ambiguity, in some cases even deliberately created ambiguity. On a different conceptual level, we have illustrations of difference and unity as crucial dimensions of effective teams, of complex situations reduced to a cogent simplicity. We recognize something paradoxical in all of these: that is, they describe what appear to be two 'opposing', perhaps apparently mutually exclusive, themes.

Definitions of paradox usually involve some notion of contradiction or opposing forces. Perhaps the best summary of the appeal of some notion of paradox was made by Jackie Mason, Jewish Rabbi and humorist, who said 'only paradox can do justice to life's injustices'. However, there are many more formal attempts to divine some core definition of the term. Putnam (1986) identifies different categories of paradox, including 'the pragmatic paradox, contradictions (which) are mutually exclusive alternatives that evolve over time' (p. 153); Berg and Smith (1987) identify three aspects, 'self-reference, contradiction and vicious circle', which are all necessary for paradox; Van de Ven and Scott Poole (1988) argue 'paradox is the simultaneous presence of two mutually exclusive assumptions or statements; taken singly, each is incontestably true, but taken together they are inconsistent' (p. 21); Quinn and Cameron (1988) offer 'the simplest definition, going back to the Latin root, [which] says that a paradox is an apparent contradiction' (p. 290). And many more besides. Indeed, consulting the *Oxford English Dictionary*, we find definitions of paradox as a 'seemingly absurd though perhaps really well-founded statement' or 'statement contrary to received opinion'. And this perhaps is the key to our understanding of paradox: that is, it arises from *the statements we make*, (i.e. our interpretations of situations) rather than being inherent in the situations we observe. And as we will go on to explain, the problem of paradox becomes that of the analyst rather than the practitioner because it is the analyst who constructs these apparently 'absurd though perhaps well-founded' statements whereas the practitioner, in our analysis, does not.

Van de Ven (1983) points out:

> Most administrative theories begin with or search for internal consistencies in the nature of man and organizations and relegate contradictions, as indicators of either poor theory or anomalies, to an area outside the bounds of theory. Correspondingly, most administrative theories are static and are rightly criticized for their inability to explain the dynamics of change and development in organizational form and individual behaviour. (p. 622)

He notes five key paradoxes which Peters and Waterman (1982) observed in individuals as well as drawing out his own set of organizational paradoxes which he identifies in their work. Peters and Waterman, however, did not offer a clear analysis of paradox in their book, *In Search of Excellence*, other than making their much quoted observation that 'excellent companies have learned how to manage paradox'. Even in their chapter, entitled 'Managing Ambiguity and Paradox', they manage to leave much ambiguity as to what this managing process might refer.

In calling for a theory of paradox, Van de Ven goes on to suggest it would involve a 'dynamic, tension-strung view' centred on 'transforming leadership, corporate culture and organizational evolution' (p. 624).

To some extent, we might agree with Van de Ven. Our data could be interpreted in terms of leadership, culture and evolution to give a 'dynamic, tension-strung view', rich in examples of paradox. But the result would still be two-dimensional rather than multi-dimensional. More importantly, it would not be given in the language used by respondents and nor would it help to convey the 'whole' process of managing as they described it. Indeed, at one point in our research, we made a conscious decision *not* to present respondents with examples of contradictory ideas they might have just expressed or to suggest to them that there might be something paradoxical in what they were saying. On occasions when we had done this, the response was one of 'Well, I suppose you could put it like that but ...'. To do so would seem to be constraining them to make a choice which in reality does not seem apparent to them.

We suggest, though, that it is extremely difficult, certainly for analysts, to avoid the 'either/or' framework of theorizing. For example, Quinn and Cameron (1988) describe three kinds of ways to deal with paradox: paradox as contradiction; paradox as negative dynamic process; and paradox as a positive, dynamic process, based on ideas of 'flow' and peak performance generated through the paradoxical state. From this, they produce a model which seeks to describe eight general sets of effectiveness criteria, both positively and negatively: for example, the positive criteria of stability, control, continuity which in negative terms lead to habitual perpetuation, ironbound tradition. The key positive values are also paired up into polarities such that stability, control and continuity are placed at the polar opposite of innovation, adaptation and change. Their thesis is that:

> Long-term survival depends upon the balancing of polarities through transformational strategies ... Thus, the skilled manager can pursue one or more values in the positive zone while remaining sensitive to the need to consider polar values. By building creative tension between polar values, the manager can occasionally reach peak performance or the flow state, and then eventually move back to routinization and control. (p. 306)

Although this 'competing values model' is quite complex, together with its explanation it is extremely orderly – simply a matter of balancing polar opposites and making sure your balance remains in the positive rather than the negative zone. And so their discussion of paradox concludes almost where it starts – with an either/or analysis of organizing: either you centralize or decentralize, control or not control, or in the case of their model, either you value more stability/less innovation or more innovation/less stability.

However, from an empirical point of view, we find a strong pragmatic theme underlying the and/and essence of paradox. (see also chapter 5.) That is, for practitioners, it is not a matter of asking, 'Does this paradox model get it right?' or 'Does it accurately represent the world?'. Rather, it is more a question of asking 'What would it be like to believe that?' or 'What would happen if I believed that?'. For the Pragmatist, the answer to the first question might be 'Yes, the paradox model gets it right' but it does not help you to deal with the situation. But if you were to *believe* in the paradox model, the second set of questions would probably lead to paralysis or at least considerable stress, having to cope with apparently opposing strains or dimensions. Hence the Pragmatist chooses not to believe this: that is, rather than believing something as contradictory and complex as paradox, our respondents choose to focus on what for them is relevant in that situation, which could be that the system of increased unit autonomy works most effectively if it is well controlled. In essence, they pare down the salient features to a minimum in order to cope, to simplify, to impute *some* kind of order and to make the issues of managing and their solution workable. And this is done within the context of their own specific organizational situations. Hence, for the Pragmatist, debates about how to deal with paradox (that is, to resolve it or to live with it and manage it, which are the core frame to much of the work on organizational paradox, see Scott Poole and Van de Ven (1989)) are in effect irrelevant. How can you be said to be managing paradox when you do not conceive of two dimensions or elements or aspects of a situation to be paradoxical? The other key problem, it seems to us, of many contemporary analyses of paradox is that they tend to take a static view of isolated phenomena and label them paradoxes. If you then return these to their organizational context, you find they constitute part of the unfolding, developing biography of organizational action. From the pragmatic viewpoint, the past does embody an order of some kind as its constituents are fitted together and perhaps even revised or reviewed to make up some coherent pattern of past experience, an explanation, which is crucial for present action. Unless you can make some sense of past experience, it does not help in the learning/developing process by which you deal with the present and from which the pragmatist 'mounts an attack' on the future. And it is this crucial time dimension which tends to be absent from theorizing about paradox. Van de Ven and Scott Poole (1988) provide an interesting and well-argued analysis of 'paradoxical requirements for a theory of organizational change' in which they conclude:

This essay has not adequately considered different conceptions of time. Clearly, the model of time researchers adopt – whether chronos or kiros, continuous or granular time, reversible or irreversible time – will have a major impact on both the description and explanation of development. Development of these issues should represent high priorities for further work. (p. 59).

We think our analysis helps to take a step further in this direction. In their terms rather than chronos (calendar time), our time dimension is more one of kiros ('time gauged in terms of peak experiences'). However, they go on to illustrate kiros 'as in the planting and harvesting periods of a growing season' (p. 21), while we prefer to stress the explanatory nature of our time dimension. That is, peak experiences are not immutable or ecologically determined as are planting and harvesting: they can be revised and re-viewed in the light of later experiences. And more importantly, we argue that paradox exists in the analyst's statements rather than in the 'doings' of the practitioner. So while the analyst has a problem in allowing two apparently contradictory statements to coexist, the practitioner faces no such conflict. Hence it is on this analytical level that the concept needs to be attended rather than trying to seek 'resolutions' through the 'doings' of practitioners.

8 We use the term 'punctuation' as developed by Weick: 'Any set of punctuations, however reasonable, is arbitrary. Punctuation simply means "chopping the stream of experience into sensible, nameable and named units" (Weick, 1976b, p. 280) (Weick, 1977, p. 194).

9 In the terms of Watzlawick et al. (1974), it is 'the meaning attributed to the situation' which is changed as a result, 'and therefore its consequences, but not its concrete facts' (p. 95).

10 For a full discussion of stories and story-telling see chapter 5.

11 So clearly we have to apologize to any of our readers who feel they have 'better' or 'more comprehensive' or whatever versions of the events we recount. It is inevitable and indeed to some extent, a healthy sign of difference. (How awful if you could all recite the same story!) We might even suggest that, were we to visit our contributors now, they too might use slightly different phrasing to their music.

In this way we are talking of 'the doing of organizing': by focusing attention, the explanations in effect control the range of response to events which become signified as key. From the field of medicine, Brody (1987) notes:

The primary human mechanism for attaching meaning to particular experiences is to tell stories about them. Stories serve to relate individual experiences to the explanatory constructs of the society and culture and also to place the experiences within the context of a particular individual's life history.

And so again, we see the interweaving of action and structure, meaning and response, stories and 'objective' organizations. One consistent feature of our data is the ability of all contributors to tell stories. (Indeed, the popular business press thrives on such material; see Peters and Waterman (1982).

In a similar vein, Dr Oliver Sacks, the famous neurologist, recently remarked:

> I think one cannot describe psychological processes without this kind of phenomenological detail. Without it we actually cannot understand what it is to be alive. For example, a lot of things to do with disease belong to the comic-dreadful mode. Ordinary clinical discourse is not too good at catching this. It's not that one wants to import plot or character or meaning into clinical narrative. But it's already there. My patients come to me with stories. They have predicaments. They have plights. They come in searching for ways of dealing with these things. There is something essentially dramatic in all this. (Interview with John Ryle, *Independent on Sunday*, 28 January 1990)

12 This notion of explanation is not to be confused with the idea of organizational myths. Pondy (1983) discusses the role of metaphors and myths in the process of sensemaking in organizations and we largely follow his argument. The distinction between explanations and myths as we see it is that explanations have a wholistic, immediate and temporal quality and relevance, while myths are more partial, enduring and unchanging.

13 Kanter (1984) writes about the 'prehistory' of change and notes:

> Organizational change consists in part of a series of emerging constructions of reality, including revision of the past, to correspond to the requisites of *new players and new demands*. Organizational history *does* need to be rewritten to permit events to move on. (In a sense, change is partly the construction of such reconstructions.) (p. 287)

From our point of view, we suggest that the metaphor of 'organization as explanation' is a more useful framework for shifting the emphasis from change as the focal object to reconstruction of constructions as being the focus of attention. That is, it is in the process of explaining that organizational history may come to be reviewed and revised rather than as part of the organizational change process.

14 For instance, Tony Mitchard's speech to the unions at Avon Rubber had a time and a place and no doubt several interpretations. The predominant one which we came across has been described earlier. In Mitchard's analysis it was a significant turning point in a period of major change

which had officially begun when he assumed full control as Chief Executive and began to 'orchestrate' his team. Inevitably the interpretation given at other times and/or by other people could not only attribute different meaning to the event but also give a different significance in the sequence of events as well as marking the change process differently. In our analysis, based on the data we collected/were given, the appropriate response to the event was one which signified it as a turning point which put steel in Tony Mitchard's spine and convinced him to edge further along this path.

15 Quinn and Cameron (1983). Interestingly though, only one of the nine models they surveyed dealt with the ultimate stage of the lifecycle, organizational decline and death.
16 Beckhard and Harris (1987, p. vii).
17 Beckhard and Harris (1987, p. 29).
18 Gorbachev published *Perestroika* in 1987 to explain the new political thinking and to help 'strengthen international trust': in effect, to communicate his vision internationally. In June 1988, an All-Union Conference of the Communist Party of the Soviet Union took place in Moscow: the first in 49 years, it was itself a consequence of *perestroika*. Its main focus was to discuss *perestroika* and the way ahead. Hence the book of 1987 was already out of date and a revised edition was published in 1988, which included Gorbachev's closing speech to this Conference. In the 1988 edition he adds:

> I said in the Conclusion of the original edition that this book is not yet finished, nor could be finished without the deeds, the practical action that would bring its goals into being. Now, a year later, the resolutions of the Party Conference – which are designed to achieve the next phase of our New Thinking – are the realization of the new chapter of *perestroika*.

As the subsequent events of the last two years illustrate, new chapters are being constantly written in and by the individual and collective actions of the peoples of Eastern Europe and the Soviet Union (and external audiences such as ourselves as we respond to those events). And there is even a curious paradox noted by contemporary commentators of Gorbachev, who, on the one hand, is advocating openness and restructuring and, on the other, is acquiring the greatest centralized power base of any Soviet leader since Stalin.

19 Quinn (1980).
20 Quinn (1982, p. 613).
21 Kanter (1984, p. 289).
22 Quinn (1982, p. 626).
23 Quinn (1982, p. 616). The seeds of some of these ideas have been around in the literature for a long time. For instance, Wrapp (1967) describes executive behaviour as 'muddling with a purpose':

> The successful manager, in my observation, recognizes the futility of trying to push total packages or programs through the organization. He is willing to take less than total acceptance in order to achieve modest progress towards his goal. Avoiding debates on principles, he tries to piece together particles that may appear to be incidentals into a program that moves at least part of the way toward his objectives. (p. 80)

24 The quotation is from Giddens (1976, p. 115). In any discussion of organization (that is, groups of people together seeking to achieve common purpose), there is inevitably the need for some analysis of the relationship between individual and collective action. Unfortunately, it is frequently absent from organizational theorizing: it is generally assumed that somehow (perhaps by some additive model) individual purpose becomes common purpose (see Coleman, 1986). Indeed, the question of how purposive actions of individuals combine to produce social outcomes is the core of what is commonly known as the micro/macro debate in social science to which Knorr-Cetina and Cicourel (1981) provide an excellent contribution.

Giddens argues that 'structure is both the medium and the outcome of the human activities which it recursively organizes' (1987, p. 61). Thus he addresses not only the *reproduction* but also the *production* of practices.

> The communication of meaning in interaction involves the use of interpretative schemes by means of which sense is *made* by participants of what each says and does. The application of such cognitive schemes within a framework of mutual knowledge depends upon and draws from a 'cognitive' order which is shared by a community; but while drawing upon such a cognitive order, the application of interpretative schemes at the same time *reconstitutes* that order. (1976, p. 122)

We have argued throughout for the need to have some relatively stable process of sharing meanings – the reconstitutive aspect of order – together with some room for random response, for difference – the constitutive aspect of order. And Giddens' theory embraces the notion of 'structure-in-process', as 'structure' is both re-produced and produced through interaction. He develops the concepts of mutual knowledge and common sense as the interlocking means by which reasons are held by actors to be valid: that is, 'how far an agent's stated reasons in fact express his monitoring of what he did' and 'how far his explanation conforms to what is generally acknowledged in his social milieu as reasonable conduct' (1976, p. 114). And our data provide much evidence of these two notions. In his later writing, he goes on to bring these together in his notion of 'practical consciousness':

Agents can sometimes express their reasons for what they do in verbal or discursive form. Human beings can in some degree give accounts of the circumstances of their action. But this by no means exhausts what they know about why they act as they do. Many most subtle and dazzlingly intricate forms of knowledge are embedded in, and constitutive of, the actions we carry out. They are done knowledgeably, but without necessarily being available to the discursive awareness of the actor. To speak a language, an individual needs to know an enormously complicated range of rules, strategies and tactics involved in language use. However, if that individual were asked to give a discursive account of what it is that he or she knows in knowing these rules, etc., he or she would normally find it very difficult indeed. Any analysis of social activity which ignores practical consciousness is massively deficient. (1987, p. 63)

In essence, this describes the taken-for-granted element of shared meaning, the mutually expected response patterns which constitute the structure of organization, and guide our actions and understanding of 'the' organization – its history, context, implications, etc. (as Polanyi might suggest, it is the things 'about which we know more than we can tell'). This way, the theory of structuration describes the process whereby layer upon layer of social action builds up to become 'structures' of organization which take on an 'objectified' or 'objective' quality. And while we recognize that our analysis has for the most part implicitly assumed structuring and structuration to be the means by which organizing both persists and changes, we must be clear that we have not provided a 'structurationist' account of organizing, as we have strictly confined our observations to the senior executive team in each enterprise.

25 Recall the previous reference to persistence and change as 'accomplished by and consisting in the doings' of Reckitt and Colman, (chapter 4) and also the quotation from Barnard with which we began chapter 1.

26 Robbins and Duncan (1988, p. 206).

27 Robbins and Duncan (1988, p. 224).

28 Once again we question the notion that actions taken in organizations are so logical and orderly and suggest that, true to Weick's (1977) notion: 'An organization can never know what it thinks or wants until it sees what it does' (p. 195). Thus we question the logic which suggests a triggering of the need for action as a prerequisite for some 'vision'.

29 Sederberg (1984, p.169).

30 'What if ...?' kinds of questions are discussed in more detail in chapter 5.

31 Some theorists talk of management philosophies which are taken to inform particular styles of managing. For example, Goold and Campbell (1987) identify three main styles out of a total of eight in their study of

large diversified organizations. Having described the three key styles, they note:

> These are very different philosophies of how to develop a winning strategy: of how to motivate a management team; of how to succeed competitively. The assumptions behind each style are different and incompatible, but each set of assumptions can be valid, in the right business circumstances and with the right management group. (p. 297)

While we understand the case they are making we do not share their enthusiasm for prescription or categorization. Nor do we feel that the notion of philosophy, 'the principles underlying any department of knowledge', adequately captures or conveys either the important developmental emphasis or the raw but very human dimension of *beliefs* which underpin ideology. Indeed, perhaps the term 'faith' in the sense of 'that which is believed', is more appropriate but we feel that 'ideology' better expresses the developmental link between learning from past experience through current action to future possibility, rather than the more enduring/unchanging sense of faith. We also wish to explore more closely the blending of personal and organizational ideology which provides the 'push', the artist's sense of emergence, with all the implied uncertainty and risk involved, rather than the sense of 'pull' implied in implementing a 'philosophy' or practising a faith. We also realized early on in our data analysis that to develop a framework of managerial styles would require as many categories as we have contributors.

32 Peters and Waterman (1982) identify 'hands-on, value driven' as one of their eight criteria of excellence and give many examples of how their excellent organizations exhibit this quality. By shared values, they mean 'basic beliefs, overriding values' (p. 281) and while they highlight the key role of the CEO/leader (the 'unique individual' who 'grooves' organizational beliefs (p. 283)), they do add that 'it is the team at the top that is crucial' (p. 290).

> Creating and instilling a value system isn't easy. For one thing, only a few of all possible value systems are really right for a given company. For another, instilling the system is backbreaking work. It requires persistence and excessive travel and long hours, but without the hands-on part, not much happens it seems. (p. 291)

These extracts seem to sum up the complexity of the subject: they talk of values and beliefs interchangeably, of unique individuals and shared values, strong leadership creating and instilling value systems, etc. In addition, while recognizing Barnard's influence on understanding the management process, they also talk about values and purposes interchangeably (pp. 97–8), which is not quite how Barnard used the terms (see later in this chapter). However, we stress that these themes *are* complexly interrelated which is why we prefer to talk of ideology, a concept which embraces value and belief, comprising some system of faith or conviction which is enacted and communicated, to which people are *converted* rather than a particular configuration of components in a value system to be instilled in organization members.

While the distinction is a subtle one, there is an important difference between conversion and instilling. That is, instilling values is a continuous, never-ending part of the doing of organizing. The concept of ideology, as used by organizational theorists, is most commonly proposed as some means of maintaining organizational culture; for example, organizational ideology as 'systems of thought that are the central determinants of the character of organizations' (Harrison, 1972, p. 119) or 'a set of fundamental ideas and operative consequences linked together in a dominant belief system often producing contradictions but serving to define and maintain the organization' (Abravanel, 1983, p. 274). But here we are talking about the doing of organizing writ large: explanation and communication, shaping meaning and channelling response, in the process of changing (some aspect of) their enterprise. For this reason, communications are more than the slow infusing or instilling of values: in the process of changing, people have to be actually converted, persuaded to accept a new (dimension to) ideology.

33 Schein (1985).
34 The concept of ideology triggers a vast area of debate, drawing on philosophy, political science and the sociology of knowledge. This is neither the time nor the place to embark on charting a path through this minefield: indeed, it could consume an entire book. However, we wish to associate our approach more with the work of people such as Berger and Luckmann (1966) than as the concept has been adopted into organization literature by theorists such as Abravanel (1983). Berger and Luckmann suggest that 'when a particular definition of reality comes to be attached to a concrete power interest, it may be called an ideology ... The distinctiveness of ideology is that the *same* overall universe is interpreted in different ways, depending upon concrete vested interests within the society in question' (1966, p. 141).

In the sense that realities thus defined are social in origin and social in persistence (Berger and Luckmann), this definition embraces values and beliefs which in essence underpin the central ideological 'propositions'. However, at this point we begin to differ in that we are not talking of ideologies in the sense of some self-consciously rationalized set of propositions. Nor are we trying to distinguish between different kinds of ideologies or even different ideological levels, e.g. non-, pre- and meta-ideological levels (Abravanel, 1983, p. 275). Rather, we are suggesting some set of core values which may be considered *as* an ideology in the sense that it proposes a powerful definition of reality which guides and shapes current and future actions and responses.

35 Weick (1979, p. 135).
36 On this basis, we would not advocate formal 'value statements', describing core organizational values. Values are *demonstrated* through action, that is, what one chooses to attend and how one gives such attention, from which can be inferred what it is which is valued rather than some additive notion of items called values. And for this reason we suggest they are generally part of the taken-for-granted in organization: implicitly known and demonstrated through action. This is why they surface at times of change. The expression of difference or variance causes one to make (if only tacitly) comparisons with the past: raising the question of what does this 'change' signify compared with what has been/is and, indeed, this in part informs the learning process (see chapter 5).
37 Pondy (1978) describes something of this in the context of leadership:

> The real power of Martin Luther King was not only that he had a dream, but that he could describe it, that it became public, and therefore accessible to millions of people. This dual capacity (surely it is much more than a mere trait) to make sense of things *and* to put them into language meaningful to a large number of people gives the person who has it enormous leverage. (I must confess to racking my creative insight to the breaking point to find the right phrase to describe this capacity, but the effort was, sad to report, in vain!) (p. 95)

We suggest that the late Lou Pondy's difficulty in finding the right phrase to describe this capacity stems from the idea that it is more than just a single capacity: it is a confluence of imagination and ability, of sense and sensibility, which has a time and a place, in a tradition and a context.
38 Barnard (1938, pp. 281–2).
39 Quotes from Metal Box, Coats Viyella, Glynwed.
40 Not only do these examples illustrate something of the way in which meaning is shared and responses are shaped but also the way in which these integrate into a consensus decision-making process. Unlike the classic theories of consensus decision-making such as Schein (1969) describes, there is no obvious sounding out of differing viewpoints and then testing for the 'sense of the meeting' (p. 56), rather consensus begins to emerge long before the actual decision in the process of shaping responses and controlling stimuli.
41 George Davies, ex-Chief Executive of Next, was at one time hailed as leader of the 'High Street Revolution', and then subsequently and abruptly removed from office in the kind of struggle which is music to the ears of gossip columnists. About a year later, he gave a lengthy interview to John Humphrys on Radio 4, during which he was asked how it was that someone whose background and training was in accountancy had been able to demonstrate such imagination and creativity in revolutionizing the High Street. Davies' response was immediate and simple: 'I see pictures in the figures.'

Barnard also has something to say on this when talking about businessmen and accountants who can within seconds 'get a significant set of facts' from a balance sheet. 'These facts do not leap from the page and strike the eye. They lie between the figures in the part filled by the mind out of years of experience and technical knowledge' (p. 306). These 'gaps in between' surface again in chapter 5, note 43.

42 As Quinn (1982) suggests; with some initial prompting, 'the seeds of understanding' can be sown.

43 Peter Medawar (1984) refers to the exercise of imagination as being, in effect, to suspend disbelief. In a sense, this is what our data describe. To break away from 'persistent, habitual experience' of the doing of managing in a particular context requires managers to suspend disbelief in alternatives: to catch the imagination does not necessarily require active belief, rather for a moment disbelief is suspended. Actually to express some imaginative idea in terms of action may require active belief, but the initial challenge is to *capture* the imagination. The seeds of these ideas are found already in our text and continue to develop through chapter 5.

44 A classic case of Poggi's (1965) famous dictum: 'A way of seeing is also a way of not seeing.'

45 This is a tricky notion as it means people: people have faith, beliefs and convictions, underpinned by values as opposed to a simple case of 'organizational vision'. Hence it raises questions of the individual executive and the collective executive team, in turn reflecting the idea of corporate values and organizational visions. Many of the analyses of organizations, particularly those comparing Japanese and American organizations, highlight differences in core shared values. For instance, Pascale and Athos (1981) describe examples of this, using the McKinsey 7 Star model as their framework. They note that shared values (or superordinate goals, as it was then known) 'provide the glue that holds the other six – strategy, structure, systems, style, staff and skills – together' (p. 178).
But what these kinds of models have great difficulty in capturing or even addressing is the developing and interweaving process by which individuals and collective together 'grow'. It is more than just a simple notion of evolution and involves issues such as ability to be self-critical, to learn, to evaluate and achieve/not achieve, the context and timing of evaluation and re-evaluation, to admit mistakes and reshape aspirations, beliefs and values, all of which feeds into the 'active shaping of experience', the control and range of responses and both the individual and collective/organizational process of developing and 'changing'. We suggest a strong underlying theme of learning and will return to this later in chapter 5.

46 See chapter 3, on consensus decision making.

47 March (1981, p. 563).

48 We happily note that even attempts to incorporate chaos theory in modelling exchange rate behaviour are still limited in their ability to predict behaviour patterns.

Trivial events can completely alter the entire path of the exchange rate, generating dynamics unrelated to observable events. This does not mean that exogenous disturbances have not been important in driving the exchange rates. However, it warns against the tendency to look for 'news' behind every exchange rate movement that we find difficult to explain. (De Grauwe and Vansanten, 1990, p. 1)

49 Sederberg (1984, p. 184).

50 It is a difficult point to make because clearly our respondents made many of the formal decisions of organization in the usual way – with committees and proposals and evaluations of alternatives. Yet we have much evidence of a more fluid means by which ideas are shaped and decisions made. Indeed, there is something of Starbuck's (1985) idea of 'acting first and thinking later', although we hesitate to put it in such staged terminology:

> People make many of their decisions, perhaps a great majority of them, after they have begun to act and have seen some of the consequences of their actions. When they begin courses of action, people normally see themselves as following the only sensible courses, not choosing among several plausible courses. They may not even realize that they are embarking on distinct courses, partly because organizations decompose big actions into multiple increments and partly because the individual actors in organizational actions merely follow banal programs. But looking back, the people can see that alternative courses did exist, and so they must have chosen. Thus, decisions are often retrospective re-enactments that misrepresent actual sequences of events ... All actions evoke retrospective rationalizations, and these retrospective rationalizations grow stronger as the actions are repeated.

We demur from some of this, particularly the idea that retrospective re-enactments misrepresent actual sequences of events. In the framework which we have been developing, we suggest that, rather than events unfolding, it is more a case of executive Pragmatism which, with hindsight, can iron out the creases.

51 Quotes from Beazer, Coats Viyella.

52 Quote from Prudential.

54 No-one actually spoke about planning departments and few contributors, i.e. members of the inner circle, were actually entitled directors of planning. Clearly, though, plans and strategies were much in evidence. What we conclude is that while the formal aspect of planning and evaluating strategy is important in the formal aspect of decision, it is the informal process of shaping and nudging which is more immediate in its consequences as it affects organizational purpose. More on this a little later.

54 Henry Mintzberg (1987) also uses an artistic analogy in developing his

ideas of 'crafting strategy'. He suggests that as potters shape their clay based on past experience of what has and has not worked and ideas of what might be done differently this time, so too do managers craft strategy. Their clay is the strategy which they shape in their organizations. Some of his inferences about this process do echo ideas we are developing but there is an important distinction. For us, there is more than one pair of hands shaping and modelling the material and the clay is not some sense of organization strategy, it *is* organization. If we wished to use the term strategy we might suggest it could encompass that set of beliefs and experimental ideas about what *might* work in the process of shaping organization: that is, how we might choose to shape our clay.

55 Although Barnard does go on to note that it is possible for organizations to 'overreach' themselves, as growth affects the effectiveness and efficiency of organization. (1938, p. 159)

56 Quotes from BTR, Glynwed.

57 So, for example, at Hanson, return on capital was an important guide to evaluations of purposes whereas at BTR the key ratio was return on sales. At Glynwed, Gareth Davies signalled a set of performance criteria – as one director put it, 'the dials on your dashboard as you are driving along ... that say you are in reasonable nick' – which included return on capital, working capital and margins on sales.

Once again though, we stress that these are just *some* of the manifestations of growth: they are not objective measures of growth *per se*.

58 Quote from Beazer.

59 More on the process of 'pushing back the limitations' in chapter 5.

60 Barnard (1938, p. 82).

61 Barnard (1938, p. 86). Vaill (1982; 1989) draws on Barnard in developing the term purposing, by which he means: 'that continuous stream of actions by an organization's formal leadership that has the effect of inducing clarity, consensus and commitment regarding the organization's basic purposes' (Vaill, 1989, p. 29). For him, it is to do with the 'establishment, clarification and modification' of purposes. We are not so sure though that this is quite what we find in our data. There is not that much emphasis on clarity in terms of statements of purpose, mission or vision. Nor is it necessarily the case that what might be taken as the executive notion of overall purpose is clearly communicated to all members of the organization. Indeed, Vaill's definition seems to reify purpose as distinct from purposing and in this we have to disagree with him. Certainly, one might suggest that organization purpose is indeed inferred from the actions of the formal leadership: in this sense, it might be inferred from the kinds of things they communicate. But it is in the process of *communicating* that such issues of consensus and commitment and perhaps some degree of clarity are achieved.

62 See Perrow (1977, 1986).

63 Barnard (1938, p. 89).

64 Again an example of Giddens' theory of 'structuration'.

65 Barnard (1938, p. 89).
66 He later admits to being much influenced by A. N. Whitehead's *Process and Reality* (1929).
67 Barnard (1938, p. 195).
68 There is a subtle distinction here in what Barnard is saying as opposed to the more usual conception of decision, for example, as proposed by March and Olsen (1976): 'a decision process transforms the behaviour of individuals into organizational action' (p. 11).
69 Barnard (1938, p. 231).
70 Barnard (1938, p. 233).

Chapter 5

1 We have argued elsewhere against the component parts approach to the 'Making of Managers' (Pye, 1988). We suggest the same is true of teams: that the component parts can never adequately express the 'tacit dimension' – 'about which we can know more than we can tell' (Polanyi, 1967).
2 Quotes from Coats Viyella, Reckitt and Colman.
3 Barnard (1938, p. 215).
4 Quote from Coats Viyella.
5 Different people mean different things by the term process theory and they go about their explanations of what they mean in quite different ways. Mohr (1982) considers process theory by contrasting it with variance theory. 'In variance theory, the precursor (X) is a necessary and sufficient condition for the outcome (Y). In other terms, if X, then Y, and if not-X, then not-Y … In process theory, the precursor (X) is a necessary condition for the outcome (Y) … The precursor in a process theory contains three types of elements – (1) necessary conditions and (2) necessary probabilistic processes, which together form the core of the theory, and (3) external, directional forces that function to move the focal unit and conditions about in a characteristic way, often herding them into mutual proximity' (pp. 37–45).
And he goes on to elaborate and argues that much organizational theory confuses the two kinds of theories and blurs the distinctions between the two categories of theoretical propositions. This, he claims, frustrates theory: 'It becomes an obstacle, a distraction, a derailer of purpose' (p. 61). Interestingly, though, he concludes: 'Although each (variance and process) theory must be an integral, inviolate whole as theory, splintering and recombining is eminently possible and desirable in application' (p. 70).
And therein lies the rub. He seems to be proposing pure theoretical types as might be found in pure scientific research and then acknowledging that in practice, one actually needs a bit of both. If organization theory is supposed to be empirically based, then the pure types notion in the sense Mohr is describing is irrelevant if it fails, as he suggests, to adequately

model the practice. Yet, in so doing, he highlights a key problem in many of the debates about process theory, which is picked up by Van de Ven (1987): that is, the lack of '1. a clear set of concepts about the object being studied; 2. systematic methods for observing change in the object over time; 3. methods for representing raw data to identify processual patterns; and 4. a motor or theory to make sense of the process pattern' (p. 330). He goes on to consider 'how these four requirements might be met in order to study processes of strategic organizational change over time'.

His paper raises some interesting issues. One which is particularly relevant to our analysis is the continuing assumed need for definition and categorization. That is, in many ways his analysis is framed in the language and thinking of variance theory – with a clear *set* of concepts, systematically observed over time, tabulated into some processual pattern and 'driven by an explicit motor or theory of change processes' by which he means alternative choice processes, i.e. rational, contingency, incremental, random and structuration.

If, as we have argued, the nature of executive process is one of the developing of an integral whole, the guiding frame is one of change: things change, people change, situations change and in so doing they develop, they expand, they mature, whatever. The point is that what you set out with to define and measure in the beginning may be re-shaped, re-formed or even re-written during observations over time. Likewise, tabulating process patterns again allows only linear interpretation and flattens what is, empirically speaking, a vast, complex, inchoate whole. In his conclusion, he points to:

four requirements of a good theory of change:
- to explain how structure and individual purposive action are linked at micro and macro levels of analysis
- to explain how change is produced both by the internal functioning of the structure and the external purposive actions of individuals
- to explain both stability and instability
- to include time as the key historical metric. (p. 340)

While we agree these four criteria are important to a processual analysis of change, we suggest that it is not possible to achieve these by meeting the four requirements with which he set out. To achieve the explanations he is requesting means we must break out of the kind of analysis which, even though processual in intent, is still spoken in the language and framed by the thinking of variance theory. We hope that in our exploration of a rather different language and approach, based on 'doing' and a 'vocabulary of practise' (see later in this chapter), we have at least broken with some of the traditions which are so deeply embedded in the practice of organizational theorizing.

6 *Brewer's Dictionary*.
7 Rorty (1982, p. xiii).
8 Rorty (1982, p. xiv).

9 So Rorty points out, 'the natural approach to such sentences (of universal truths), Dewey tells us, is not "Do they get it right?", but more like "What would it be like to believe that? What would happen if I did? What would I be committing myself to?" ... James' dictum about truth says that the vocabulary of practise is uneliminable, that no distinction of kind separates the sciences from the crafts, from moral reflection, or from art.'

10 In particular, the pragmatic principles of experience are well worth exploring, as they expressly dismiss the idea of experience as simply content or subject matter to concentrate on 'the *process* which in the end turns out to be a medium and a means'. Hence, Dewey, for instance, talks about ideas which are gathered *from* experience rather than forced *into* experience.

'For Dewey, experience is the name for what results, a process and a funded product, from the interaction situation: experience is *simultaneously* both doings and sufferings or undergoings. Consequently, the experiencing subject is at once both agent and patient, receiving what is presented to it and responding in ways appropriate for a being who seeks to sustain itself in a precarious world' (Smith, p. 81).

11 Smith (1978, p. 115).

12 In this case, we are confronted with senior executives with reputations and biographies of successful achievement in organizations. From this, we infer something of their ability as managers. It is perhaps, though, not quite as arbitrary as it sounds. A common theme amongst contributors was expressed as the ability to ask questions: that is, although perhaps not technically expert in a particular area or issue, they can ask pertinent and challenging questions of potential converters in 'making up their minds' about alternative solutions.

13 'Unshakeable facts' was supposedly the catch-phrase of Harold Geneen, Head of ITT, and analysed in Pascale and Athos (1981). Although by some measures, he was considered to be successful in directing ITT, his style was apparently authoritarian and based on fear. When he left, he had no adequate successor and in that sense, he had failed to develop the continuity and interdependence of what we take to be effective executive team work.

14 Peters and Waterman (1982) have had much to do with drawing wide attention to the subject of managing ambiguity in organizations: 'managing ambiguity and paradox' is the first of their eight attributes of 'management excellence'. It is a subject which has been around in the literature for a long time, particularly in the work of people like Weick (1969) and March (1978), as well as even Barnard (1938), although perhaps not expressed in contemporary vocabulary. But it is only more recently that, as rationalist assumptions have begun to wane, such voices have at last been heard by a wider audience.

There are still some, particularly in more practitioner-oriented work, who deal with ambiguity as indicating less effective communication: that is, effective communication means clarity and openness. And even in literature, which is more oriented towards managing rather than communication, there is still a tendency to imply that ambiguity is a new phenomenon which relates to 'messy, poorly defined, administrative situations':

> The world of managers and administrators is becoming more complex, interconnected, unsettled and ambiguous ... Poorly structured problems ... are *substantively* different from well defined ones and disaster awaits the manager who mistakes one for the other. (McCaskey, 1988, p. 14).

We suggest that it is not the manager's world which is becoming more ambiguous, rather it is the organizational analyst who is at last beginning to recognize ambiguity. But it is not a matter of identifying some situations to be ambiguous and others to be clear and making one's choice accordingly. Rather, in taking an interpretative, interactionist view of behaviour, ambiguity is simply part of the meaning attributed by individuals, not something which is inherent in particular problem situations or even discourse itself.

As Eisenberg (1984) points out in an interesting paper on ambiguity as strategy in organizational communication:

> Clarity (and conversely, ambiguity) is not an attribute of messages, it is a relational variable which arises through a combination of source, message, and receiver factors ... *clarity is only a measure of communicative competence if the individual has as his or her goal to be clear.* (pp. 229–30).

While we are not suggesting that our respondents make deliberate use of ambiguity as strategy in their doing of managing, as Eisenberg argues, we welcome this symbolic view of social order which recognizes that ambiguity 'can promote unified diversity which is essential to the process of organizing' (p. 232). This approach accords with the pragmatic theme which we find expressed in our respondents' comments which, as we go on to argue, emerges in asking 'what if ...?' kinds of questions rather than 'is it? or is it not ambiguous?'

15 See chapter 4, note 7.

16 Morgan, *Images of Organization* (1986).

17 Sederberg, *Politics of Meaning* (1984, p. 129). As we have said in a note to chapter 4, this notion of explanation is not to be confused with the idea of organizational myths. Pondy (1983) discusses the role of metaphors and myths in the process of sensemaking in organizations and we largely follow his argument. The distinction between explanations and myths as we see it is that explanations have a wholistic, immediate and temporal quality and relevance while myths are more partial, enduring and unchanging.

18 Sederberg (1984, p. 131).

19 Italo Calvino, *Italian Folktales* (1975), quoted in Lester (1987).
20 Lester, *The Tales of Uncle Remus* (1987).
21 Polanyi *The Study of Man* (1958, p. 11).
22 Interviewed on *Kaleidoscope*, BBC Radio 4, October 1989.
23 Arthur Miller recently made some interesting points in an article he wrote, shortly before *The Price* was staged in London.

> Scholarship seems more and more interested in parting the curtains that conceal the genesis of artworks, and I often wonder if the impulse behind all this unveiling is a desire to steal a spark of creative fire for anyone at all to make his own. It is almost as though anyone could make art if he could only penetrate the mechanics of the process by which artists do what they do. Needless to say, if I knew how a play comes to pass I would cause one every few months, but unfortunately I don't, it is just too complicated.
> Writers are forever being asked if a character is based on a real person, a fictional town on an actual one. (The answer is usually 'yes' but what difference does it make?) I find a subtle reductionism in this to journalism. I am often tempted to reply that everything in our heads is based on something outside our heads, but that the real question is whether, interesting though the gossipy information may be, there is any particular wisdom to be found in knowing how real the basis of a work may be. Does its derivation from reality make it better art? If it did, our almost daily TV docu-dramas would be the very crests of high creation. (*The Guardian*, 25 January 1990)

Although it was probably not Arthur Miller's intention the two key points he makes here are quite relevant to management. There is much effort spent in attempting to steal sparks of creative fire, as evidenced by the fads, gurus and burgeoning field of 'how to do it' books. Furthermore, the quest to find out where ideas came from or what prompted an action or decision is equally fruitless, in as much as it is no guarantee that it might be replicated. The only difference such wisdom might make is in what can be learnt from it – a subject we return to later.

24 Polanyi, 'Life's irreducible structure' (1968). Sederberg also says something similar, although our preference is for Polanyi's analysis.
25 Polanyi (1968, p. 1311).
26 Quote from Coats Viyella.
27 For instance, they gave of their time to talk to and be talked to on development courses, industry initiatives, government bodies, management researchers, etc.
28 An interesting illustration of persuading key 'others' to believe a particular telling of a story is found in the recent press reflections on the battle between Lonrho and the Al-Fayed brothers for control of the Harrods store. It has gradually emerged, after long investigation by the MMC and the DTI which originally pronounced them as suitable owners of the Harrods group, that the Al-Fayed brothers do not have the wealthy Arab

background and connections that 'people' had been led to believe. Amongst the many problems this apparently presents, the most important seems to be that 'people' no longer know how to respond in the light of this information (including the business press, government and city analysts). Does this confirm the view of those who always felt they were simply asset stripping? or does it simply mean that none of what they say can be trusted? or does it mean that some people made assumptions which they are now having to revise? or does it just mean that their intentions (and presumably their abilities as managers) remain the same, but that this is not founded on great personal wealth?

29 Sederberg (1984, p. 134).
30 Michael Goold and Andrew Campbell, in *Strategies and Styles* (1987), identify BTR as having a style based on financial control. It is interesting to note that the current Chief Executive of BTR, John Cahill, does not have a formal accountancy background.
31 Although Barnard does not have much to say specifically about trust he does talk about cohesiveness and in particular, addresses the relationship between formal and informal organization. In essence, he says you cannot have one without the other but he adds: 'informal organizations are necessary to the operation of formal organizations as a means of communication, of cohesion and of protecting the integrity of the individual' (1938, p. 123).
32 Brian Beazer made very explicit reference to judgement:

> At the end of the day, all success in business is only made by three issues ... One is hard work ... The second essentially is economy of operation. But the most important quality in business at my level is sadly neither of those things. And I say sadly because, being a sort of Calvinist, I would hope that it was hard work and economy of operation, but it isn't. It's judgement. What is required is judgement. You've got to have judgement to be in the right things at the right time.

33 Quote from Beazer.
34 Polanyi, *Personal Knowledge* (1964, p. 50).
35 Barnard (1945, p. 204).
36 Our original brief was presumptive and assumptive: 'to establish what kinds of competenc(i)es contribute to effective performance in a variety of organizations and at specific senior levels of managerial responsibility'. That is, we took it for granted that the basic theme made sense and we assumed that notions of competence, effectiveness and performance could be suitably distilled in this approach. And we are pleased to say we were very wrong. We had ignored the cardinal rule of organizational analysis which is 'never make assumptions' (or presumptions). Consequently, though, we cannot now offer prescriptions or lists of competencies required for effective managerial performance. Nor can we define

effective performance in order to deduce competence. And we seriously doubt the arguments of those who claim they can.

37 In some senses, this is an inevitable consequence of trying to define globally something which is 'known' through individual performance: trying to prescribe universal criteria for evaluating something which is judged primarily through response to particular performance. There is, however, much interest in the subject and in the UK this is particularly generated through the energies of the National Forum for Management Education and Development (NFMED) – replacing the Council for Management Education and Development (CMED) – and the debate around the Management Charter Initiative (1989). Their approach to the subject is very much rooted in practical application and seeks to develop three different levels of management qualification in an attempt to encourage professional standards of management competence.

In one of their recent documents (September, 1989), they define management competence as 'the ability to perform management functions effectively in the work place' (p. 11). As they go on to explain:

> The importance of the competence approach to training and qualifications is that it provides a measure of what people can actually do rather than what they know or understand. It means that you can drive a car safely rather than knowing how to do it in principle. (p. 11)

While we do not share the same distinctions between what people do and what they know or understand, the analogy with car driving is very useful, making both their point and ours too. Certainly, it is one thing to know the theory of safe driving and quite another to drive safely. But likewise, there is a world of difference between driving a Formula One Racing Car safely and being the careful custodian of a Morris Minor en route from Oxford to Stratford-upon-Avon. Perhaps even more importantly, though, your ability to negotiate such paths safely – be it Brands Hatch Racing Circuit or the A34 – is in part dependent upon other drivers or road users in general. No amount of driving skill will protect you from a car whose driver fails to stop at the cross roads where you have right of way and he doesn't. Likewise, no amount of driving ability will save you from crashing if your brakes suddenly fail or the engine catches fire.

So we come back to our core theme that such competence is known through performance and evaluated through response to performance. While we might like to believe in some shared universal criteria for recognizing ability to do managing in whatever context it might occur, from our evidence and experience we do not believe this to be possible. And to some extent, from our respondents' comments there is even a hint that what they celebrate in other successful doers of managing is their 'difference'. This arises again later in this chapter.

38 Mintzberg, 'If you're not serving Bill and Barbara, then you're not serving leadership' (1982), in Hunt et al., *Leadership: Beyond Establishment Views*.

39 Meindl et al. (1985).
40 As we noted in chapter 3, many of our respondents stressed that theirs was a team effort, suggesting that it is analysts rather than practitioners who struggle with this relationship between individual and team.
41 For a recent example, see Morgan, *Riding the Waves of Change* (1988).
42 Morgan (1988, p. xi).
43 In trying to develop an analytical framework for our data, the best we could visualize was some multi-dimensional framework where different dimensions criss-crossed and interwove. But even this we agreed would still be inadequate, as it seemed that the way our data come alive exists in the spaces in between the dimensions. These messy, interrelated and sometimes *opposing* dimensions are held together and shaped, providing the distinctive complexion of each manager. But it is not the dimensions themselves, the particulars, which determine the outcome: it is what happens in between, in the interrelating of dimensions as they fashion a 'whole'.
Arthur Koestler (1981) provides a lovely analogy for this kind of understanding:

> We do not live in laboratories where the rules of the game are laid down by explicit orders: in normal life, the rules control our thinking unconsciously – and there's the rub. When talking, the laws of grammar and syntax function below the level of awareness, in the gaps between the words. (p. 3)

However, it is what goes on in the gaps in between which gives such talk its recognizable and understandable quality. The same is true of competence. In trying to answer the question, 'what is competence?' one is tempted to say, 'it's to do with this, this and this, but also the gaps in between'. Certainly from our data, whatever 'it' is seems to function below the level of awareness, although contributors 'know' and recognize 'it' when they see it. However, it is not simply the possession of some lists of abilities or qualities – there is no absolute quality or measure or conception of competence. There is no definitive measure of ingredients which defines or predicts competent performance: rather, it is relational, which is perhaps why it is so elusive a concept to comprehend and why one's attention is drawn to the 'gaps in between'.
44 Quote from Lucas.
45 Quote from BTR.
46 Constable and McCormick (1987), for instance, used the phrase as the title for their report on management education and development.
47 The phrase was heard in a play by Frank McGuinness, called 'Scout', which was broadcast on BBC2, 8 September 1987.
48 William James, letter to W. Lutoslawski, 6 May 1906, quoted in Garfield, *Peak Performers* (1986).
49 James (1907), *Pragmatism*, quoted in Smith (1978, p. 46).

50 For instance, Murray Stuart described some of the 'lessons' which he took from his experience of cost-cutting in the turnaround of Metal Box.
51 Bruner, *On Knowing* (1964, pp. 159–60).
52 Briskman (1981) informs much of our discussion of creativity and we point here to some of the core themes of his paper. He deals with the relationship between creative product and process and argues that we can only identify creative people and creative processes through our identification of their products as themselves creative. As he argues:

> Before a novel problem-solution can be given the honorific title 'creative', it must be evaluated positively as meeting certain standards. Moreover, these standards will normally themselves be incorporated in the background of prior products, in the tradition against which the problem-solution has emerged. In other words, from the point of view of the background itself, the creative product surpasses that background in a positively evaluated way, in a way meeting certain stringent requirements or standards already inherent in that background.' (p. 144).

His explanation resembles very closely that which we have found in our data. Those who can lead or steer their organizations through successful changes are attributed 'creative' or at least 'effective' executives. The change processes are seen as 'novel' or 'creative', certainly successful. Yet these attributions still depend on the actual product, the achievement of some change in state to be evaluated positively as 'creative'. And in this respect, the criteria for assessment are not some arbitrary, abstract(ed) theoretical or global standards, but instead arise out of the tradition or 'background of prior products'. Hence, the novel or creative product must 'transcend' this tradition from which it emerged.
Briskman also deals with a crucial point which arises time and again in discussions of creative achievement. He starts by noting that 'a journalist once asked Picasso: "What is creativity?" Picasso answered, "I don't know, and if I did I wouldn't tell you"'. He goes on: 'It is, I believe, crucial to see that the problem is to explain the possibility of creativity, *not* its necessity. For if we were to actually succeed in explaining the necessity of creativity, or the necessity of specific creative achievements, then in a sense we would have explained too *much*' (p. 130)
Again, this is very much at the heart of our subject: what our accounts describe is the possibility of effective performance, not its necessity for indeed, to be able to predict such achievement would be to explain too *much*.
53 Quotes from Hanson, Beazer, Coats Viyella, Reckitt and Colman.
54 One might suggest that ConsGold were doggedly perseverant in their resistance to takeover by Minorco, but it left them completely exposed to and unable to defend against takeover by Hanson.
55 Barnard (1945, p. 204.)

56 For example, Kotter (1982). Bennis and Nanus (1985), and McCall et al. (1988).
57 Klemp and McClelland (1986, p. 36).
58 McCall, Lombardo and Morrison (1988).
59 M. Csikszentmihalyi *Beyond Boredom and Anxiety*, (1975) M. Csikszentmihalyi and I. S. Csikszentmihalyi *Optimal Experience*. (1988).
60 M. Csikszentmihalyi (1975, p. 253).
61 George Kelly *The Psychology of Personal Constructs*. (1955).
62 Aldous Huxley, quoted in Weick (1979).
63 These ideas also refer back to chapter 2.
64 Of course, on a broader note it is quite possible to use such learning opportunities to inculcate some new directions for behaviour and indeed, this is often the aim of more formal learning situations. While this relates back to some of what was said on the subject of communication in chapters 2 and 4, the point remains clear that it is up to the individual to make what he/she will in the process of learning and actually to shape responses in performance through what has been learnt.
65 Quotes from Marks and Spencer, Avon, Metal Box.
66 This should *not* be taken as a mandate for regular changes in Executive personnel. Quite the contrary. (Persistence and change again.) Rather, we are talking about changing the pattern of limitation, both individual and collective.
67 Cameron (1986, p. 543).
68 Cameron (1986, p. 546).
69 Quote from Metal Box.
70 Barnard (1938, p. 238).
71 Barnard (1938, p. 253).
72 Barnard (1938, p. 253).
73 Barnard (1938, pp. 256–7).
74 We wish to be clear that the point we are making here is not that of Belbin (1981) and his concept of team roles. Over many years of studying management teams, he identified eight team roles and some basic characteristics of effective or winning teams. The latter include a 'good' chairman, one strong plant (creative individual), a fair spread of mental abilities, a spread in personal attributes offering wide team-role coverage, a good match between members' attributes and their team responsibilities, and an ability to recognize and adjust to imbalance in team-role distribution.
    It is perhaps quite possible to analyse our teams using his framework and to predict some level of effectiveness. However, we are not casting our team members as 'role-players' in the sense that Belbin does. We prefer to take a rather more fluid approach which recognizes that the executive team is but one of the areas they work in and that their performances are as much symbolic as they are task specific in the team-role sense. That is, they create and shape meaning individually and collectively in the doing of managing, organizing, leading and organizing writ large, not just in the

more limited sense of performing a team-role. So where we talk of spreading the range of limitations and pushing back the boundaries, we refer to a metaphorical level rather than a literal one, which we take to mean the cumulative process of experience and learning, demonstrated in performance – retaining our emphasis on process and temporality. This is not quite the same as Belbin's more prescriptive definitions which attempt to predict success.

75 Quote from Reckitt and Colman.
76 Barnard (1938, p. 322).
77 Einstein, quoted in Briskman (1981, p. 141).
78 Bronowski (1978, p. 14).

References

Abravanel, H. (1983) 'Mediatory myths in the service of organizational ideology'. In L. Pondy, P. J. Frost, G. Morgan and T. C. Dandridge (Eds), *Organizational Symbolism*. Greenwich, CT: JAI Press.

Arden, J. (1988) *The Books of Bale*. London: Methuen.

Arnheim, R. (1985) 'The double-edged mind: Intuition and the intellect'. In E. Eisner (Ed.), *Learning and Teaching the Ways of Knowing*. Chicago: Chicago University Press.

Avolio, B. J. and Bass, B. M. (1988) 'Transformational leadership, charisma and beyond'. In J. G. Hunt et al. (Eds), *Emerging Leadership Vistas*. Lexington, MA: Lexington Books.

Barnard, C. (1938) *The Functions of the Executive*. Cambridge, MA: Harvard University Press.

Barnard, C. (1945) *Organization and Management*. Cambridge, MA: Harvard University Press.

Barnes, L. B. and Kriger, M. P. (1986) 'The hidden side of organizational leadership'. *Sloan Management Review*, 15, Fall, 15–25.

Beckhard, R. and Harris, R. T. (1987) *Organizational Transitions*, 2nd edition. Reading, MA: Addison-Wesley.

Belbin, R. M. (1981) *Management Teams: Why They Succeed or Fail*. London: Heinemann.

Bennis, W. and Nanus, B. (1985) *Leaders: The Strategies for Taking Charge*. New York: Harper and Row.

Berg, K. and Smith, D. N. (1987) *Paradoxes of Group Life*. San Francisco: Jossey-Bass.

Berger, P. and Luckmann, T. (1966) *The Social Construction of Reality*. Harmondsworth: Penguin Books.

Braybrooke, D. (1964) 'The mystery of executive success re-examined'. *Administrative Science Quarterly*, 8, 533–60.

Briskman, L. (1981) 'Creative product and creative process in science and art'. In D. Dutton and M. K. Krausz (Eds), *The Concept of Creativity in Science and Art*. The Hague: Martinus Nijhoff.

Brody, H. (1987) *Stories of Sickness*. New Haven, CT: Yale University Press.

Bronowski, J. (1978) *The Visionary Eye: Essays in the Arts, Literature and Science*. Cambridge, MA: The MIT Press.

Bruner, J. S. (1964) *On Knowing.* New Haven, CT: Yale University Press.

Calvino, I. (1975) *Italian Folktales,* tr. Sylvia Mulcahy. London: Dent.

Cameron, K. S. (1986) 'Effectiveness as paradox. Consensus and conflict in conceptions of organizational effectiveness'. *Management Science,* 32(5), 539–53.

Chatwin, B. (1979) *In Patagonia.* London: Jonathan Cape.

Coleman, J. S. (1986) 'Social theory, social research and a theory of action'. *American Journal of Sociology,* 91(6), 1309–35.

Constable, J. and McCormick, R. (1987) *The Making of British Managers.* British Institute of Management Report.

Csikszentmihalyi, M. (1975) *Beyond Boredom and Anxiety.* San Francisco: Jossey Bass.

Csikszentmihalyi, M. and Csikszentmihalyi, I. S. (1988) *Optimal Experience.* Cambridge: Cambridge University Press.

Daft, R. L. and Weick, K. E. (1984) 'Towards a model of organizations as interpretation systems'. *Academy of Management Review,* 9(2), 284–95.

De Geus, A. P. (1988) 'Planning as learning'. *Harvard Business Review,* March–April, 70–4.

De Grauwe, P. and Vansanten, K. (1990) 'Deterministic Chaos in the Foreign Exchange Market'. Discussion Paper No. 370, January, Centre for Economic Policy Research.

Deutsch, M. (1962) 'Cooperation and trust: some theoretical notes'. In M. R. Jones (Ed.), *Nebraska Symposium on Motivation,* Lincoln, NE: University of Nebraska Press.

Dewey, J. (1934) *Art as Experience.* Extracts reprinted in A. Hofstadter and R. Kuhns (Eds) (1964) *Philosophies of Art and Beauty.* Chicago: Chicago University Press.

Ducasse, C.J. (1929) *The Philosophy of Art,* New York: Scribner.

Eisenberg, E. (1984) 'Ambiguity as strategy in organizational communication'. *Communication Monographs,* 51, 227–42.

Eisner, E. (Ed.) (1985) *Learning and Teaching the Ways of Knowing.* Chicago: Chicago University Press.

Eliot, T.S. (1935) Burnt Norton. In *The complete Poems and Plays of T. S. Eliot* (1969). London: Faber and Faber.

Frost, P. J., Moore, L. F., Louis, M. R., Lundberg, C. C. and Martin, J. (1985) *Organizational Culture.* Beverly Hills: Sage.

Garfield, C. (1986) *Peak Performers.* London: Hutchinson.

Giddens, A. (1987) *Social Theory and Modern Sociology.* Cambridge, Polity Press.

Goffman, E. (1959) *The Presentation of Self in Everyday Life.* Garden City, NY: Doubleday

Goold, M. and Campbell, A. (1987) *Strategies and Styles.* Oxford: Blackwell.

Gorbachev, M. (1987) *Perestroika.* London: Fontana/Collins.

Graham, J. W. (1988) 'Transformational leadership: fostering follower autonomy, not automatic followership'. In J. G. Hunt et al. *Emerging Leadership Vistas.* Lexington, MA: Lexington Books.

Hage, J. and Dewar, R. (1973) 'Elite values versus organizational structure in predicting innovations'. *Administrative Science Quarterly*, 18, 279–90.

Hambrick, D. C. (Ed.) (1988) *The Executive Effect: Concepts and Methods for Studying Top Managers*. London: JAI Press.

Hambrick, D. C. and Brandon, G. L. (1988) 'Executive values'. In D. C. Hambrick (Ed.), *The Executive Effect*. London: JAI Press.

Hambrick, D. C. and Mason, P. A. (1984) 'Upper echelons: the organization as a reflection of its top managers'. *Academy of Management Review*, 9, 193–206.

Harrison, R. (1972) 'Understanding your organization's character'. *Harvard Business Review*, May–June, 119–28.

Hofstede, G. (1980) *Culture's Consequences: International Differences in Work-Related Values*. London: Sage.

House, R. J. (1977) 'A 1976 theory of charismatic leadership'. In J. G. Hunt and L. L. Larson (Eds), *Leadership: The Cutting Edge*. London: Feffer and Simons.

Hulme, T. E. (1953) 'Speculations'. In E. Vivas and M. Krieger (Eds), *The Problems of Aesthetics*. New York: Holt, Rinehart and Winston.

Hunt, J. G. and Larson, L. L. (Eds) (1977) *Leadership: The Cutting Edge*. London: Feffer and Simons.

Hunt, J. G., Sekaran, U. and Schriesheim, C. A. (1982) *Leadership: Beyond Establishment Views*. Carbondale: South Illinois University Press.

Hunt, J. G., Baliga, B. R., Dachler, H. P. and Schriesheim, C. A. (Eds) (1988) *Emerging Leadership Vistas*. Lexington, MA: Lexington Books.

James H. (Ed.) (1920) *The Letters of William James*. Boston: Atlantic Monthly Press.

James, W. (1907) *Pragmatism*. London: Longman.

Kanter, R. M. (1984) *The Change Masters*. London: Unwin.

Kelly, G. (1955) *The Psychology of Personal Constructs*. New York: Norton.

Klemp, G. O. Jr. and McClelland, D. C. (1986) 'What characterizes intelligent functioning amongst senior managers?'. In R. J. Sternberg and R. K. Wayner (Eds) *Practical Intelligence*. Cambridge: Cambridge University Press.

Knorr-Cetina, K. and Cicourel, A. V. (1981) *Advances in Social Theory and Methodology: Toward an Integration of Micro- and Macro-Sociologies*. London: Routledge and Kegan Paul.

Koestler, A. (1981) 'The three domains of creativity'. In D. Dutton and M. J. Krausz (Eds), *Concept of Creativity in Art and Science*. The Hague: Martinus Nijhoff.

Kolb, D. A. (1983) 'Problem Management: learning from experience'. In Srivastva, S. and Associates (Eds) *The Executive Mind*. San Francisco: Jossey-Bass.

Kotter, J. P. (1982) *The General Managers*. New York: Free Press.

Lakoff, G. and Johnson, M. (1980) *Metaphors We Live By*. Chicago: University of Chicago Press.

Lester J. (1987) *The Tales of Uncle Remus*. London: The Bodley Head.

Luhmann, N. (1979) *Trust and Power*, Chichester: Wiley.
McCall, M. W., Lombardo, M. M. and Morrison, A. M. (1988) *The Lessons of Experience*. Lexington, MA: Lexington Books.
McCasky, M. B. (1988). 'The challenge of managing ambiguity and change'. In L. R. Pondy, R. J. Boland and H. Thomas (Eds) *Managing Ambiguity and Change*. Chichester: Wiley.
McDonald, A. (1972) 'Conflict at the summit: A deadly game', *Harvard Business Review*, 50(2), 60.
National Forum for Management Education and Development (1989). Management Charter Initiative – Question and Answer Briefing, September,1989.
Mangham, I. L. (1988) Effecting Organizational Change. Oxford: Blackwell.
Mangham, I. L. and Overington, M. A. (1987) *Organizations as Theatre*. Chichester: Wiley.
March, J. G. (1978) 'Bounded rationality, ambiguity and the engineering of choice', *Bell Journal of Economics*, 9, 587–608.
March, J. G. (1981). 'Footnotes to organizational change', *Administrative Science Quarterly*, 26, 563–577.
March, J. G. and Olsen, J. P. (1976). *Ambiguity and Choice in Organizations*. Universitetsforlaget: Bergen, Norway.
Medawar, P. (1984) *Pluto's Republic*. Oxford: Oxford University Press.
Meindl, J. R., Ehrlich, S. B. and Dukerich, J. M. (1985) 'The romance of leadership'. In J. G. Hunt, U. Sekaran and C. A. Schriesheim (Eds.) *Administrative Science Quarterly*, 30, 78–102.
Miller, G. and Simons, H. W. (Eds) (1974) *Perspectives on Communication in Social Conflict*. Englewood Cliffs, NJ: Prentice-Hall.
Mintzberg, H. (1982) 'If you're not serving Bill and Barbara, then you're not serving leadership'. In Hunt J. G., Sekaran, U. and Schriesheim, C. A. (Eds) *Leadership: Beyond Establishment Views*. Carbondale: South Illinois University Press.
Mintzberg, H. (1987) 'Crafting strategy'. *Harvard Business Review*, 65(4), 66–75.
Mintzberg, H. and Waters, J. A. (1983) 'The mind of the strategists'. In Srivastva, S. and Associates (Eds) *The Executive Mind*. San Francisco: Jossey Bass.
Mohr, L. B. (1982) *Explaining Organizational Behaviour*. Francisco: Jossey-Bass.
Morgan, G. (1980) 'Paradigms, metaphors and puzzle solving in organization theory'. *Administrative Science Quarterly*, 25, 605–22.
Morgan G. (1986) *Images of Organization*. Beverly Hills: Sage.
Morgan G. (1988) *Riding the Waves of Change*. San Francisco: Jossey-Bass.
Morgan G. and Smircich, L. (1980) 'The case for qualitative research'. *Academy of Management Review*, 5, 491–500.
Pascale, R. T. and Athos, A. C. (1981) *The Art of Japanese Management*. Harmondsworth: Penguin Books.
Peckham, M. (1979) *Explanation and Power: The Control of Human Behaviour*. New York: Seabury Press.
Perrow, C. (1977) 'Three types of effectiveness studies'. In P. S. Goodman, J.

M. Pennings and Associates (Eds), *Organizational Effectiveness*. San Francisco: Jossey-Bass.

Perrow, C. (1986) *Complex Organizations: A Critical Essay*, 3rd edition. New York: Random House.

Peters, T. and Waterman, R. (1982) *In Search of Excellence*. London: Harper and Row.

Poggi, G. (1965) 'A main theme of contemporary sociological analysis: Its achievements and limitations', *British Journal of Sociology*, 16(2), 283–94.

Polanyi, M. (1958) *The Study of Man*. Chicago: University of Chicago Press.

Polanyi, M. (1964) *Personal Knowledge*. New York: Harper and Row.

Polanyi, M. (1967) *The Tacit Dimension*. New York: Routledge and Kegan Paul.

Polanyi, M. (1968) 'Life's irreducible structure'. *Science*, April–June, 160, 1308–12.

Pondy, L. (1978) 'Leadership is a language game'. In M. W. McCall and M. M. Lombardo (Eds), *Leadership: Where Else Can We Go?* Durham, NC: Duke University Press.

Pondy, L. (1983) 'Union of rationality and intuition in management action'. In S. Srivastva and Associates (Eds) *The Executive Mind*. San Francisco: Jossey-Bass.

Powell, A. (1951) *Dance to the Music of Time: 1 A Question of Upbringing*. London: Heinemann

Putnam, L. (1986) 'Contradictions and paradoxes in organizations'. In L. Thayer (Ed.), *Organization-Communication: Emerging Perspectives I*. New York: Ablex Publishing.

Pye, A. (1988) 'Management training: acts of faith, scenes of competence'. *Journal of General Management*, 13(4), 74–87.

Quinn, J. B. (1980) *Strategies for Change: Logical Incrementalism*. Homewood, IL: Irwin.

Quinn, J. B. (1982) 'Managing strategies incrementally'. *OMEGA*, 10(6), 613–27.

Quinn, R. E. and Cameron, K. (1983) 'Organizational life cycles and the criteria of effectiveness'. *Management Science*, 29, 33–51.

Quinn, R. E. and Cameron, K. S. (Eds) (1988) *Paradox and Transformation*. Cambridge, MA: Ballinger.

Quinn, R. E. and Kimberly, J. R. (1984) 'Paradox, planning and perseverance: Guidelines for management practice'. In J. R. Kimberly and R. E. Quinn (Eds), *Managing Organizational Transitions*. Homewood, IL: Irwin.

Robbins, S. R. and Duncan, R. B. (1988) 'The role of the CEO and top management in the creation and implementation of strategic vision'. In D. C. Hambrick (Ed.), *The Executive Effect: Concepts and Methods for Studying Top Managers*. Greenwich, C.T: JAI Press.

Rorty, R. (1982) *Consequences of Pragmatism (Essays: 1972–1980)*. Minneapolis: University of Minnesota Press.

Rowe, A. J. and Mason, R. A. (1988) *Managing with Style*. San Francisco: Jossey-Bass.

Sapienza, A. M. (1987) 'Image making as a strategic function'. In L. Thayer

(Ed.) *Organization-Communication: Emerging Perspectives II*. Norwood, NJ: Ablex Publishing Corporation.

Sargent, A. G. (1981) *The Androgynous Manager*. New York: AMACON.

Schein, E. (1969) *Process Consultation*. Reading, MA: Addison-Wesley.

Schein, E. H. (1985) *Organizational Culture and Leadership*. San Francisco: Jossey-Bass.

Schon, D. A. (1983) *The Reflective Practitioner: How Professionals Think in Action*. New York: Basic Books Inc.

Scott Poole, M. and Van de Ven, A. (1989) 'Using paradox to build management and organization theories'. *Academy of Management Review*, 14(4), 562–78.

Sederberg, P. (1984) *The Politics of Meaning: Power and Explanation in the Construction of Social Reality*. Tucson, AZ: University of Arizona Press.

Simon, H. (1989) 'What is intuition?'. In W. H. Agor (Ed.), *Intuition in Organizations*. London: Sage.

Simons, H. W. (1974) 'The carrot and the stick as handmaidens of persuasion in conflict situations'. In G. Miller and H. W. Simons (Eds), *Perspectives on Communication in Social Conflict*. Englewood Cliffs, NJ: Prentice-Hall.

Smith, C. S. (1980) 'Structural hierarchy in science, art and history'. In J. Weschler (Ed.), *On Aesthetics in Science*. Cambridge, MA: MIT Press.

Smith, J. E. (1978) *Purpose and Thought: The Meaning of Pragmatism*. New Haven: Yale University Press.

Spender, S. (1951) *World within World*. London: Faber.

Srivastva, S. and Associates (1983) *The Executive Mind*. San Francisco: Jossey-Bass.

Starbuck, W. H. (1985) 'Acting first and thinking later: Theory versus reality in strategic change'. In J. M. Pennings and Associates (Eds), *Organizational Strategy and Change*. San Francisco: Jossey-Bass.

Starbuck, W. H. and Milliken, F. J. (1988) 'Executives' perceptual filters'. In D. C. Hambrick (Ed.) *The Executive Effect: Concepts and Methods for Studying Top Managers*. London: JAI Press.

Tannenbaum, R. and Davis, S. A. (1969) 'Values, man and organizations'. *Industrial Management Review*, 10, 67–86.

Tomas, V. (1958) 'Creativity in art'. *Philosophical Review*, 67, 1–15.

Torbert, W. (1983) 'Cultivating timely executive action'. In S. Srivastva and Associates (Eds), *The Executive Mind*. San Francisco: Jossey-Bass.

Turbayne, C. M. (1970) *The Myth of Metaphor*. Columbia: University of South Carolina Press.

Vaill, P. (1982) 'The purposing of high performing systems'. *Organizational Dynamics*, Autumn, 22–39.

Vaill, P. (1989) *Managing as a Performing Art*. San Francisco: Jossey-Bass.

Van de Ven, A. (1983) 'Review of T. Peters and R. Waterman "In Search of Excellence"'. *Administrative Science Quarterly*, December, 621–4.

Van de Ven, A. H. (1987) 'Central problems in the management of innovation'. *Management Science*, 32(5), 590–607.

Van de Ven, A. and Scott Poole, M. (1988) 'Paradoxical requirements for a theory of organizational change'. In R. E. Quinn and K. S. Cameron (Eds) *Paradox and Transformation*. Cambridge, MA: Ballinger.

Vickers, G. (1965) *The Art of Judgement*. London: Harper and Row.

Vickers, G. (1980) 'Rationality and intuition'. In J. Weschler (Ed.), *On Aesthetics in Science*, Cambridge, MA: MIT Press.

Watzlawick, P., Weakland, J. and Fisch, R. (1974) *Change: Principles of Problem Formation and Problem Resolution*. New York: Norton and Co.

Wechsler, J. (Ed.) (1980) *On Aesthetics in Science*, Cambridge, MA: MIT Press.

Weick, K. (1969) *The Social Psychology of Organizing*, 1st edition. Reading, MA: Addison-Wesley.

Weick, K. (1977) 'Repunctuating the problem'. In P. S. Goodman, J. M. Pennings and Associates (Eds), *New Perspectives on Organizational Effectiveness*. San Francisco: Jossey-Bass.

Weick, K. (1979) *The Social Psychology of Organizing*, 2nd edition. Reading, MA: Addison-Wesley.

Weick, K. (1981) 'Psychology as gloss'. In R. A. Kassachau and C. N. Cofer (Eds), *Psychology's Second Century*. New York: Praeger.

Weick, K. (1983) 'Managerial thought in the context of action'. In S. Srivastva and Associates (Eds), *The Executive Mind*. San Francisco: Jossey-Bass.

Weick, K. (1985) 'The significance of corporate culture'. In P. J. Frost, L. F. Moore, M. R. Louis, C. C. Lundberg and J. Martin (Eds), *Organizational Culture*. Beverly Hills: Sage.

Weick, K. E. and Browning, L. D. (1986) 'Argument and narration in organizational communication'. In J. G. Hunt and J. D. Blair (Eds), *1986 Yearly Review of the Journal of Management*, 12(2), 243–59.

Whitehead, A. N. (1929) *Process and Reality*. New York: Free Press.

Wolff, K. H. (1950) *The Sociology of Georg Simmel*. Glencoe: Free Press.

Wrapp, H. E. (1967) 'Good managers don't make policy decisions'. *Harvard Business Review*, Sept/Oct. 91–9.

Zaleznick, A. (1988) 'Making managers creative: The psychodynamics of creativity and innovation'. In R. L. Kuhn, *Handbook for Creative and Innovative Managers*. New York: McGraw-Hill.

Zand, D.E. (1972) 'Trust and managerial problem solving'. *Administrative Science Quarterly*, 17, 229–39.

Zohar, D. (1990) *The Quantum Self*. London: Bloomsbury.

Zukav, G. (1979) *The Dancing Wu Li Masters: An Overview of the New Physics*. London: Hutchinson.

Index